FOAL

EAT, LIVE, LOVE, DIE

Betty Fussell

EAT, LIVE, LOVE, DIE

Selected Essays

Introduction by Alice Waters

COUNTERPOINT

Library of Congress Cataloging-in-Publication Data

Names: Fussell, Betty Harper, author.
Title: Eat, live, love, die : selected essays / Betty Fussell.
Description: Berkeley, CA : Counterpoint, 2016
Identifiers: LCCN 2016020225 | ISBN 9781619027855
Subjects: LCSH: Gastronomy. | Food. | Food writing.
Classification: LCC TX633 .F87 2016 | DDC 641.01/3--dc23
LC record available at https://lccn.loc.gov/2016020225

Cover design by Kelly Winton
Interior design by Neuwirth & Associates

COUNTERPOINT
2560 Ninth Street, Suite 318
Berkeley, CA 94710
www.counterpointpress.com

Printed in the United States of America
Distributed by Publishers Group West

10   9   8   7   6   5   4   3   2   1

To Eve in the Garden,
who dared take The First Bite

CONTENTS

CONTENTS

INTRODUCTION

by Alice Waters

THE THING I'VE always loved and appreciated about Betty Fussell's writing is her curiosity about where things come from. She's like an anthropologist who is interested in the roots and sources of things, and their evolution. Her perspective is down-to-earth and straightforward, and she knows intuitively that, at the foundation of all inquiry, there are basic human qualities that need to be acknowledged and celebrated. No matter what she's focusing on, her palpable desire to make sense of the world and explain it to us makes her a pleasure to read.

Part of this pleasure, I'm sure, is due to her candid and unfussy style. Her direct language illuminates, without pretension. Reading one of her essays, on any subject, is like listening to a well-spoken and wise old friend at a dinner table, a raconteur who makes you feel comfortable and then draws you in and enlightens you about things you had not even realized you had an interest in. Like all good teachers, Betty seduces intriguingly, then explains clearly, and, finally, inspires.

I remember the first time she visited Chez Panisse many years ago. Betty was one of the first journalists who came to write about us when things were starting to really take off. I knew she was a friend of some of my great mentors, friends and heroes—James Beard, Julia Child, Elizabeth David, Marion Cunningham, and Edna

Lewis, to name a few—so I had an idea of her standards, and I was more than a little intimidated. But Betty got it right away. She saw pretty clearly what we were doing at the restaurant; and she understood that the story wasn't just about the food on the plate, but the bigger picture of how we were looking for the roots of taste and trying to figure out how to honor those roots while also making them relevant to the times we were living in.

Only a certain kind of writer has the sensitivity and ability to describe what she sees in such an appealing, grounded, and serious way. As a body of work, these essays are an astonishment, ranging from her first brisk food and travel pieces to measured and intimate reflections on time and loss. The essays are provocative, forthright, and far-seeing. Here is the record of a writer who has never lost her nose for history and her ear for honesty, and one who has never, ever stopped looking for connections.

PREFACE

WHAT HAPPENED? Never had a good sense of time, but jesus-christ! Yesterday I'm wiping applesauce off my baby's cheeks and today I'm wondering when she'll retire. For years I didn't wear a watch because I wanted to stop time. Now time stops me dead. Tic-Toc.

Always lived from moment to moment, but always wanted more. Like keys on a piano. Black/White. But what mode? Major/Minor? What beat? 3/4—4/4? What scale? 7-tone/12 tone? Find the piano, then the keys.

But who sets the metronome? Composer, performer, director? Who sets the limits of the composition, performance, event? The limits of day/night, summer/winter, bright star/black hole, life/death? Tic-Toc.

The terror of In/Out. And so we eat. Not just to survive, but to chitter-chatter, twitter-tweet. About food, sex, danger, safety, flight, the wind and the rain. Like geese, chimps, dolphins. We honk, hoot, whistle. We play dead, wrestle, chase. We bump our uglies together, whether feathered, furred, or finned. We feed our kids and teach them to fly, swing, swim. And then what? And what for?

Are we the only critters who ask? The only ones who scratch stones or mark caves or shape clay to tell someone, anyone, that Kilroy was here? For a moment . . . beyond this moment? Make mud pies, fly a kite? Are we the only ones to give Time the finger?

In my forties I wanted for my epitaph "She did it the hard way." Nearing my nineties, I'd be happy with "She was."

Good lord, what a time it took to put my Tic-Toc terror into words. Explanation was never my strength. I grew up on movies, not books. Images, song and dance.

Sunday-school Jesus in pastels. Long beard, skinny body, hands hammered into wood. For what? For us sinners. How come? Satan seduced, Eve and Adam fell. Praise be to God. Jesus saves. Here We Gather at the River. Tell Me the Stories of Jesus. I Come to the Garden Alone.

But never ever dance. Satan's work. Shirley Temple a Devil? Movies don't count. Movies are not real. God's Word is real. Movies are not Words. Movies are fairy tales for children.

As a child my stories were all from the Bible, the movies, church pageants, and high school plays. How I loved plays. They snatched me from my cradle like Moses in the bulrushes and made me a changeling child.

I'd hit 40 by the time I began to write real words. By then I'd married a professional writer/teacher, typed and edited his manuscripts, raised two children, entertained like crazy, finished a doctorate in English Lit, taught Shakespeare, performed in community theaters, traveled as family all over Europe, lived in Princeton, London, and Provence.

And along the way I found Julia Child and the pleasures of making at home in Princeton what we were eating in Cimiez. Like Julia, I wanted to tell other people about it. Not through how-to technique but how food checks time. The way travel does. The way play-acting does.

Through my writer husband, I learned how tricky it is to put life into words. He was born with a Remington typewriter in his mouth.

I was born with a 35 millimeter reel unspooling in my head. To him, I was wasting my (his) time by my silly attempts to write since I had no talent for it.

But I was too excited to shut up. Traveling, I'd put boots on the ground of the Swiss alps of Shirley Temple's Heidi. I'd walked through the Tower of London head high as Hepburn's Mary Queen of Scots. I'd sped through the birch forests of Russia faster than Dietrich's Catherine the Great

And everywhere we went, we ate. Foods I'd never seen, smelled, or chewed before. Hot runny cheese dripping from toast on a fork, pudding of sheep's innards and oatmeal boiled in the skin of a sheep's stomach, thick blood-red soup of beets and cabbage with a white blob of sour cream.

I was thrilled that food was the only native language I needed anywhere. Anyone would talk to me by sign and face language if I pointed to a grilled fish in some Italian bistro. Or raised a glass of beer in Munich or of ouzo in Athens.

To find words in American English to convey my excitement was another matter. My academic training was profoundly counterproductive. I'd published in academic journals where I had to eliminate all personal opinion or, god forbid, emotion in order to make the fuzzy humanities as cold as science.

Now I must delete everything I'd learned in school. How do real people talk? What kind of words in what kind of order? What for? Move them, said my mentor-critic husband. Make it dramatic.

I was proud as hell of my first published piece in a big-time national magazine, slick and glossy. The old *Holiday* in 1969 paid me for writing about Real Chickens and how they grew in Bresse, where I'd interviewed a chicken farmer in my pidgin French and a formidable chef in a white bandana, La Mère Brazier.

I was lucky as hell to catch the Last Wave of travel magazines in the '60s and '70s, now defoamed or defunct. I also caught the New Wave of women's magazines like *Lear's*. And the evolution of Women's pages in newspapers from society gossip and recipes to upscale titles like the "Living Section" of the *New York Times*.

I became the *Times*'s food editor for New Jersey and learned, with pain, how to write restaurant reviews in 750 words and rank eateries with one to four stars.

I loved the challenge and hated the job. It was specific to place. Manhattan standards of connoisseurship in food and drink had nothing to do with the real life of real people in the state of New Jersey. I got hate letters from chefs to whom I'd awarded less than four stars. I got heartbroken letters from couples who'd saved for years to celebrate their Big Night Out at a place I ranked "Fair." I got telephone threats on my home phone from the Mafia.

But even my semi freelance position on the *Times* gave me credibility. In a corridor state turning rapidly from rural to industrial, I learned about the fragility of real food everywhere. I interviewed Italian mushroom growers, Swedish cranberry harvesters Hungarian sausage makers, Russian kulich bakers.

When I moved in 1980 to Manhattan, once the kids had grown and I'd left my husband, I worked like a madwoman for the next 30 years—writing. Writing 15 hours a day, learning the craft of essays and books.

My first book was about the movies: a silent-movie comedienne *Mabel Normand, "The First I-Don't-Care Girl."* And what a gal she was, dead at 29, two years after I was born. My second book was about writers, writers who'd taught me about food in words and in person. M.F.K. Fisher, James Beard, Julia Child, Craig Claiborne—most of them westerners, all of them translators of French cuisine into American cookery. Hot diggity. I was home.

And in the '80s and '90s no matter what you wrote about food, somebody wanted to print it. Money was thin, but other rewards were fat. Especially for someone obsessed by history—whether of literature, theater, movies, high culture, or pop culture. At that time, to invade the clannish world of chefs and restaurants and recipes as a "food historian" was, in America, as oxymoronic as "fresh frozen."

Of course my first food books were panned by publishers because they were about "how come?" rather than "how to." Where are the recipes? *Publishers Weekly* asked, reviewing *The Story of Corn*.

But by the end of the '90s, established publishers were going over the cliff like lemmings. Every damn one of my 11 books had a different publisher because my latest publishing company had either dropped dead or been sold to a conglomerate.

I recite their names like a litany for the dead: Ticknor & Fields, Times Books, Viking, Dutton, Harcourt Brace, Alfred A. Knopf. Even Farrar, Straus had dropped the Giroux. In my head the bells toll for magazines named *Diversion*, *Off Duty*, *Au Jus*, *Lear's*, *Culture-front*, *Savvy Woman*, *Journal of Gastronomy*—and my true love, *Food Arts*. Gone with the world of linotype. *Requiescat in pace.*

Enter the blog, the tweet, the twitter, a new global world of quick bytes and selfies. Instantaneously. Look at me now. Now. NOW. Scary for someone whose Grandma forbade her to look in mirrors because that was Vanity, enemy of God. Someone whose stepmother told her she was ugly. Whose husband saw only himself. Who didn't really see herself in a mirror until she was 55 and old enough to join AARP.

When food is the lens, you can see all the contradictions of self and time right there on your plate. And with each bite, you bite into your past, memories of your family, your tribe, your race, your tree-swinging ancestors. And into your future, your kids', your country's, your globe's.

Eating is the great connector. Of fellow creaturehood. An act of love as well as of murder. Of sharing and of suicide. Chewing to the waltz of past, present, future. Breakfast, lunch, dinner. Repeat. Laugh between bites.

How to capture that rhythm in words? Not just the two-step of the heart's beat Thump/thump. The lung's breath In/out. But the cycle/recycle of waltz or polka on the dance floor of morning-noon-night. A common dance. A little girl dances on her daddy's feet. A granny in her wheelchair taps her foot.

Eating, living, loving, dying—this is our dance to the music of time. Birds do it. Bugs do it. Even the Black Holes of the cosmos do it—Deep Throats swallowing and spitting out galaxies like the messy eaters they are. I could split a gut laughing, but I need that gut for my Last Dance before I too am swallowed up and spat out elsewhere.

BETTY FUSSELL
Casa Dorinda, Santa Barbara, CA
Fall 2016

FOOD IS . . .

Eating My Words

◾

FOOD IS NOT a subject in the way that the great subjects of literature like War, Love, Death, Sex, Power, Betrayal, or Honor are subjects. Neither is food an object, in the way that a Car, a Washing Machine, a Computer, a House are objects—generic commodities that we desire and consume. Rather, food is an action, more primal than speech and more universal than language. And for humans, there's the rub. While everything in the created universe eats, not everything speaks. Wind and water eat stone, night eats day, black holes eat light—silently. We find words to address these actions, but long before we ever arrived on the scene or said a word about it, every link in the terrestrial food chain, as in the cosmic chain, was chomping away and changing one thing into another. It's one of those givens we like to avoid because we don't fancy our table companions or dining conditions. We don't like to be reminded that if dung were not caviar to the dung beetle, the earth would be covered in shit.

Nor do we like to be reminded that we are steak tartare to worms or, if we thwart their slow munch, a grillade to flames. We want to be exempt, special, excused. We don't want to be reminded that in the game preserve staked out for us, we are flesh and blood like our fellow animals, subject to the same feeding frenzies but with inferior teeth. In terms of brains, we may be first among mammals, but we are mammals nonetheless, and as such we cannibalize our mothers in order to live. Each of us, no matter how noble his sentiments at a later stage of development, drinks mother's blood from the time he is a tiny egg clinging hungrily to a uterine wall. Long before speech, the drama of communication begins in the womb and is merely amplified with baby's first intake of breath that ends in a howl, acknowledging in premonitory outrage that life-long separation of the feeder from the fed. From birth on, what comes out of the mouth and what goes in are inextricably mingled because there is only the one orifice for both feeding and speaking, not to mention kissing. Was that a mistake in engineering or a brilliant subversion of human pretense?

Elias Canetti asks whether it wouldn't have been better to have one orifice for food and another for words. "Or does this intimate mixing of all our utterances with the lips, teeth, tongue, throat, all those parts of the mouth that serve the business of eating—does this mixing tell us that language and eating forever belong together, that we can never be nobler and better than we are?" But what if we ask the question another way? Does this intimate mixing of language and eating suggest that both are forms of knowledge and communication, that ingesting what is outside us with lips, teeth, tongue, and throat is intimately related to excreting from within the cries, sighs, babbles, and prattles that are eventually transformed into words and sentences in the cauldrons of the human mind and imagination? Could we go further and suggest that the lineaments of the mouth lick into shape the very images that the mind of man conceives in his struggle to find sound bites and transform them? The crunch of teeth biting into an apple shapes the image of the father of mankind, who hungers and thirsts after righteousness with actual lips and throat. Does not this intimate mixing suggest that the human animal is forever a bewildering compound of body parts and spirit sensors, a belcher of hymns, an angel that farts, and that wise eaters and speakers will savor the mixture?

For is not the mouth our primary mediator in distinguishing what is without from what is within, as we suck first our own and then other people's fingers and toes? We learn to say "Mama" out of hunger, for both speaking and eating express similar actions of hungering, desiring, gathering, preserving, communing, laughing, fearing, loving, and dying in the long agon of separation and connection. Even a mouth eating in solitude—and silence—is engaged willy-nilly in discovering and communing with what is outside itself, which its hunger transforms by taking the outside literally in. We eat the world to know it and ourselves. If we fail to distinguish outside from in, we are stamped with a name and a story: Narcissus, hungering to eat himself, imaged in a pool, opened his mouth and drowned.

Eating, like speaking, reconnects through the imagination what reason has learned to disconnect through the senses. In this way, eating is a form of magic. When Shakespeare's Leontes discovers in *The Winter's Tale* that the statue of his Hermione is alive, he exclaims, "If this be magic, let it be an art lawful as eating." Eating, like speaking, mediates between opposite worlds, forging a bridge over the natal chasm between mind and body, images and substances, symbols and things that reason works hard to keep apart. Even as a noun, food suggests the action of ferrying meaning across species, across ontological continents, ensuring that despite the logic of appearances, you *can* turn a sow's ear into a silk purse through the "turn" of trope, or the "transfer" of metaphor, through speaking pictures, or images in action.

Food is always image and icon as well as substance. Semioticians explained decades ago how food, cooking, and eating create a tripartite language of their own through which a culture expresses itself, and this language dances between the literal and the figurative in the way that we usually expect of speech but not always of food. Despite laboratory analyses, mother's milk is never simply the sum of its biochemical or molecular parts, no more than a bottle of milk is. Who's holding the breast or the bottle or the baby, and where? Are mother and baby sitting on the grass in suburban sunshine or are they flat on a canvas surrounded by drapery and haloed cherubs? Are they on a railway platform herded into a cattle car by soldiers in uniform? Food always condenses a happening, a plot, which unfolds like any enacted drama in the spotlit present, surrounded by shadows of the past.

The most ancient originating plots in the Western world, in fact, hinge on the relation of food to language. Before the Madonna there was Eve, and before Eve there was Nin-ti, the Sumerian mother goddess whose story, told in the world's first written language, Sumer, is a food story. After the water god Enki ate eight of Nin-ti's magic plants, the goddess cursed eight of his bodily organs with death, then relented and restored the god to life. Nin-ti's name was a pun, which meant both "rib" and "to make live." In the language of Sumer, Eve's name also meant "rib," but the language and the food got muddled in the translation from Sumer to Hebrew, so that in the Hebrew story the lady Eve was given life by the rib of man, whose death was caused by the woman's eating of a magic plant. Despite the gender and cultural reversal from mother goddess to father god, the paradox of the human animal remains intact: that which gives him life also kills him, and his tragedy is that he knows it.

Human life is so bound up with food—the sounds, textures, smells, tastes, emotions, ideas, and rituals of the one so meshed with the other—that to take a slice of life at any point is to cut into a full loaf, a pie, a roast, a terrine of meaning. Personal and cultural memories are so integral to eating and speaking that simply to name a food is to invoke the lifetime of a person—and a culture. We don't need Proust's madeleine. We have Twain's cornpone. Even when the nominal subject is a single food, such as coffee or oysters or beans, it is also about place and time and occasion and memory and need, just as it is about politics and economics and trade and war and religion and ceremony. While the first person singular is the instinctive voice in which to express our thoughts and feelings about food, the point of view will be as diverse as the position of the speaker: social critic, gardener, connoisseur, athlete, chef, housewife, farmer, dentist, historian, garbageman, politician, pastor, poet. All walks of life eat, in every corner of the world, whether in Nigeria, Bombay, Austria, Israel, Kyoto, or Iowa. Although attitude and tone of voice may play every key from rhapsodic to obscene, both the particularities of food and the universality of hunger keep the speaker, or writer, rooted in common ground.

Food, like language, forever unites the concrete with the universal, and a writer's attitude toward food will appear in how he manipulates the nervy relation between substance and symbol, jittery with dramatic tension, that dictates the behavior of us all. The materialist asserts the primacy of flesh: "*Erst kommt das Fressen, damnn kommt die Moral*," sings Brecht. The spiritualist denies or subjugates the flesh: "*I need nothing. I feel nothing. I desire nothing*," writes Wole Soyinka in prison on the eleventh day of his fast. The ritualist transforms substance and symbol alike into physical sensation: "The gamey taste and smell of ripened cheese is sexual, and provocative; the smell is maternal still, but now it is the smell of cyclical time," writes Paul Schmidt. The satirist mocks symbols of fabricating ridiculous substance: "The correct drink for fried bologna *à la Nutley, Nouveau Jersey*, is a 1927 Nehi Cola," writes Russell Baker.

Writings about food are necessarily as diverse as writings about any art of life and as illuminative of the things that matter because food is connected to everything. Homer, whether speaking of epic wars or journeys, never neglected food and drink. He specified in detail how to roast and salt the joint of meat and how to mix wine with water to invite the gods in. Greek gods ate and drank in the company of man long before Christians turned their God into cooked food to be eaten by men. That changed the nature of the feast, of course, although there is nothing new in gods who existed to be eaten. Think of Prometheus with his eternally gnawed, eternally renewed liver, wherein man's lips and tongue tasted forever the sour of cyclical time, the bitter of eternal hunger, the sweet of immortality, the salt of death.

In imaging the unavoidable and appalling fact that life eats life, the Ancient Maya invented a language in which men and gods were made of the self-same food in an eternal interchange of substance. A literal ear of corn growing in the fields was also the finely shaped head of the sacrificed young corn god with his hair of green leaves. To eat corn was to eat one's mother, father, sister, brother, and ancestor gods. Substance and symbol were so intimately mixed in the mouth of man that life and death were as mingled as body and soul, as eating and speaking. Maya speech wrapped the cosmos in a language of verbal and visual food puns, so that eating and speaking were alike actions of punning. To eat a kernel of corn, the substance of life, was to swallow a drop of blood, a sign of death. The Maya sign, or glyph, for bread abstracted the cornhusk wrapper and the ball of corn dough of an actual tamale, so that both speaker and eater alike shared in the bread's layered meanings of "sacred offering," "sacrificial blood," "something precious," "day." Every kernel of corn condensed the plot of the *Popul Vuh* and its hero, the sacrificed god

Hunahpu, whose decapitated head in the calabash tree, after he and his twin brother outwitted the Lords of Death, impregnated Blood Woman who gave birth to man from her body of corn.

And so then they put into words the creation,
    The shaping
Of our first mother
    And father.
Only yellow corn
    And white corn were their bodies.
Only food were the legs
    And arms of man.
Those who were our first fathers
    Were the original men.
Only food at the outset
    With their bodies.

Nothing else can do for man's mind and imagination what food does because it is the one and only thing that accompanies every single man, Maya, Christian, Muslim, Buddhist, on his journey from cradle to grave. If his first sound is a cry for milk, his last may be a whimper for sugared tea or a spoonful of Jell-O. Sans teeth, tongue, or throat, he still must open the veins of his body to the outside world to sustain life, whether or not he is conscious of that mechanized connection. His final image may not be of the loved face hovering over his bedside at all, but of a wished-for muffin or martini, as real and intense as the griever left behind.

Never underestimate the power of food to summon images and dictate lives in the here and hereafter. Why are the graves in almost every ancient culture stuffed with containers for food and drink to accompany the corpse on its journey between worlds? As in life, so in death, food remains our most faithful attendant on the ferry across the river Styx, giving comfort and sustenance to the frightened soul soon to swallow and be swallowed by a realm where outside and inside have no meaning and where that peculiar mixture of eating and speaking will vanish in the emptying out of appetite and the entering in of silence.

Introduction to *A Slice of Life: Contemporary Writers on Food*
(Bonnie Barranca, editor), 2007

CULTURES

"If You Lack Turtles, Try Buffalo Hump."

EUROPEANS LAUGH WHEN Americans claim regional diversity and provincial specialties in their cooking. They laugh the way *National Lampoon* laughed at "The Cooking of Provincial New Jersey": traditional Coke, Twinkies, Rice-a-Roni, Hostess cupcakes, frozen fishsticks—"21 cuisines, one great taste." Words like "regional" and "provincial" belong properly to Europe, China, and other civilizations that took root and blossomed over the centuries in the same plot of earth. American cooking cannot be regional in this sense, but it is vernacular, as vernacular, uprooted, and upstart as American jazz.

With American cooking, a word like "authentic" is as useless as "regional." A Big Mac, after all, is authentic American Road Food, for which Americans stationed in Borneo or Mozambique yearn as nostalgically as for a Chicago deep-dish pizza or a Philadelphia soft pretzel. When a Frenchman demands authenticity as the criterion for a native dish, I recite my favorite recipe from a Northwest Gitksan Indian for moose or caribou, which begins, "Get a good-sized piece of heavy tinfoil, big enough to wrap your roast in. Get a package of onion soup mix, any good brand." And if the Frenchman persists in his folly, I remind him that Edward S. Curtis, the great photographer of North American Indians at the turn of the century, always carried with him a box of long-haired wigs to guarantee the authenticity of his aborigines.

We need new words to describe the cooking and culture of a "new" world of émigrés and immigrants, in which the first émigrés arrived some 40,000 years ago. We need new syntax to capture the monstrous size, mobility, and speed that go with the American territory and the American table, where "all semblance of European structure," as Cyril Connolly once said, "vanishes." We need new forms to express a cooking culture that is continuously moving and changing, that is entirely hybrid, atomistic, versatile, improvised, and gloriously askew.

It's cooking based on authentically improvised substitutes. If you lack mincemeat, advised the ladies of the parish guild of Deerfield, Mass., in *The Pocumtuc Housewife* of 1805, use dried apples or dried pumpkin or grated carrot or boiled raisins or cracker crumbs: "A little ingenuity added to almost any material that comes to hand, will make a tasty pie." If you lack Christmas dinner, as Ginnie Mae Finger did in Texas in the 1860s, then climb on a horse with Mother and Father and go hunting for "Christmas dinner lunch" of buffalo, turkey, and deer. If you lack turtles for soup, try buffalo hump, advised Susan Magoffin, who traveled the Santa Fe trail in 1846 and found buffalo-hump soup "far superior to any soup served in the best hotels of Philadelphia or New York."

Hodge-Podge of Peoples and Food in Motion

No place on earth contains such a hodge-podge of peoples and food in motion in a landscape as radically diverse as ours. But if we don't have static culinary regions, still we can chart a culinary map by drawing a circle around our borders and cinching the middle with a belt. We can map at least seven borderlands—the Northeast,

Middle Atlantic, Deep South, Delta South, Southwest, Northwest, and Great Lakes—that encircle the heartland of the Corn Belt.

We can even chart a topography of provender characteristic of each place: cod, clams, and lobsters in the Northeast, oyster and crabs in the Middle Atlantic, shrimp and rice in the Deep South, crawfish and cane in the Delta South, chili peppers and squash in the Southwest, salmon, apples, and artichokes in the Northwest, lake fish and dairy stuff in the Great Lakes, and in the Corn Belt, what else but corn?

Ethnic topography, however, complicates our map, since we find Sephardic Jews in Texas, Danes in California, Vietnamese in Arkansas, and Lithuanians in Michigan. These graftings of peoples and places produce curious results. It was a German in Braunfels, Texas, who first packaged chili powder. It was a pair of Armenians in Oregon who devised the confection called Aplets and Cotlets. It was Portuguese fishermen in California who refined our sourdough bread.

And yet we do find ethnic groupings that historically grafted old-world methods onto new-world ingredients to create lasting traditions of their own. British émigrés to New England brought with them iron pots to cook their chowders and stews and boiled puddings. German émigrés to Pennsylvania brought the sweet-sour preservatives of their homeland and the baked goods of their tile ovens. English and African transplants to the South established a high-low style of country cooking that combined pit-fire barbecues with Elizabethan syllabubs. Arcadian French, Spanish, and Caribbean natives developed the highly spiced flavors of Creole and Cajun cooking in the Delta. Native Pueblo Indians, crossed with Spaniards, maintained the chili, bean, and squash cooking of their ancestors in the Southwest. In the Northwest, Chinese met Gitskan Indians, Russian trappers, and Japanese fishermen to reap Pan-Asian harvests from Pacific gardens and seas. Scandinavians and Germans settled the Lake country to make beer and cheese. American-born Anglo-Saxons brought factories and sanatoria to the prairies to can corn and pork and invent health food.

Festal Traditions

These ethnic particularities surface most during holidays and holy days when people celebrate continuity rather than change. But even here festal traditions crop up in unexpected ways. In the Archdiocese of Detroit, for example, Catholic descendants of the "Mushrat French" still alleviate the tedium of meatless days during Lent by stewing up muskrats as "pretend-fish." In Northern New Mexico, Navajos still celebrate Christmas with a 100-pound Navajo cake of roasted corn, sprouted wheat, brown sugar, and raisins, enclosed in corn husks to bake overnight in a fire-heated earth pit covered with coals.

Even with a national food feast as standardized and traditional as Thanksgiving, there are plenty of local surprises. I recently did a roundup of America's 50 states, in which I asked 50 women for their Thanksgiving specialties. "We just have traditional fare," many of them said, "nothing special." Nothing special turned out to mean yams with Macadamia nuts in Hawaii, wild goose with lingonberry sauce in Alaska, artichoke pickle in South Carolina, quahog pie in Rhode Island, noodles and mashed potatoes in Indiana, crawfish dressing in Louisiana.

To understand American cooking, a European must listen as closely to the dialects of our vernacular as he listened to the dialects of our jazz. He must listen to the voices of American men and women as they cook at home. Here's the voice of Bertha Schiller, born in Brooklyn in 1895, talking about her cabbage soup: "Now I like the breast flanken, you know flanken. . . . Maybe your butcher will give you knee bones, but if you can't get the knee bone, get any bone. Get at least 2 ½ pounds of meat and bones, whatever they give you. Whatever it is, it is . . . I like to kosher cook it—soak it for half an hour in plain cold water, then drain it and salt all around for an hour, then you know it's gonna be tasty."

Here's the voice of Mary Frashure Allen, a young lawyer who moved with her husband David onto a small farm outside of Clarksburg, West Virginia, where they grow fruits and vegetables and store their harvest in the double-walled cut-stone cellar house built by Rubin Kemper in 1880. "In the fall we harvest MacIntosh apples and black walnuts for turkey stuffing for Thanksgiving dinner. The work involved in husking and shelling a bucket of black walnuts makes eternity seem short-lived, but the reward is in the flavor."

Here's the voice of Irene Giroir, a mother of six and a grandmother of 15 in Houma, Louisiana, telling how her son-in-law deep fries their Thanksgiving, Turkey. "My son-in-law he deep fries the turkey in a big deep pot in the backyard. He gets the grease good and hot and then it takes maybe 20 minutes for the whole turkey to cook. When you cook the whole thing the meat is moist and the skin as crispy as can be. When you drop the turkey in, it falls to the bottom, and when it starts to float, it's done."

The media and marketing voices of American cooking are noisy but they don't tell half of it, not even of the cooking of provincial New Jersey, where I have sampled native venison sausage and Concord grape pie and freshly smoked bluefish. In America, there are so many gustatory mouths, so many vernacular voices. "He that hath ears to hear, let him hear."

Radcliffe Quarterly, 1988

America the Bountiful

■

IF ANYONE ASKS me what's American about American cooking, I say, "Baked Alaska." The history, the name, the concept of baking a meringue-covered ball of ice cream is as American as Huck Finn. First, the dish was "invented" not by a cook, but by a scientist, born in Massachusetts in the 18th century and knighted in England as Count Rumford, whose experiments in thermodynamics included the discovery that egg whites resisted heat. Second, the dish was marketed by those clever Swiss immigrants in the 19th century who "invented" New York's first fancy French restaurant, Delmonico's. Exploiting America's guffaws when William Henry Seward purchased a frozen wasteland half the size of Europe, they called the dish, "Alaska-Florida." So the dish celebrates, in name and substance, America's crazy contradictions in geography, climate, places, and peoples with the gusto of a joke. America loves edible jokes. The tall-tale comedy of baking Alaska in an oven is like Paul Bunyan digging the Grand Canyon with his toothpick.

American cooking is like no other cooking because America is like no other land. A French person looks at American cooking and says there is no such thing because it is not French. A Chinese person looks at American cooking and chops it fine with a cleaver to make it Chinese. But their histories, structures, cultures and cuisines are not ours and not to be compared. No one anywhere is like us. We are the world's biggest polyglot conglomerate, an impossible folly, and we laugh at both our monstrous size and our monstrous mixtures. We are the land of Big Macs and Blue Sazeracs, Cajun Martinis and Chili Dogs, Crepes Suzettes *alla casa* and Chow Meins *du jour*. And why not? What better way to embody the hyperbole of a nation that, from Alaska to Florida and Hawaii to Maine, links glaciers to swamps, earthquakes to hurricanes, Eskimos to Creoles, Nisei to Tex-Mexicans? What better way than by the polyglot bounty we put on our plates?

For 400 years people have come to this hemisphere from the rest of the world to set up tent or shop because the riches of our land and seas were beyond belief. The earliest colonists to the shores dubbed New England complained that their ships were "pestered with cod." Explorers of Northwest shores were appalled at the prodigal Grease Feasts of native potlatchs spawned from a superabundance of fish oil. Nineteenth-century European tourists were alarmed not just by the abundance but by the size of American oysters. Said novelist Thackeray, "I felt as if I'd swallowed a baby."

After Columbus, the Americas served as supermarket to the world, supplying both natural and processed foods in unprecedented quantity, with the usual results. From the 18th century on, American depopulated its Floridian seas of turtles by supplying every royal banquet, and especially the annual Lord Mayor of London's Banquet, with green turtle soup. America depopulated its mighty rivers of sturgeon by supplying Europe as late as the turn of the century with 100,000 pounds of caviar annually.

Before Columbus, the abundance of fish, game, fruits, roots, vegetables, tubers, pulses and grains had nourished the building of civilized centers as ancient as those of Egypt and Babylon. In Mexico, Montezuma's corn sustained a population in the city of

Tenochtitlan of 300,000, five times larger than the population of London at that time, the time of Henry VIII. Even today such native cultures are hard for Americans to grasp because we like to think of civilization and its culinary arts as arriving in the wilderness with the arrival of our forebears, whenever they came, or with the arrival of ourselves.

But only in America do we separate Nature's bounty from man's art, identifying the former as indigenous and the latter as imported. It's an unnatural and irrational division, as our current bounty of cities, arts, markets, gardens, chefs and culinary styles attest. For four-and-a-half centuries post-Columbian America identified civilization with Europe. Only after World War II, when modern America began to catch up with its new global identity, has that definition changed and changed radically. As we enter a new century, America has stamped the rest of the world with our larger-than-life style and polyglot mix through American images on a screen, American sounds on a stereo, and American signature foods and drinks.

In every sense America is the king of pop; and while many deplore the culinary pop culture of Big Macs in Moscow and Cokes in Beijing, they are no more anomalous than pizzas in Peoria and sushi in Santa Fe. We're the land of the hybrid, as well as the land of the free, and in the last 40 years we've turned hybridization into high art. Look at the way we've melded pop high culture in painting, dance, music, theater, film. Now it's time for food. For the first time we have not one, but two generations of native-born and -trained American chefs, who are in the process of changing the food we put on our plates and the way we think and feel about it.

From America's rich assemblage of regions east, west, north, south and middle, we have for the first time a unique amalgam of American chefs with names as ethnically diverse as D'Amato, Del

Grande, Donier, Goldstein, Gross, Hamersley, Malgieri, Miller, O'Connell, Tropp, and Trotter, names that may suggest where their great-grandparents came from but that will tell you nothing of where they settled. But talk to any of them and they will tell you how much it matters where they are now. America is planting its own definitions of culinary regionalism, as young winemakers plant vineyards in the Hudson Valley, as cheese-makers herd goats in Vermont, as gardeners sow ancient strains of corn in New Mexico and seed kiwi in California.

American chefs are recreating America's culinary map the way television has recreated the nation's weather map. Every day our screens flash the dialogue between "the national picture" and "the weather where you are." We can see the way jet streams from Hawaii and cold fronts from Alaska shape the weather in New York. So too we can see the way culinary streams and fronts from all points of the compass shape the weather of particular chefs at specific points on the map, the weather where they are now. The interchange is constant and pervasive. When a Wolfgang Puck or a Jean-Louis Palladin lands in this country, with his *batterie de cuisine* intact, he is struck by a hailstorm of accents, a Brooklyn honk, a Texas twang, an Alabama drawl, but they're all part of the same map.

Our native-born chefs are right now in the process of creating a vocabulary of cooking that was once the exclusive patrimony of the French in Europe and the Chinese in Asia. Just as the American language is not, except to a Colonel Blimp, an inferior and vulgar dialect of British English, but rather an explosive and constantly changing language of its own, so America's culinary language is not a barbarous dialect of French cuisine but an innovative, fluid, imaginative, evolving language, composed of a hundred vernaculars charged with energy.

How could it be otherwise when America's structures are defined not by the conventions and hierarchies of classical European art but by the egalitarian mayhem of native jazz? Our regions are not French provinces or Italian duchies bounded for millennia by Paleolithic peaks and valleys. Our regions are defined by the traditions of nomads and Gypsies, 20 mule teams and Superchiefs, helicopters and superjets. We eat up space like bounty hunters, like video-game Pac-men. We are always on the move, back and forth across continents, up and down and across classes. Our generosity, our largesse, is legendary, but it goes with the territory, which is vast.

No wonder that when the American kitchen came of age, its icons would be a Bunyanesque pair born larger than life, both with global appetites befitting bodies over six feet tall. For four decades each helped create the climate that enables our new generations of cooks and eaters not only to thrive but to take pride and pleasure in the savoring of America with all our senses, minds and hearts. Appropriate to Americans, the world calls Julia Child, "Julia," and James Beard, "Jim." Like the dish once called "Alaska-Florida," "Julia-Jim" symbolizes the American bounty we celebrate at the 1994 James Beard Awards. Jim, and Julia, gave us a taste for, and now their inheritors are giving us a taste of, America on the plate. America the bountiful.

News from the Beard House, 1994

True Grits

∎

THEY SAY HOMINY'S back, but since many people today have never heard of it, who knew it was gone? Yet 100 years ago, from Portland, Maine to Portland, Oregon, hominy was a common word that Americans used to describe dried field corn that had been made fit to eat by removing its tough outer hide. And demand for it was so great that any city worth its salt had a hominy man, like the fish man or the ice man, who wandered the streets in a horse-drawn cart, selling hulled corn by the quart. In New Orleans, the locals called him the "grits man," and he sold both "big hominy" and "small hominy," which is to say, both whole kernel hominy and ground hominy, or grits.

Around this time, much of the country (except for Charleston, South Carolina, which decried the tautology) began to call grits "hominy grits." Charlestonians scorn what they call "bucket hominy," which was often made in a backyard bucket and was a staple of the poor during the Depression. When Charlestonians say "hominy," they mean freshly ground grits, to which both rich and poor are chauvinistically partial. And there's the rub. Today, most grits are no longer made from hominy at all, and while most people think they know what grits are, they're not so sure about hominy, however much the two words—and products—have recently begun to appear interchangeably on the menus of fashionable big city restaurants.

Today, grits means any coarsely ground (not hulled) corn, and many associate it with poverty food of the South—a blob of bland white tasteless pap that accompanies everything from biscuits and red-eye gravy to ham hocks and collard greens. Hold it, grits lovers! I, too, am fond of grits, but not the instant or quick gruel I'm usually served. Good grits, made from cornmeal with taste and texture, derived from artisanally grown and artisanally ground corn, are as rare as any other product that bravely flaunts its quality in a quantity-based world.

That's why the arrival of an heirloom corn product is making a big stir, as it should. The quality is in the corn's genes, which haven't been manipulated in a laboratory but have evolved in the field over centuries, selected by farmers who loved them for their character and flavor. Every variety of corn has its own flavor, and native Americans knew well how to breed selectively to intensify it. One of the most favored varieties among Northeastern groups was Iroquois hominy corn, described by British colonists as an eight-rowed, 14-inch cob, 1 ½ inches around, and creamy white in color. Today, professor-cum-farmer Dr. John Mohawk of the Seneca Turtle Clan and his wife, Yvonne Dion Buffalo, are working with Iroquois on the Cattaraugus Reservation near Buffalo, New York, to restore this endangered species. As vital as Dr. Mohawk's knowledge of traditional native farming is, his knowledge of history is greater; he serves as director of the Program in Indigenous Studies and co-directs the Center for the Americas at State University of New York at Buffalo.

To grow such corn the old-fashioned way is to take to the interstate in a horse and buggy rather than a Mercedes. This corn is handheld all the way. It's grown organically, and because it isn't bred to grow ears at a uniform height or at a uniform time for mechanical harvesting, it must be handpicked. It's also hand-husked, dried in corn cribs, and hand-shelled by the grower. The kernels are brought to the small cabin where Dr. Mohawk's parents once lived and are turned into three traditional native corn products: roasted corn flour, whole grain hominy, and tamal flour. The tamal flour, if it were ground into a coarse meal instead of a fine flour, would constitute old-fashioned grits.

The simplest preparation of the three, but the one with the most distinctive culinary effect from a chef's point of view, is to roast the corn meal or flour in a big iron pot over the stove. Just as with dried nuts or herbs, toasting or roasting releases oils and intensifies flavor. Roasted cornmeal smells and tastes earthy and enticing as roasted nuts. Since heat cooks the oil in the kernel's germ, roasting is also a good way to preserve the ground meal, as native Americans well knew when they used roasted cornmeal for their traveling, or "journeying," corn.

One sniff of an opened bag of Iroquois roasted corn flour tells you why Bobby Flay is now using it for his corn rolls and for dusting fish at Mesa Grill in Manhattan and why Michel Nischan of Heartbeat in the W New York hotel is using it to dust soft shell crabs. It's the cornmeal Kary Sparks shaped into johnnycakes topped with caviar and oyster seviche when she was at the recently closed Quilty's, that Charlie Trotter in his take-out venue Trotter's To Go in Chicago has turned into a dessert cake with organic cream icing, and that pastry chef Joseph Murphy, now at Blue Fin in Manhattan, put into Iroquois corn cakes with blueberries, nectarines, and toasted almonds when he was at Gotham Bar and Grill. With this meal, cookbook author Deborah Madison has devised a simple loaf cake, mixing corn and wheat flours with butter, sugar, eggs, yogurt, and pine nuts, to be served with fresh fruits. Kevin von Klause and Judy Wicks of the White Dog Cafe in Philadelphia construct savory corn cakes topped with smoked trout hash and toasted hazelnuts. Robert Stritzinger of the Corn Dance Café in Santa Fe features it as Iroquois roasted white cornbread sticks, flavored with fresh corn kernels and sweet and hot peppers. Also in Santa Fe, Napoleon Lopez of Cafe Pasqual prefers it for his sweet-and-savory tamales, the masa flavored with orange juice and maple syrup to enclose a *salsa rojo* of tomatoes and chiles d'arbol, bananas, fresh corn, cheese, and raisins, all of it wrapped in banana leaves. Dr. Mohawk himself enjoys it as polenta, or cornmeal mush, flavored with scallions, garlic, sweet and hot peppers, mushrooms, and oregano, with a toasted pumpkinseed/epazote sauce.

The second Iroquois product is whole hominy, in which kernels of the same dried variety as flint corn have their hulls removed by boiling them with slaked lime (limestone dissolved in water to make calcium hydroxide). The Iroquois, Algonquin, and other Woodland groups living in the forests of the Northeast used wood ash to create a similar alkali (potassium hydroxide) for the same end: to soften the skins so they could be rubbed off. Skilled basket weavers, the Iroquois developed sets of woven bark washing baskets, which they used as sieves in which to wash the hulls away in a stream. They also wove different grades of sifting baskets for pounded hominy, which then became grits.

The Iroquois used whole hominy in soups and stews with game, beans, squash, roots, and vegetables. Just as New England colonists co-opted the word hominy, from the Algonquin *rockahominie* (parched corn), to mean skinned corn, so they adapted succotash from the Narragansett *misickquatash* (corn ear) to mean corn stew. The first stews at Plymouth Plantation in Massachusetts were most likely close to the generic Iroquois soup/stew of hominy, beans, and wild game or fish, before evolving into a kind of New England boiled dinner of corned beef, fowl, potatoes, and white turnips, in addition to the nutritive hominy and beans.

Does this remind you of Southwestern posole? It should, because that splendid soup/stew, which long ago extended Mexico's cultural legacy north of the present border with the United States, takes its name from the Spanish word for whole hominy. To be accurate, posole is the "half-cooked hominy" (as Chicago restaurateur and Mexican food authority Rick Bayless calls it) that the Aztecs called *mixtamal*, and skinning corn was the first vital step in preparing staple bread dough (masa), whether for tortillas or tamales. The starchy large kernelled *maiz cacahuazintle* is the one favored in Mexico today, but many types of blue, red, purple, yellow, and white field corns are available in this country, usually from the Southwest, under posole labels.

As a dish, posole reflects a *criolla* mingling of Spanish pork, onions, garlic, and cabbage with Indian hominy and chiles. But using Northeastern Iroquois corn provokes one to rethink the flavors of hominy stew. While Bayless is using the Iroquois hominy for some of his Mexican dishes at Frontera Grill, Peter Hoffman at Savoy in New York City takes a more open-ended approach, mixing it with stewed diced carrots and tomatoes, shredded cabbage pickled with lime juice, and cilantro to serve as a bed for chile-rubbed grilled chicken. Leslie McEachern at Angelica's Home Kitchen in New York City serves up a vegetarian stew she calls "three sisters posole," adding to the hominy three kinds of beans plus winter squash, celery, carrots, turnips, herbs, jalapeños, and canned organic tomatoes. One of Dr. Mohawk's favorite stews is hominy with oyster mushrooms, flavored with root vegetables, basil, and parsley. In the Southwest, Joseph Wrede at Joseph's Table in Taos, New Mexico, has been experimenting with stuffing roasted quails with hominy and chipotles and serving them in a roasted lobster *crema*. Back north, in the fashionable Ilo in Manhattan, Rick Lankkonen is nesting jumbo quail on a bed of hominy.

When finely ground, hominy becomes masa, which, when dampened, turns into tamale dough. If the kernels are cooked longer and ground finer, the flour is used to make tortillas. Unless you're accustomed to working with wet Mexican doughs, however, the texture can be tricky, so it may be easier to use the third Iroquois product. This is tamal flour, in which the corn, once hulled, is dried again in food dehydrators and then milled into flour. Freshly ground tamal flour resembles the supermarket *masa harina* (hulled corn flour) the way a freshly baked focaccia resembles Wonder bread.

Like roasted corn flour, tamal flour has an intense flavor all its own, reflecting its lime processing, but it can be used interchangeably with the roasted flour. The one is nuttier, the other "cornier," but the beauty of either is that each is ground to order so that what you're tasting is the full flavor of fresh corn intensified by drying. Joe Realmuto of Nick & Toni's in East Hampton, New York, is using the tamal flour for tamales at La Fondita, his new Mexican restaurant in Amagansett. Susan Spicer of Bayona in New Orleans chooses it for her tamales of smoked Portobello mushrooms. Paul Wade of Montagna at The Little Nell in Aspen is turning it into lobster tamales with roasted tomatillos and crème fraîche as well as griddle cakes to accompany roasted Colorado lamb prime ribs. Mollie Katzen of Moosewood Restaurant in Ithaca, New York, prefers it for savory tamal griddle cakes with chipotle cream.

No matter how good the product, how can chefs be alerted to its existence, particularly if it begins on a small Indian reservation near Lake Erie? Nothing better demonstrates the need for organizations connecting farmers directly to chefs than the successful marketing of Iroquois corn by Bioneers and the Collective Heritage Institute, an environmental nonprofit group founded by Ken Ausubel (formerly head of Seeds of Change in Santa Fe). The institute has been working with Native Seeds/SEARCH in Tucson, Arizona, which the ethno-botanist Gary Nabhan was instrumental in starting more than a decade ago. If such groups ring enough bells, maybe restaurants like Manhattan's Clove will have to be more cautious in its menu language. Chef Rebecca Rubiel explains that the "hominy" on her menu is really soft grits, with kernels of sweet corn added. Why does she call it hominy? "My dad says he hates grits," she says, "but he loves hominy. People don't know what it is, so it adds an air of mystery."

That may be true for now, anyway. But who knows? Maybe we'll be buying quarts of fresh hominy soon from the hominy man.

Food Arts, 2002

When Corn Was King

■

The wind blows, The corn leans.

—CARL SANDBURG, "Ripe Corn"

IN JANUARY OF 1888 the wind blew the corn shocks flat in a blizzard that banked snow sixteen feet high across the prairies and left so much ice that six months later folks used it to freeze their ice cream on the Fourth of July. My grandfather in Edgerton, Kansas, scarcely noticed the wind that year or the blizzard because he was courting a school teacher from Bergholz, Ohio. He married her in May the year following, and in October, when the corn was in, the bridal couple took a trip up-river to Sioux City, Iowa, which had been spared the worst effects of the drought of 1887, the tornadoes of 1886, and the plagues of grasshoppers and locusts in the years before that. Mindful of the Bible and its stories, the fathers of Sioux City had thanked Providence in 1887 in a Grand Harvest Jubilee Festival by erecting the Eighth Wonder of the World, the world's first Palace of Corn.

Nearly a century later, in 1984, I stood on North Main Street in Mitchell, South Dakota, where the wind blows and the buildings lean, so that you wonder how anything upright could survive at all, let alone the World's Only Corn Palace. Mitchell is an hour's drive west of Sioux Falls across land so flat and bare that a shack is a relief to the eye. A Palace—of onion domes painted with buffaloes and

topped with flags, of turrets swathed in slough grass, of walls tapes-
tried in corncob mosaic—is clearly an illusion, if one did not know
that a Palace had been standing here since 1892. Some might call
it "vernacular architecture," but all I could think of was my grandfather building his first house of prairie sod in a land so hostile that
the United States Government had challenged homesteaders: "The
government bets you 160 acres of land against $18 [about 11¢ an
acre] that you will starve to death before you live on it five years."

The year my grandfather married, Kansas, Iowa, and Dakota were
still the West. Dakota was still a battleground between heathen and
Christian in a conflict that would not be settled until the Battle of
Wounded Knee in 1890. In Kansas and Iowa farmers were still mis-
sionaries preaching, like Henry Agard Wallace's grandfather, the
gospel of Calvin and corn according to the masthead of the magazine *Wallace's Farmer*, "Good Farming . . . Clean Living . . . Right
Thinking." Corn was the lifeline, the brick and mortar, the food and
wine of the New World. The Corn Mother for the heathen was Corn
King for the imperialists. And as the empire builders conquered the
plains with guns and ploughs and railroads in the second half of the
nineteenth century, corn became the foundation of prairie culture
as well as its commerce.

In the 1880s the corn boom was on, as the western edge of
the Corn Belt bulged with upstart cities and pushy railroads and
a booster press that proclaimed the glory of territories fighting to
become states, towns fighting to become cities, and cities fighting
to become capitals and county seats and railroad centers. In this
battle corn was a weapon, because corn meant not only grain but
pork, oil, starch, syrup, the beginnings of modern agribusiness.
Between 1840 and 1900 corn acreage increased tenfold to reach
one hundred million acres. Corn ears increased tenfold to become

giants a foot long, ten inches round, weighing two pounds each. This mightily expanding kingdom required an art and an architecture to symbolize its power. London had its Crystal Palace; St. Paul, Minnesota, its Ice Palace. Sioux City would have its Corn Palace. "St. Paul and Montreal can have their ice palaces, which melt at the first approach of spring," the Sioux City *Daily Journal* declared on August 21, 1887, "but Sioux City is going to build a palace of the product of the soil that is making it the greatest pork-packing center of the northwest."

The Festival committee commissioned an architect, E.W. Loft, to cover the county courthouse with a corncob pavilion, but the architect's plans, like the city, soon doubled to include the armory and the Goldie Roller Rink. Newspaper poets vied with Longfellow for the title of Corn Laureate. Longfellow, in *Haiwatha*, had celebrated the Ojibwa corn god, Mondamin:

> *All around the happy village*
> *Stood the maize fields, green and shining,*
> *Waved the green plumes of Mondamin.*

Now the Sioux City *Journal* took up the theme, if not the meter, in homelier Corn Poems:

> *The time is now at hand*
> *In this great and glowing land,*
> *Where side by side we stand,*
> *And clasp each other by the hand,*
> *and shout and sing*
> *CORN IS KING.*

In the spirit of Coleridge, the Kubla Khans of Sioux City dreamt of Moorish domes, arches, cupolas, pinnacles, and minarets linked by flying buttresses and banners. They thatched their turrets with corn blades and husks. They turned cob and kernel, grain and grass into "brick" and "tile" to cover the walls with allegorical friezes. "Along the upper line of the front ran a shiny border of oats," a reporter wrote, "interspersed with the dark seed of the sorghum plant and flaming red corn." The Ladies Decorative Association discovered in corn a native "medium of artistic expression." With only "an ear of corn, a handful of grasses, a bunch of weeds, a wisp of straw," the ladies created for the Palace interior a map of the United States in multicolored kernels, the state seal of Iowa in cattails, Miller's "Angelus" in corn mosaic, a wax Ceres robed in husks on a stairway of golden grain. The *New York Times* noted that everything in the Palace but the iron nails came from Iowa cornfields, "blended and arranged as to form magnificent specimens of rustic art."

Over the streets of the town, arches flamed with the colors of globes lit by gas jets. Two hundred Omaha, Sioux, and Winnebago Indians paraded in costume, and Cornelius Vanderbilt and Chauncey Depew arrived by special train in time for the corn dance in the armory.

The success of the first Palace led to four more Palaces of ever more elaborate décor, pageantry, and publicity. The 1890 Palace was a "Mohammedan mosque with Iowa trimming." The Ladies of the Lilac History Club created in corn a portrait of Dante and of Romeo and Juliet on a moonlit balcony. King Corn and his retinue mounted floats to display the history and triumph of corn. A Corn Palace Train traveled to Washington, D.C., to boost corn at the inauguration of Benjamin Harrison.

If the Palace of 1891 was the grandest, it was also the last. The Big Floyd River rose and wiped out both cornfield and boosters, but Sioux City's ill wind blew good to Mitchell, South Dakota. "Sioux City has abandoned her Corn Palace," a local merchant announced. "Why not build one here?" In 1892 Mitchell had three thousand people, seven churches, and three newspapers and was all of twelve years old. Mitchell, despite its youth, was battling Plankinton to become state capital, and in 1891 Plankinton had boosted itself with a Grain Palace. Louis Beckwith, a realtor, decided it was time for Mitchell to act: "We are a lot of Stroughton bottles [bumps on a log] to sit here doing nothing and let Plankinton establish its grain palace. We must have something that will be a booster for Mitchell." Within sixty days, the community had garnered $3,700 and built a palace, which opened on September 28, 1892, with a May Pole Dance of "sixteen of Mitchell's loveliest ladies" encircling Ceres, goddess of grain.

Ceres was not amused, however, for Mitchell lost its bid for state capital and even its Corn Palaces to a six-year drought. Iowa, meanwhile, renewed its supremacy in the kingdom of corn at the 1893 World's Columbian Exposition in Chicago, where Iowa's corn architecture dazzled the nation. A journalist was captivated by the Pompeiian style of spandrels "done in tessellated panels of many colored corns," a journalist explained, and by a frieze depicting a grape vine, "the leaves being made of corn shucks and the fruit of purple-colored popcorn."

At the Exposition, Iowa's Corn Palace was rivaled by Illinois's Corn Kitchen, presided over by the formidable Sarah T. Rorer of the Philadelphia Cooking School. Kansas made its bid for corn supremacy four years later, when Atchison staged its first Corn Carnival in 1897 and proclaimed, "King Corn is supreme." A brainchild of the editor of the Atchison *Globe*, E.W. Howe, the carnival was halfway between a county fair and a street fair and as close to an orgy as any Presbyterian had ever seen.

It was a Kansas Mardi Gras. King Corn led a procession of chariots and floats that included a monster ear of corn constructed from thirty-six bushels, weighing five thousand pounds, with windows cut in the sides from which fifty-six children peeped like John-a-dreams. Ladies and gentlemen fashioned corn costumes *cap à pied* of tassels and shredded husks. The "Corn Milliner of Kansas," Mrs. H.J. Cusack, sent a dainty corn bonnet to the wife of President William McKinley. Crowds roamed the streets buying bags of shelled corn from Mammies to hurl like confetti until "the streets became veritable mills for the grinding of the corn." Boys held red ears of corn above the heads of girls they wanted, and had license, to kiss. The Burlington Railroad boosted a corn erection four stories high for an age innocent of the phallic symbol.

Since Atchison was near Edgerton, I hope my grandfather took his two young sons one year to the Carnival, which lasted well into the next century. It lasted long enough, in fact, to be overtaken by a caricature of prairie boosterism in the Tall Tale postcards of 1905 to 1915. The surreal photomontages of Archer King of Table Rock, Nebraska, and of William Martin of Kansas City, Missouri, translated the spirit of the carnival and the tall tale into visual parody. Narrative jokesters told tales of the farmer who straddled a corn stalk to harvest it, but the stalk grew so high so fast that his friends had to feed him by shooting biscuits from a shotgun. Now visual jokesters showed photographs of a farmer sawing a single ear of corn into logs under the message, "The Way We Do It Here."

Perhaps Mitchell's Corn Palace survived the booster age because Mitchell had nothing else to boost. In 1904 the town hired John

Philip Sousa's band to play the week of their corn festival at the cost of $7,000 a day, but Sousa, seeing the size of the town, refused to leave the train until he was paid in cash. Perhaps tourists continued to flock to the Palace over the decades to hear Ernie Young's Gold Girls, the RKO Leahs, Jimmy Dorsey, Paul Whiteman, Harry James, Lawrence Welk, Guy Lombardo, Duke Ellington, The Three Stooges, Jack Benny, Pat Boone, Bob Hope, and Rich Little because there was no other Palace to go to.

Today the Palace is as anachronistic as a dinosaur bone. Five years ago an arsonist burnt the Palace to the ground, so its minarets are now made of fiberglass and its foundations of brick and concrete. But corn art is not dead in Mitchell, and Jim Sellars, who runs the Palace, explains its contemporary methods and craft. Although the four primary corn colors are still white and yellow dent, red Indian, and Bloody Butcher flint, farmers today crossbreed corn to produce hues of pink, orange, calico, brown, green, smoky gray, and black. The corn must be picked at the right point of moisture and the cobs cut to the right thickness so they won't curl but will become more solid as they dry. "If they're cut right, the kernels won't blow out even in a high wind," Jim says, "and in Mitchell the wind blows quite hard."

Birds and squirrels "erode" the panels of the outside walls, which are renewed yearly from the designed projected onto tar paper, nailed on panels of wood, and numbered by color for corn. Kids "erode" the panels inside in the excitement of the basketball tournaments that occupy the auditorium between corn festivals. For twenty-five years, Dakota's foremost Indian painter, Oscar Howe, designed the panels inside and out according to the year's theme—Allied Victory, Pilgrim Days, Relaxin' in South Dakota, 75 Years of Mitchell Progress. Today the Palace consumes one hundred thousand cobs a year and two thousand bushels of sorghum, Murdock, buffalo grass, broom grass, milo, sudan grass, slough grass, and "just plain weeds" to link America's empire of corn to corn empires of the past.

Mitchell is on the site of an eleventh-century Sioux village that was part of an ancient civilization of corn. My grandfather would have thundered had anyone said that the Mitchell ladies of the May Pole were sisters of those Aztec maids who loosened their hair, like corn silk, to dance to the corn goddess, Xilomen. My grandfather would have also roared had anyone said that the chosen Aztec maiden lay as willingly on the sacrificial altar of Xilomen as Isaac under the knife of Abraham. He would have taken a razor strop to anyone who suggested that the Aztec harvest feast of corn and chopped human meat bore some resemblance to the Presbyterian Communion feast long ago bowdlerized on the prairies into grape juice and small cubes of white bread.

For my grandfather, history was Biblical history, and he saw America's kingdom of corn not in terms of New World savages but of Old World Israelites. When my grandfather finally escaped the winds, blizzards, droughts, tornadoes, and locust plagues of the prairies by pushing west to California, he took his history with him to tell his grandchildren tall tales of Indians, houses of sod, and palaces of corn. He told them in the style of "O Mitchell of the Palace grand, Shall I relate thy story?" But he would have understood an ancient proverb of the Sioux, "A people without history is like wind on the buffalo grass."

Journal of Gastronomy, 1985

Corn Porn

■

YOU THINK CHILE'S hot? You think chocolate's sexy? Forget it. The true blue porn food, as American as aphrodisiasts have always known, is corn. "People have tried and they have tried," says Garrison Keillor, "but sex is not better than sweet corn."

But it's not just that slaveringly sweet and milky kernel-by-kernel crunch up and down the juicy sweet corn cob, back and forth and around and around, masticating with your whole mouth, lips, teeth, gums and tongue; nibbling, scrunching, licking and sucking. No. It's the nature of the plant itself, and not just sweet corn but any old kind of corn. Corn was born for sex.

Look at it botanically. Like us, corn divides sex into male and female, separate and distinct. Vain-glorious male tassel on top, showing off its multiple pollen-laden anthers. Modest female ear below, emerging shyly from the leaf sheath at the node of the stalk, hiding its ovarian womb within a tight cocoon until puberty, when each embryonic kernel sends forth a strand of silk that bursts through the green cocoon's tip in a dazzlement of long silky pubic hair.

In sex timing is everything. The male tassel must hold its load of fertilizing pollen until the female silks have reached their maximum extension. Then . . . then . . . then all at once, the tassels ejaculate clouds of sperm (14 to 19 million pollen grains per plant)! Since only one grain per kernel is all that is needed (figure

400 to 800 kernels per cob), what could possibly motivate this egregiously wasteful expenditure other than the altogether human need for sexual excess? Corn mating is over within 24 hours, time enough for each silk to embrace a dot of pollen dust, which slides down the silk like an oiled toboggan to fertilize the waiting virgin sac within the cob.

How corn got this way remains a mystery. Attempts to solve the mystery generated the Great Corn War of a few decades ago when geneticists had at each other with staves and stalks. One botanist explorer devised the Catastrophic Sexual Transmutation Theory, better known as CSTT, to show how a cousin of corn that was still growing in the wild—perennial teosinte—suffered a radical sex change millennia ago. According to CSTT, a sudden evolutionary leap caused the male tassel spike of teosinte to transmute into a female ear of corn. Other theories suggested that the process occurred through a gradual transformation of hard spike into soft cob without a sex change but by selective breeding. Passions over this matter still run high. Says one geneticist of the inventor of CSTT, "He's the catastrophe."

Sex matters to corn more than to most plants because corn is given, as one of our puritan forefathers put it after intense scrutiny in his garden, to "wonderful copulation." Corn will screw anything that moves, if it looks like corn. Because of its "jumping genes"— and that's the discovery that won Barbara McClintock a Nobel Prize in her 81st year after six decades of scorn from her male peers— corn hybridizes like crazy. Put a red corn plant next to a white one and you'll get mixed eats of pink, white and red. Cross-pollination say botanists. Promiscuity, the Puritans denounced.

But hot-headed modern scientists are only the most recent of corn's ancient line of pornographers. Since man first helped to create corn in Mesoamerica some 5,000 years ago, the domesticators have served as both pimps and midwives. Pimps because they create new varieties by putting breeders in the same bed. Midwives because corn as we know it is a "botanical monstrosity." It has so many kernels compacted on the same cob that, unless seedlings are transplanted, they crowd each other out and die. This is a grain that, unlike wheat or rice, must be planted kernel by kernel. This is a vegetable that, until after World War II, had to be harvested ear by ear. The horny hand of man guaranteed that the relation of corn to grower has remained intensely intimate.

The Olmec, the Maya, the Toltec, the Aztec had no trouble figuring this out. Corn, or maize as the Arawak Indians called it in the Caribbean isles that Columbus stumbled on, was the major sex symbol of the Western Hemisphere. The resemblance to human sex parts were obvious and created a world of visual and verbal puns. The Chimu in Peru (think sixth to seventh century AD) made clay pots that looked like corn cobs that looked like penises. They painted pots with indented corn kernels that looked like vaginas. They painted couples copulating in the non-missionary position with stylized penile parts interchangeable with stylized corn cobs. They made Popeye a few centuries later in William Faulkner's *Sanctuary* look like a hillbilly piker.

All the native major civilizations of the New World grew up on corn. It was both food and drink, depending on how finely it was ground, how much water was added and how much it was toasted or otherwise cooked. They almost always cooked dried corn first with lime in order to remove the hard skins from the kernels and make them easier to grind, When they ground and toasted their kernels three times round, travelers carried the powder in a little bag, like trail mix, for instant food and drink.

They added finely ground corn to all their nonalcoholic drinks, like foaming chocolate deliciously flavored with chili. And to their alcoholic brews, like *balche* (made, like mead, with fermented honey), *pulque* (made with fermented agave juice) and *mescal* (the ancestor of tequila).

Besides all their usual corn mushes and breads, they also fermented corn to make a kind of sourdough bread and they fermented corn to make beer. Fresh corn beer, called *chicha*, is still the drink of choice in Peru, and if you're lucky enough to get to Cuzco when *Inti Raymi* (summer solstice) is celebrated, you can spend an altitude-elevated week bombed on *chicha* with all the rest of the inhabitants, for whom this annual *chicha* fest is a moral and religious duty.

Corn was not just the life blood of these ancient communities, corn was the symbolic blood of the whole bloody universe. In Maya myths of origin, man and his gods were fashioned out of corn dough and their veins ran with a kind of liquid gruel of white corn called *saka*, as well as with blood. The Olmec were letting blood sacrificially, with sharp corn-shaped obsidian perforators, from royal penises over two thousands years ago. The Maya let the blood of their rulers (both from carefully cut penises and tongues) to feed the World Tree of the Cosmos, the sap of which was blood and *saka*, the tree itself imaged as a colossal corn plant with its roots in the primordial sea of Water Lily Monster and its top surmounted by Sky Serpent. The Aztec carved out living hearts from their human sacrifices, organized on a scale that many more recent war mongers might envy, and offered them to their Warrior-Sun god to guarantee the life of their commune. They called such rituals "husking" or "harvesting" the heart.

The logic is irrefutable. In an agricultural commune, you can see everyday that life feeds on life, that death breeds life and that sex also breeds death. It's easy enough for corn to become a symbol of all three transformative moments: birth, copulation and death, as T.S. Eliot put it. The Aztec at their annual Midsummer Corn Festival in honor of *Xilonen*, goddess of young nubile corn, went mad for a month of singing and dancing and general screwing around until it was time to lead the pretty girl who'd been chosen to represent the goddess that year, up the pyramidal steps of the altar and to lay her head on the calendar stone. The blood from her severed head was sprinkled ritually on little blobs of corn dough that everyone ate, and her torso was flayed so that the dancer representing Xipe Totec, god of renewal, could wear her skin inside out and dance up a storm to the general jubilation of all. Hollywood hasn't even gotten close to this kind of porn.

So the next time you're cruising by a Mexican restaurant and wondering whether to tank up on some tacos and tamales and a batch of nachos and maybe some enchiladas and certainly all the *cerveza* you can drink, go to it feeling sexy. You can even do it alone. It's as good as safe sex and it's certainly the cheapest porn show in town.

Au Jus, 1997

The Cowboy and the Machine

I DIDN'T GROW up eating beefsteak. I was a child of the Depression, and our fancy meat for Sunday-noon dinner was boiled chicken or boiled beef tongue, or else a shoulder of lamb, boiled until cuttable with a spoon. Steak was a luxury for the rich, and when I ate my first steak at seventeen, in the company of college chums fed up with our dorm swill, I didn't know how to cut it. I'd never before had to eat meat with a knife in order to get a bite-size piece. Nor did I know how to chew it. The meat we cooked at home, including the rare holiday treat of Swiss steak in the pressure cooker, was designed to give way at the first touch of my grandparents' dentures. My family were enthusiastic proponents of the Puritan principle that all food aspired to liquid, so that you could flush it out of your body as rapidly as possible. Maybe this was just an elaborate rationalization for not being able to afford steak.

I did grow up American, however, in a small town in Southern California, shaped by two kinds of stories, one Spanish and the other British.

It was the same hybrid, I would discover, that had produced, over the course of five hundred years, American beefsteak. Bred from both Spanish and British traditions, as well as from both Spanish and British cattle breeds, American beefsteak is more characteristic of our hybrid national identity than apple pie (which came from the English), popcorn (from the Native Americans), or the hamburger (German). True, every country has its beef, branded with chauvinism. England has its bully roast beef, evoking not only the coziness of hearth and home, but also "the marrow of political freedom," as historian Simon Schama would have it, whereby the Society of Beefeaters proclaimed that "Beef and Liberty" would vanquish the effeminate French. France, in turn, has its *entrecôte et frites*, typifying in its full-bloodedness, as literary theorist Roland Barthes would have it, "the very flesh of the French soldier." Argentina has its *parrillada*, evoking the fierce independence of the gauchos on the vast and lawless pampas. Japan has its soft-as-butter Kobe, treated as a work of art by aesthetic islanders devoted to the refinements of umami.

We Americans have a very different take on steak, because we have a very different history. The destiny of American beef was shaped by the 100th meridian, which in the nineteenth century came to represent the divide between the wet East and the dry West, just as the Mississippi River had earlier represented the divide between British-colonized territory and Spanish territory. But our minds and imaginations shape geographical facts, and our differing expectations create different landscapes.

What my British ancestors saw when they imagined the West was a larger England, with forests and meadows just like those of the eastern seaboard Colonies. What the Spanish saw was a larger Spain, with desert highlands and mountains like those of Mexico. I'm sure that all a British yeoman wanted was a cottage for his family and just enough land to plow, while all a Spanish herdsman wanted was a nice hacienda with peons serving the *patrón*. While Britishers looked forward to the egalitarianism of a new world founded on Reason, Spaniards looked back to the feudalism of an old world serving God, pope, and king. One vision was utopian and utilitarian, the other monarchic and nostalgic.

And so the crazy mixed-up iconography that shaped me was the result not just of one collective fantasy but a pair of conflicting fantasies, with a push-pull as permanent as taffy. What child of the twentieth century did not grow up worshiping cowboys? Yet the cowboy himself is a hybrid. We got our mythic Western cowboy from Spain, a man on a horse herding cattle; but he's got the moral stance of a Britisher, a man who does what's right. This mixed-breed loner is both an underdog fighting for the common man and nature's nobleman, superior to others, a knight in chaps. But the beauty of icons is that they get to have it both ways, which is how they ride out the contradictions of history. The historical cattle drives lasted a mere twenty years in the second half of the nineteenth century, but that was long enough to fix the iconography of the cowboy as a peculiarly American fantasy of power that clothes violence in virtue.

In fact, even when actual cowboys were herding cattle from Mexico to Wyoming, it wasn't they who controlled the destiny of the herds. It was the barons back East who owned the cattle, the railroads, the markets, and most of the land. If the cowboy's weapon was a gun, the Technocrat's was the steam engine. The Iron Horse was another icon of power fueling our romance with the Machine, which has been every bit as vital to the raising of American beefsteak as the cowboy's lariat and saddle. We try to keep these myths, separate but equal, running on parallel tracks that double the great disconnect between pasture and plate. But they belong together, as our very first cowboy motion picture showed in 1903, when "Broncho Billy" Anderson shot up the screen in *The Great Train Robbery*, while Edwin S. Porter cranked the camera.

One of the reasons steak is the most American of our dishes is that, in addition to being fast, steak is classy. It's an icon of something "special," whether a backyard barbecue or a night out on the town. It's part of our democratic code that everyone shall win and all shall have prizes. Steak is one of those prizes.

Steak is its own category, the pinnacle of the American food chain. Last year, a research team claimed that steak eaten "as is" was the single most popular beef dish in America. "As is" presumably means unprocessed, untreated, unflavored, unmarinated, un "value-added"—the red muscle and bone thing in itself—sold in single packs labeled rib eye, sirloin, tenderloin or filet mignon, porterhouse, T-bone, and strip steak, ready to be unwrapped and thrown on "the barby." Significantly, low-income consumers ate steak nearly as often as high-income consumers and ate more beef of all kinds than high-income ones did. The high price of steak is one reason the U.S. beef market is the largest revenue generator in our entire agricultural industry ($49 billion in 2005). The average consumption per person of all cuts of beef in 2005 was 66.1 pounds, second only to chicken, at 84.3 pounds per person. A beefsteak, however, may cost eight times as much as chicken, so if price is not the major determinant, what is?

Not surprisingly, one answer is gender. Steak is not only guy food, but he-man food. I remember World War II as a time when we civilians ate no red meat because it all went to our fighting boys, to whom the U.S. Army issued nearly half a pound of animal protein each day. Russell Baker has described this as "beef madness . . . when richly fatted beef was force-fed into every putative American warrior;" but beef was less fatted then than now, and our warriors were delighted to be fed any meat that wasn't Spam. But while few American men nowadays get to be warriors, despite the number of wars around the globe, they still eat the lion's share of the beef. In 2005 men aged 20 to 39 ate the most beef and the most steak, a substantial 86 pounds of beef per person, and out of that, nearly 25 pounds of steak. Women of the same age group ate about 52 pounds of beef, of which only 11 pounds was steak. "The more men sit at their desks all day," the nutritionist Jean Mayer points out, "the more they want to be reassured about their maleness by eating those large slabs of bleeding meat which are the last symbol of machismo."

Our word "steak" evolved from *stik*, Old Norse for stick, and for meat stuck on a stick, *steik*, which is as close to caveman cooking as you can get. A steak means No Pot Needed, only fire. That keeps steak masculine, at home on the open range, not the cast-iron one indoors. Consequently, steak is not about recipes but about hunting, hunting down that really good piece of cow, whether by mail or greenmarket or supermarket or one of the few remaining butcher shops or, if you're lucky, from a friend who raises his own.

Of course there's also a strong indoor steak tradition. Perhaps the definitive steakhouse—at least for New Yorkers—is Peter Luger's in Williamsburg, Brooklyn. When you enter Peter Luger's, you walk into a bar—a long wooden bar under bare wooden beams next to a room with bare wooden tables and bench booths and brass chandeliers. You don't ask for a glass of house red or a wine list. You ask for a martini straight up. Or beer—pint or pitcher. The ceilings are tin, the floors strewn with sawdust. You don't ask for a menu, and you don't expect the waiter to introduce himself by name and tell you his life story. The waiters have been here for decades and scorn such guff. The entire ritual was set a century before you walked in the door. Men in shirtsleeves, women in housedresses, huge families packed with fat kids yelling loudly as they tuck in. You relax. You feel good, privileged, king of the fort. Everything is big: the chewy onion rolls, the thick-sliced tomatoes and onions in the salad slathered with Luger's special steak sauce, the 1 3/4-inch porterhouse sliced and sizzling on a platter so hot it can cook, the sides of German fried potatoes and creamed spinach, the bowl of whipped cream next to the apple strudel or chocolate mousse or pecan pie. You are in for a Big Evening and you pay in cash.

Joseph Mitchell in the 1939 *New Yorker* piece "All You Can Hold for Five Bucks" recounted a typical Peter Luger's conversation: "At a table near the kitchen door I heard a woman say to another, 'Here, don't be bashful. Have a steak.' 'I just et six,' her friend replied. The first woman said, 'Wasn't you hungry? Why, you eat like a bird.' Then they threw their heads back and laughed." One 2007 blogger just didn't get it. "The place is a barn," she wrote, complaining about the poor wine list, the lack of menu, the arrogant waiters. "I prefer a finer atmosphere." The American steakhouse was born for no other reason than to give "finer atmosphere" the finger.

As a Westerner who'd gone east, I was still and forever caught up in the romance of beef. I felt that when I ate steak, I was sinking my teeth into the myth of the Frontier—the Marlboro cowboy busting his bronc, the cast-iron skillet on an open fire, the smell of tobacco and burnt coffee, a soft neigh or two from a tethered horse, the clank of a metal spur, the wheeze of a harmonica, a black sky full of stars. Mine was part of the national imagination, suckled on thousands of Western novels and movies, serenaded by millions of country-western songs, clad by the fashioners of boots and jeans, ritualized in rodeos, pastoralized in dude ranches, and nourished by billions of pounds of American steak. Americans, I decided, eat steak more lustily than pot roast because steak is fast, mobile, improvised, casual, egalitarian, reliable, raw, bloody, and violent—and it tastes best outdoors.

It represents both freedom and independence, and the camaraderie of campfires. It's the closest we can get to yoking the raw and the cooked, the savage and the civilized. It invokes "Home on the Range" with a pang of longing far closer to the national heart than "The Star Spangled Banner." It goes with beer or wine, bourbon or tequila, and (God help us) Coke or iced tea. If it's pricey, it's also good value, because all that protein sticks to the bones. Muscle builds muscle, blood feeds blood. Steak denies our faith in evolutionary progress and returns us to our dark and dirty primordial roots. Let the ascetic and self-righteous weep for the lobster and the clam, ignoring the rape of beets and berries. Like a movie Western, steak ritualizes our appetite for violence and purges us of its need. Let the never-too-thin or too-rich of Eastern cities devour limp fish and vacuous chicken, white and bloodless as paper. Real American men, women, and children eat steak because it is red with blood, blood that pumps flavor, iron, vitality, and sex into flaccid bodies. For women, steak is better than spinach. For men, it's better than Viagra. With steak, it's easy to get carried away.

Meatpaper, 2012

Hamburgers

■

THE NOSTALGIA OF Americans abroad for their national dish is inexplicable to the non-American unless he recalls with Mark Twain the exiled Scot who yearns for his haggis and the Fijian for his missionary. What the GIs away from home sigh for and their children cry for is the first bite into a rich, juicy, tender hunk of beef bulging in a crusty fresh roll, accented by a crisp lettuce leaf, a thin slice of onion, and perhaps a slice or two of sour pickle and ripe tomato. And please, no smothering under soggy fried onions or drowning in ketchup.

In America the hamburger's popularity is not difficult to explain. Its origin is. Like many an American tycoon, the hamburger got its start as a poor immigrant in the New World. Its birthplace, however, remains obscure. Residents of Hamburg disavow any kinship between the American hamburger and their *Deutsches Beefsteak*, a ground-beef patty mixed with onions and cooked in gravy. How then are we to explain the name? One unlikely theory suggests that "hamburger" came to the German port in the late 19th century in the form of steak tartare, when trade with the Russian Baltic provinces was heavy. But I suspect that Russian Tartars would as quickly disavow steak tartare as Hamburgers hamburger.

Whatever its background, a grilled meat patty on a bun most probably originated in the New York delicatessens and short-order restaurants created by the mass of German immigrants in the mid-19th century. The food served was cheap. At Blake's Doughnut Parlor at the turn of the century you could buy two hamburgers with All-U-Kan-Drink Coffee for five cents.

And so was born the hamburger joint. But hamburger could not abound without refrigeration for the transport and storage of meat. And for that we must thank an industrious German, Gustavus Franklin Swift. By his invention of the refrigerator railroad-car in the 1870s, Swift was the first man to ship dressed beef from midwestern Chicago to New York.

As the popularity of the hamburger spread, England contributed her bit in the hamburger's rise from raffishness to respectability. J. H. Salisbury, the 19th-century English dietitian, earned the gratitude of grease-joint owners everywhere by enabling them to call their greasy "prole" patties "Salisbury Steaks." Salisbury had incautiously recommended ground-beef patties thrice daily, "for the relief of colitis, pernicious anaemia, asthma, bronchitis, rheumatism, tuberculosis, gout, and hardening of the arteries."

Today highways from Connecticut to California cut like rivers between banks of roadside hamburger stands owned by vast businesses. Such is the Burger Chef System or McDonald's, whose neon signs proclaim the three-billionth McDonald hamburger sold to date.

Not unnaturally California is the place where the hamburger reaches its apotheosis. Here the Self-Realization Fellowship, a vegetarian sect, has created for its worshippers the Nutburger. Here for a car cult whose places of worship are drive-ins and whose drive-ins are places of worship, Bob's Big Boy Drive-in, California's largest chain, has provided a hamburger pantheon: the Mummyburger (peanut butter, guava jelly, spinach or lettuce leaf), the Aloha (pineapple ring, green pepper, and onion in sweet-sour sauce), the New

Delhi (shredded cabbage, banana slices, mango chutney), the Parthenon (feta cheese, red onion, red pepper, radish, celery, mint), the Frenchburger (caviar, cucumber, watercress, mustard), and the Flipsvilleburger (chocolate or vanilla ice cream, chocolate sauce, toasted almonds).

While some palates may boggle at this sort of rococo exuberance, it is clear that even the unadorned hamburger should not be thought of as a cheap meat dish. Rather, it is an easy-to-chew steak. The meat must be of good quality, freshly ground, and with no more than 25 percent fat to 75 percent lean. Americans tend to err on the safe side by using a cut such as topside from the chuck, because its slightly higher ratio of fat to lean provides a juicier texture and beefier taste. Other good cuts for ground beef are from the shoulder and the bottom of the round.

Since bacteria grow quickly in ground meat, the quicker the trip from the butcher to pan the better (no more than one day stop in the fridge). Never freeze ground meat, or you'll lose the juice when it thaws.

Like steak, a hamburger tastes best when crusty on the outside and rare within. To achieve this, the patties should be made from at least 4 ounces of meat and should be shaped about 1 ½ inches thick. Brush with a little oil or butter and grill with a flame hot enough to sear but not to burn. Add salt and pepper after initial searing. Handle the meat as little as possible or you'll destroy texture, and— above all—don't overcook.

If you plan to serve hamburgers in a sauce, it is well to sauté the patties in butter in a frying pan in order to catch any meat juices for the sauce. The fat-free dieter can fry the patties in a little salt sprinkled over the bottom of a very hot frying pan, but since salt draws out juice, some flavor will be lost.

Hamburger on a bun

The roll functions as a kind of edible napkin to keep one's fingers clean while devouring the meat. Consequently, you should use a soft roll no more than an inch or so thick and about 4 inches in diameter. When you taste more bread than meat, the hamburger is a dreary affair.

As for garnishes, it's hard to go wrong as long as you stick to flavors traditionally complementary to beef. This modest caveat would prevent such desperate novelties as Fanny Farmer's Hamburgers with Corn Flakes. On the other hand, the use of fresh vegetables—lettuce, onion, tomato (sometimes green pepper or avocado pear)—produces the pleasant effect of steak-and-salad. In fact, I like to toss the salad vegetables I'm using in a vinaigrette dressing for the sake of the lemon and oil taste with the meat and bread. You could use instead mustard or mayonnaise or sweet piccalilli or slices of Jewish sour pickles.

The major variation is the Cheeseburger: Grill patties on one side, turn, and cover with a slice of sharp cheddar cheese, or Swiss or American. You need a cheese with good flavor and one that melts well. Cover the cheese with the toasted top of the bun until the cheese melts and the underside of the patty is cooked.

To secure sandwiches more tidily than these, where a hearty bite may cause pickle or mayonnaise ejection, you can put appropriate garnishes between two *thin* uncooked patties, press their edges together, and grill as usual. Good combinations here are grated sharp cheese and mustard, or crumbled Stilton or Roquefort softened with a little butter, or a slice of mozzarella sprinkled with oregano and basil.

Another device is to mix your seasonings into the whole patty before cooking. You can use any combination of grated cheese, minced garlic or shallots, Worcestershire sauce, mustard, or Tabasco.

Or you can concentrate on herbs. I like especially to mix into the meat a lump of softened herb butter (chives, tarragon, thyme, basil, or chervil are good).

HAMBURGER WITH CHILI

A traditional combination for American frontier appetites is hamburger with Mexican chili sauce (very, very hot) or with Texan chili beans. The Mexican sauce is available in cans, but Texan chili should be made fresh. You can either mix the ground beef into the chili mixture or cook as usual and pour the chili over.

INGREDIENTS:

2 lbs ground beef

SAUCE:

2 cups cooked red kidney or pinto beans
3 large chopped onions
2 cloves minced garlic
3 tablespoons olive oil or 1 oz beef fat
1 ½ lbs fresh tomatoes (preferably Italian plum)
3 tablespoons chili powder or a minced fresh chili pod
1 teaspoon cumin
1 teaspoon oregano
Salt and pepper
Pinch of cayenne pepper

Soak ½ lb dried beans overnight, drain, add fresh water to 1 inch above the beans, bring to boil, and simmer about 2 hours. (The beans will be more flavorful if you add a slice of bacon cut in small pieces fried with a chopped onion and minced garlic clove.)

To prepare the sauce, wilt onions and garlic in oil or fat. If you wish to mix the meat in with the sauce, brown *lightly* in the same frying pan. Add seasonings and chopped tomatoes. Cook 1½ hours, adding a little beef stock if necessary. Add beans, bring to simmer, remove from heat, and let mixture sit for three or four hours. Since chili is better each time it's reheated, it can be prepared a day or two in advance.

If you wish to serve the sauce with hamburger patties, grill as usual, reheat chili and pour on top.

HAMBURGER AU POIVRE

If you look to France rather than the Frontier for culinary in-spiration, you'll find hamburger as adaptable as steak to such classic French sauces as Béarnaise, Diable, Madère. One of the best dishes I ever had was hamburger au poivre, served by a hostess in no way penurious who prefers to use ground meat rather than steak in this dish because ground beef better ab-sorbs the pepper and Cognac.

INGREDIENTS:
  2 lbs ground beef
  1 to 2 tablespoons peppercorns

SAUCE:
  2 tablespoons minced shallots
  4 oz beef stock
  3 oz Cognac
  2 oz butter

Form meat into four patties. Crush peppercorns, sprinkle onto both sides of each patty, and press them well into the meat. Grill or sauté meat as usual. For the sauce, sauté shallots gently in 1 tablespoon butter, pour in stock, and boil down rapidly. Add Cognac and continue to boil until liquid is reduced to 4 oz. Add remaining butter and pour over patties.

BITOK À LA RUSSE

Another good combination of flavors involves scallions, beef, and cream—similar to Beef Stroganoff.

INGREDIENTS:

2 lbs ground beef

4 tablespoons scallions or green onions

2 oz butter

SAUCE:

8 oz double cream

2 oz beef stock

¼ teaspoon ground nutmeg

Salt

Pepper

Sauté scallions lightly in 1 tablespoon of butter. Add to meat and shape into six to eight patties. Flour patties and sauté in remaining butter. Remove patties and keep warm. To the pan add cream, stock, nutmeg (salt and pepper to taste), bring to simmer, pour over meat.

Wine & Food, 1969

All About Oysters

■

"OYSTER LOVE KNOWS no bounds," says Denis Corridan of the Long Island Oyster Farms in Greenport. "People who love oysters would eat 'em if there was arsenic in 'em or part of an old boot." Oyster farms like his, of course, go to great lengths to keep their oysters free of such pollutants, nurturing the little "seedlings" in an indoor nursery, selecting the best for sea-beds vacuumed and monitored by scuba divers, plumping up their growing girls with the care once lavished on the geishas of Japan. The result is the cultivated oyster, a triumph of art over nature, designed to satiate the world's unending oyster lust.

Oyster cultivation is as old as the world's oldest profession, dating back to ancient China, Greece and Rome. But in America, large-scale oyster farming is as recent as the 1970s. Blessed with the largest oyster beds in the world, which line estuaries and bays from New Brunswick to the Gulf of Mexico in the south, Americans until this century have regarded the oyster as a wild child of the wilderness, free for the taking. Indians had been eating oysters on Atlantic shores for 10,000 years when Captain John Smith landed in Virginia to find "savages . . . roasting oysters in the half shell." These oysters were a different species from the ones colonists had eaten in Europe, the small flat *Ostrea edulis*. These were rough giants and were so named, *Crasostrea virginica*. While many found their size repellent, Thackeray, on eating his first American oyster, found himself "profoundly grateful . . . as if I had swallowed a small baby."

A century ago, oyster madness overtook America at the same rate transport overtook the land. In 1859 the mid-Atlantic and Chesapeake oyster beds alone produced 145,000,000 pounds of oyster meat, and Americans gobbled it up at the rate of 6 pounds/6 ounces per person. Those were the days when New York was jammed with oyster hawkers, oyster stalls and oyster houses advertising, "All the oysters you can eat for six cents." Before the refrigerated railroad car, oyster express wagons sped barreled oysters from Bivalve, New Jersey to Chicago and from Puget Sound to Sacramento. Housewives could afford to follow Miss Eliza Leslie's instruction in *Directions for Cookery* (1831) to, "Take a hundred and fifty fine large oysters . . ." Those were the days when Maryland formed an "Oyster Navy" to patrol the waters and shoot oyster pirates on sight.

Since the end of the century, however, our oyster production has declined at the rate of 4 to 6 percent a year while oyster lovers continue to increase. Although America is still the largest oyster producer, totaling 48,270,000 pounds of meat in 1984, we are also the largest oyster consumer, eating that same year 84,373,000 pounds. We make up the difference by imports, mostly canned and smoked oysters, from Korea and Japan. If production is down, dollar value is up, by 13.5 percent in 1984, totaling 80,000,000 for a crop that was 2,000,000 pounds less but cost $13,000,000 more than the year before. Harvesters do not benefit, however, from the increase. According to Carey Muse of Maryland's Mid-Atlantic Fisheries, oyster harvesters get about the same price today for a bushel of unshucked oysters than they got 15 years ago ($8 to $14 a bushel). That's one reason the old-time tongers are disappearing as fast as the once wild oysters of our natural beds.

Gone forever are the six-inch Lynnhavens of Chesapeake, the Bon Secours of Mobile, the Galvestons of Texas. Dozens more are endangered—the Olympia of Washington, the Girdle Tree of Maryland, the Peconic Bay of New York, the Pocomoke and Rappahanock of Virginia, the "coon" oyster of Florida's mangrove swamps. Overharvesting, chemical and thermal pollution, natural disasters and the oyster's natural enemies have all taken their toll. A parasitic disease, MSX, destroyed 90 percent of Delaware's beds in the late 1950s, a starfish invasion attacked Long Island and Cape Cod oysters in the 1960s, and last year three hurricanes ravaged Florida while crabs invaded Maine. Chronically, the oyster is victim to the slipper limpet, the cownosed sting ray, the boring sponge, the whelk-tingle, and the oyster drill, which bores a hole with its saw-toothed tongue and sucks out meat, as Euell Gibbons says, like soda through a straw. Less elegantly, the starfish pries the shell open with its suction-cupped arms, inserts its stomach and swallows the oyster whole.

The answer to America's oyster decline is the kind of oyster farming Europe has known since Aristotle and Lucullus. Aristotle reported that fishermen at Rhodes were wont to throw potsherds into the bays to provide housing for oyster "spat." He also found fishermen at Lesbos transplanting oysters from "seed beds" to "growing beds," the chief action of the oyster farmer, who must also provide the oyster with something to grow on. Oysters are so fecund (thus the aphrodisiac reputation) that a single female may lay some 5 million eggs at a time, but in the wild only 10 or 15 single eggs are likely to survive. The cloud of spawn floats free for several days while "vellegers," as the larvae are called, grow into adolescent "spat," ready to glue themselves to a stable object where they will stay put for the rest of their lives, usually around 2 to 5 years, or 10 if they're lucky.

French and Italian oyster farmers even today follow the practice of ancient Rome in setting out clay tiles covered with lime to catch the spat. Ancient Rome also devised an oyster "nest" of stone pilings surrounded by stakes and covered with twigs, a method Colonial Americans adapted without knowing it when they threw cut birches into a river mouth to catch the spawn. In contrast to this horizontal method of "cultch" (short for culture), the Japanese use a vertical method in which they tie cleaned oyster shells to bamboo stakes or to strings hung from a platform called a "bent." Typically there will be 48 strings to a platform, 140 shells to a string in this "hanging cult" method, adopted in the American west by Charlie Johnson at the largest such farm in the world in Drakes Bay at Point Reyes, California.

While today 94 percent of Europe's oyster reefs, from Scandinavia to Greece, are farmed, only 40 percent of America's beds involve some kind of farming, from simple transplanting to full-scale tray growing in highly controlled conditions. Typically it was an American, Taylor A. Pryor, who developed the first purely test-tube oyster in land-based plantations on the island of Oahu in 1982, but unfortunately his business went bust and the promising Hawaiian oyster is no more.

Characteristic of moderate farming are the Long Island Oyster Farms, which use a half-tray method. Here, seedlings are transplanted first from the laboratory hatchery to screens in a warm-water lagoon where they will be relatively safe from predators, then to carefully tended beds set with cleaned oyster shells for a year of fattening, and finally to deeper, colder waters off the tip of Long

Island for a final plumping year. At the Maritec Company on the Damariscotta River near Walpole, Maine, Belon seed oysters will spend their entire lives in trays stacked 8 feet high and floated along the estuary surface to provide the oysters with warmer waters and more plankton than Maine waters usually allow. Tray-raised oysters are obviously easier to harvest than bottom-raised ones, which were once removed by giant pliers attached to toothy jaws wielded by the tongers of the Chesapeake but are now sucked up by dredges attached to 40-bushel containers. Once harvested, unshucked oysters are readied for shipping by frequent water baths that simulate tides and fool the oyster into keeping his trap shut.

More controlled farming means more year-round harvesting where temperatures can be controlled. The old prohibition against eating oysters in summer ("r"-less) months had nothing to do with the health of the oyster or the eater, but rather with the health of the oysterman who needed to replenish his stock during spawning season, to clean his beds and take a break from oystering. Since the ideal spawning temperature is around 70 degrees, oysters will spawn longer and more frequently in warm waters like the Gulf than in the cold waters of the north, but indoor hatcheries can compensate. In the Chesapeake, where traditional oysterers have resisted farming, oysters are more subject to seasonal fluctuations. This may help account for the marked drop in Chesapeake oysters in 1984, where they supplied but 26 percent of America's total, at the same time the Gulf increased to 51 percent of the total. Pacific Coast oysters are almost entirely farmed, but their output is small, about 13 percent, because acreage is small in comparison to the Chesapeake's 310,000 aces. The Mid-Atlantic and New England coasts are increasingly farmed, but their grounds account for a mere 10 percent.

It's not an oyster's name that counts, but the environment in which it was bred. Where once an oyster was named for its place of origin, its name now indicates size, type and breeding. Blue Point once meant an oyster grown near the town of that name on Great South Bay, Long Island, but it is now raised on both sides of Long Island Sound and the name refers to size, a medium-large oyster about 3–4 inches, the "half-shell" of 2 ½ inches and the giant "Box" oyster of 6 inches. In the same way, Belon once meant an oyster grown in the mouth of the Finistère River in Brittany, but it is now grown in many parts of Europe, as well as in Maine, New Hampshire and Pigeon Point, California. Even the green-tinged Marennes, which was once restricted by law to the Marennes-Oleron district in the north of the Bay of Biscay (and which gave French vintners the idea of authenticating their wine districts by the same kind of *Appelation Contrôlée*, an indebtedness they honored by printing their first labels in green), has now been transplanted to a place as unlikely as York Harbor, Maine.

Genetics do condition an oyster's shape and quality, but all oysters belong to the same family of which there are two major species, *Ostrea* and *Crassostrea*. *Ostrea edulis* produces such famed European varieties as English Whitstables and Colchesters, Belgian Ostends, Dutch Zeelands and French Marennes, Belons, Amoricaines and Arcachons. The only variety of *Crassostrea* native to Europe is the large Portuguese oyster, *angulate*, found originally in Portugal, Spain and Morocco and transplanted by luck or accident to Brittany in the 19th century. In turn, the only *Ostrea* variety native to America is the Olympia oyster, *lurida*, once flourishing in Willapa Bay in Washington's Puget Sound, but now barely surviving in Toten Inlet and Skookym Bay. America's chief oyster, the *Crassostrea virginica*, covers the Eastern seaboard from the Malpeque and Bras d'Or of Canada, the Bristol of Maine, all the Cape Cod, Long Island and Chesapeake varieties, including such wild ones as the Kent, Chincoteague, Tangier, Paruxent, Pacomoke and Rappahamock, all the Gulf varieties including the Apalachicula, Indian River and Cedar Key of Florida, down to the Bayou Cook, Four Bayou and Barataria of Louisiana. The only other major variety of *Crassostrea* is the elephantine *gigas*, known as the Pacific oyster, native to China and Japan. This is the variety Americans imported to the Northwest from Japan in 1902 to farm in beds cultivated for the purpose in Quilcene and Willapa Bays in Washington, Tillamook and Jaquima Bays in Oregon, and Drakes Bay in California.

What matters most to an oyster's taste, texture and color is the water in which he's fed and bred, Since he is no more than a headless, footless pump, which siphons 40 to 50 gallons of water a day through its filter system to obtain food and oxygen, the oyster we eat is 89 percent water. The rest is mostly sodium chloride, phosphorous and other minerals the oyster had concentrated in his flesh according to the content and temperature of the water. The crisp texture and intensely marine taste of the Belon and Marennes come from the 3 percent salinity and relative coldness in which they thrive. The softness and mildness of a Gulf oyster comes from warm waters that are half as salty. Where a Marennes acquires its green color by feeding on microscopic algae cultivated in ponds that the French call *clarières*, a new Pacific hybrid called Golden Mantle acquires its golden color by removing it from the waters of Puget Sound.

While oyster lovers are as tongue-tied as any other lovers in trying to describe their loved one, most speak of a certain intensity, more or less coppery, "a sharp metallic flavor" or one that is "nice and gamey," as Steve Cohen, oyster buyer for Manhattan's Grand Central Oyster Bar, describes it. A former buyer, George Morcogen, told me that he looks for a white, clean, firm shell inside and for flesh with a little "pizzazz." M.F.K. Fisher looks for crisp flesh, although she is quick to add that "*crisp* is not quite right, and *flesh* is not quite right, but in the same way you might say that *oyster* is not right for what I mean."

When oysters were as plentiful as peanuts, American cooks were ingenious in devising ways to vary the daily routine of oysters on the halfshell, raw, with a squeeze of lemon and a dash of pepper, or a squirt of Tabasco and a grating of horseradish. Every region came up with dishes appropriate to its own kind of oyster and its own culinary style. Thus New Englanders scalloped oysters by layering shucked oysters with common crackers or sea biscuits to bake in emptied scallop shells. Or they threw shucked oysters in stews of milk and cream sweetened with a little onion. Philadelphians mixed their oysters in a stew with tripe, Marylanders in a stew with celery, onion and Worcestershire sauce. New Yorkers added a little chili sauce to the Worcestershire, heated the oysters in cream in a chafing dish and called it "Oyster Pan Roast," memorialized even today in the special round-bottomed aluminum pans at the Grand Central Oyster Bar.

The Deep South stuffed oysters into a thick beef steak, cut open and sewn up to make a "Carpetbagger's Steak." In the days when veal was plentiful, Southerners ground the meat and oysters together to form "Oyster Veal Sausages." In New Orleans, where oysters were more plentiful than people, every class had its favorite dish. The poor who thronged the Oyster Bars took home a "Po' Boy Oyster Loaf" of French bread cut in half, toasted and filled with fried oysters hot from the skillet. The rich who thronged the finest French and Creole restaurants ate oysters on the halfshell, baked or broiled and sauced with minced bell pepper, onion, garlic and pimento smoothed with a Béchamel and called "Oysters Bienville" in honor of Jean Baptist Le-Moyne, Sieur de Bienville, founder of La Nouvelle Orleans. Since 1899 they've also been eating oysters covered in a puree of fresh greens spiked with Pernod and named by its deviser Jules Alciatore, of Antoine's Restaurant, for a very rich man, John D. Rockefeller.

During the California Gold Rush, when oysters were as scarce as nuggets, men killed for oysters, crumbed and fried in butter, then mixed into an omelet to make a "Hangtown Fry," named for a Hangtown cook who introduced the dish to San Francisco. Later, when transplanted Pacific oysters grew as large as dinner plates, North-westerners found that the easiest way to open them was to throw them on a bed of coals and barbecue them with melted butter or strong sauce. Today, Alice Waters at Chez Panisse has so sophisticated the western barbecued oyster that she grills her oysters on mesquite and sauces them with an oyster fumet garnished with chervil and golden caviar.

For the addict, an oyster engenders a mysterious symbiosis between lover, oyster and sea, a symbiosis that reduced Lewis Carroll's Walrus and Carpenter to tears and Dr. William Kitchiner, of *The Cook's Oracle*, to compassionate benevolence in 1818. "The true lover of an oyster will have some regard for the feeling of his little favorite," Kitchener writes, "and will . . . contrive to detach the fish from the shell so dexterously that the oyster is hardly conscious he has been ejected from his lodging, . . . till he feels the teeth of the piscivorous gourmand tickling him to death." The true oyster lover, it seems, must be as truly cultivated as the object of his passion, an oyster so well-bred that although he might not relish the tickling, he would rather die than complain.

Vintage, 1986

Absolutely Smashing

■

FRENCH 75s WERE the way to go. Eggnogs were out of the question, except for doddering grandmas who wanted dessert first. Mulled wine, with floating cinnamon sticks, was for getting rid of those boring neighbors next door who laughed too loud and stayed too long and whose dog always dumped on your lawn. Fish House Punch was a possibility, but dangerous—that guy jabbing a finger into your face was suddenly flat on the floor. The advantage of the French 75 combo of brandy and champagne, for us everyday gin and whiskey regulars, was that it gave the bubbles a kick and topped a serious buzz with euphoria. For a genuinely smashing holiday season, it was by far the best way to get smashed.

Getting smashed, for my generation—the Drinking Generation of World War II—was not just for the holidays. It was a way of life. Or so we thought, we who had bonded with our mates over gin and Lucky Strikes, when hard liquor was as necessary to romance as lighting one up. Watching our guys sail from the San Francisco Bay toward Guam and Iwo Jima put a spin on the martini glasses we had clinked together the night before, maybe for the last time ever. Besides, we were still recovering from Prohibition, when anything in a bottle could be as lethal as it was illegal. To buy a branded quart of Four Roses or Canadian Club was a pathway to good health. Sure, we had cut our baby drinking teeth on beer and wine, but the beer was quarts of Acme and the wine was jugs of Gallo, white or red. Strictly for quantity, boot-camp training in how to stay upright while drunk. Graduates celebrated at the Top of the Mark with a row of martinis or Manhattans. Old Fashioneds were for sissies. Wine was for winos.

But even after we settled down and had children, our drinking rituals remained hard. Highballs were the beverage of choice before and during dinner, capped by brandy and liqueurs after. I remember an ex-Marine captain who drank martinis throughout the meal and far into the night. It was his favorite drink. Why change? No wonder our children, the products of very different drinking times and a greater diversity of mind-altering drugs, were convinced that their parents were alcoholics. When they couldn't persuade us to join A.A., they signed themselves up for Al-Anon.

It wasn't that they were against drinking, just against the way their parents drank. Take Christmas morning in my house. No child was allowed to open his presents until Mom and Dad had downed their first glass of milk punch, a blenderized concoction of bourbon, brandy, milk, vanilla and nutmeg, chilled by milk cubes from milk poured into ice trays the night before. If we were at half-mast from too much Christmas Eve, a raw egg added to the blender was good ballast for hangovers. The children got to finish the half-drunk glass of milk Santa had left on the hearth, next to the cookie crumbs.

As our children came of drinking age, they began to wean us off the hard stuff. They were exploring and conquering a brave new world of wines and beers of which we were ignorant. The Napa and Sonoma Valleys we had known were full of apples. Theirs were full of grapes. Suddenly good wines were available everywhere in America, and if you lived in northern California, you were at the cutting edge. What could be more fun, when the parents took you out to dinner, than one-upping them by intelligently discussing California Chardonnays or Cabernets with the sommelier? And just as soon as your parents learned which was white and which red, you could then move on to Sauvignon Blancs and Zinfandels.

When all our children now entertain us during the holidays, it's all about food as well as drink, or rather the do-si-do they do together. Last Christmas they served us a Blanc de Noir and salted almonds, moved on to a Riesling for the oysters, a Merlot for the turkey, and a Semillon for the mince pie with brandied hard sauce. Actually the bubbly and the brandy of a French 75 were present, but in minute quantities and entirely defused. Nevertheless, it was possible at the end of such a meal, with the long progression of all those lovely wines, to end up smashed, but the buzz was gentler, slower, longer lasting. For members of the Drinking Generation, who are vanishing as quickly as smoke rings, longer lasting is good. Very good.

7x7 San Francisco, 2002

J-E-L-L-O

■

TO A '30s child Jell-O was not a dessert but a way of life. Every Sunday I sang "J-E-L-L-O" and said "Jell-O again" with Don Wilson and Jack Benny. I snitched Jell-O packages from the cupboard to sniff them like glue, to eat the powder "raw," to dream of a dress in each of six delicious colors. Jell-O was my first cooking triumph and I scorned glittering molds that concealed cabbage, cucumbers, cottage cheese, and mayonnaise when they were supposed to have marshmallows and maraschino cherries.

I didn't know that before the 20th century "jellies" of all kinds were more often tart than sweet, whether flavored with wines and vinegars to make aspics or bitter almonds to make puddings. Since the Greeks, gelatin had been used to bind, stabilize, support, glaze, and—above all—preserve. Jellied molds were not only decorative. They also protected their contents like a plastic wrap.

From the Renaissance on, molds of baroque extravagance were the staple of any well-appointed buffet. In 1893 Delmonico's Charles Ranhofer instructed housewives in the construction of such pieces as bastion à l'Américaine. "Have a bastion mold," he begins, in which to put six chicken galantines fashioned into a fortress with gelatinate doors and crenellated turrets. And even the Fannie Farmer of 1896 suggested that wine jelly be piled in glasses and whipped on top to resemble "freshly drawn lager beer."

Until the turn of the century housewives extracted collagen, the glue of gelatin, by boiling up meat bones and tissues. Deer antlers were favored in the Middle Ages until calves feet and knuckles displaced them. Eliza Acton's directions in 1867 suggest the process required some care. Use a "*blunt*-edged" knife, she urges, to scrape the hair from calves' feet after striking the hooves sharply on a table to remove them from the leg bones held "*tightly*" in the hand. Hours were spent simmering, degreasing, and clarifying the broth with egg whites before filtering it through jelly bags or "filtering stools" to obtain a clear bright transparency. The gelatin was then dried in the form of sheets or leaves, still available in England and France, or cut into rounds for portable soup.

To save labor the Victorian housewife relied increasingly on isinglass, imported from Russia and made from the membranes of fish bladders. An American housewife in 1890 must have welcomed the granulated gelatin made and distributed by Charles B. Knox of Johnstown, N.Y., as she welcomed mechanical refrigeration and the new methods of processing that gave her canned peaches and pears.

As early as 1845 Peter Cooper had patented a dessert powder, but not until 1897, when the health food craze coincided with the development of the icebox, was America ready for Jell-O. May Wait, whose husband fiddled with cough remedies and laxative teas in Le Roy, N.Y., named the mix of sugar, gelatin, and fruit flavorings Jell-O. But the product went nowhere until bought by food entrepreneur Frank Woodward. He was already cashing in on a coffee-tea substitute called Grain-O. Like General Postum, Woodward knew that the secret of food packaging lay in advertising and mass marketing. By 1902 "The Jell-O Girl" on the 10-cent carton appeared in all the ladies magazines, in store displays and free recipe booklets, on spoons, dishes, and even automobiles. By 1925

Jell-O joined with Postum to found the billion-dollar business of General Foods.

The trademark of a Jell-O-eating moppet indicated Jell-O was so easy to make a child could do it. Soon ads indicated even a man could do it, and finally even upper-crust artists like Madame Schumann-Heink and Ethel Barrymore could do it. In the '30s when Jell-O ads began to branch from dainty desserts to recipes for molded salads and entrees, Knox Gelatin declared war. "Down with Sissy-Sweet Salads," the Knox ad proclaimed. "Don't use Gelatin Dessert Powders! They're 85 percent sugar." Today Knox stresses its purity as an odorless, tasteless, sugarless protein that is good for dieting, if not bodybuilding, and that may do good sometimes for people's fingernails.

Jell-O meanwhile stresses versatility. Its magic sweetness can transform the entire meal from soup through tuna mousse to non-cook cheesecake into one long dessert. Jell-O's combination of sugar and artificial flavoring, guarantees the success of their Kids' Stuff Recipes, featuring such Disney World fantasies as Banana Wobbles and Dessert-wiches.

In a home taste test I prepared three samples of lemon jelly made with different proportions of fresh lemon juice, sugar, water, and gelatin, to compare them to Lemon Imitation Flavor Jell-O. Since Jell-O's egg yolk color could have given the game away I blindfolded my tasters. All eight adults picked the same home-made jelly as the tastiest and best. My teenage son, on the other hand, picked Lemon Imitation Flavor. "Of course it doesn't taste like lemon," he said, "but I like it. It tastes like Jell-O."

New York Times, June 1977

4-F Food

■

FOR ME FOOD is a physical, passionate, revelatory window on the world, much more revealing than sex. If I want to recall a particular time and place, I think not of my love life but of my life in food. London, 1953—limp vegetable marrows and stiffly starched puddings. Athens, 1965—crisp grilled octopus and ouzo with ice. If that seems a narrow perspective, think of the size of a camera's lens. Food is my lens for zooming in on the particular and personal, a method of framing and focusing and of putting myself in the larger picture. Concentrating on food gives me a gut reaction to the most global, the most abstract, events. World War II, for instance. My window on World War II is food in the forties, when all of us home-front kids were 4-F.

Pomona College, 1944—Betsy Ross ice cream and black coffee. 1944 marked not only the Allied landings in Normandy in the spring but my own beachhead in Pomona College in the fall. I'd packed my bags, closed the door on the framed reproductions of *Pinky* and *Blue Boy* in my bedroom, waved goodbye to my grandparents hoeing their V-for-Victory garden, and was driven, on a half-tank of gas hoarded for this purpose, a whole 30 miles from Riverside to Claremont. Distance had nothing to do with it. I'd debarked from the shores of Jell-O and Ovaltine to land in spaghetti and red wine.

Not on campus, of course, and not that first year. Pomona in 1944, like small coed campuses everywhere, was marking time until our boys came marching home. The campus was like an extended Girl Scout camp, a rah-rah holding pen for adolescent girls too young, too prudent, or too scared to join the WACS and WAVES. I say girls because boys were scarce as sugar coupons. The seniors graduating class my freshman year numbered 91 girls and 5 boys. The *Metate* that year memorialized 14 dead.

We didn't distinguish between BMOC (I trust it still means Big Man on Campus) and MOC (Man on Campus). Men on campus were valued, as are most commodities, according to their scarcity. The men, however, paid a high cost for the benefits of this sexual ratio, which was small compensation for having been stamped REJECT. The Army labeled guys 4-F for as little as flat feet or weak eyes, but tell it to the Marines. In truth all of us on campus, boys and girls alike, had been rejected for reasons of youth or gender or health by a world at war. We were all 4-Fs together.

The food too was 4-F, since the good stuff went overseas. We proudly took vows of culinary poverty in the name of our fighting boys, but our vows were not entirely voluntary. Sugar, meat, butter, and cheese were rationed and fresh vegetables unobtainable, unless you hoed a Victory garden. So at Harwood Court for lunch we slurped canned soups (Andersen's pea was the cafeteria-line favorite) and for sit-down dinner murky casseroles distinguishable not by content but by color—the white one, the brown one, the yellow one. Salads were wedges of iceberg lettuce glopped with pink Russian dressing.

What the '90s have revived in downhome chic was for us Depression food—macaroni and processed cheese, lumpy mashed potatoes and heavily breaded meatloaf. In such a context, tamale pie with black pitted olives was a taste treat. We also treated ourselves to midnight spreads of Ritz crackers and deviled ham, while we read aloud the "dirty" part of *Forever Amber* instead of our boring assignment for Western Civ.

Friday was devoted religiously to fish, which meant that anyone with cash ate out. Without cash, I got a job at the Mish, a nearby juke-box and hamburger joint in what was exaggeratedly called the town of Claremont. Waitresses at the Mission got a free meal as part of their wages and I looked forward to pigging out on cokes and French fries and meeting some attractive guy who would ask me to dance, after hours, in the Passion Pit. After a week of leftover leftovers—best described as Mish-Mash—meager tips and no attractive pickups, I slunk back to Harwood's boiled overcooked fish, sauced with thinned library paste.

Football Fiber

Rumor was at Harwood that the boys at Frary Hall got real meat three times a week, at least if they were on the football team. The injustice of that bothered me less than my friends because I had never had real meat. I had come from a family of Fletcherizers—36 chews before you swallowed—who believed that food increased in value the closer it approached the taste and texture of water. Subscribing to the gospel of health food preached by the Kellogg brothers at Battle Creek Sanatorium, my folks believed that the whole point of food was to eliminate it as quickly as possible before it could pollute the body, which in turn polluted the soul. By a leap of logic natural to the Battle Creek faith, Cornflakes was salvation. Also Postum, Grape-Nuts, All-Bran, Shredded Wheat, Wheatena, and Post Toasties.

Meat was not necessarily sin, but it was costly. The only meat we ate, not counting the chickens raised in our own backyard and the rabbits raised in somebody else's, was an occasional Swiss steak (a cheap beef cut pounded with a meat mallet, then reduced to pulp in a pressure cooker) or a piece of lamb shoulder boiled until stringy in a pot of ditto string beans. At home, the pinnacle of meat pleasures was boiled beef tongue, still one of my favorites for its velvety texture. Then we ate it because it was cheap.

When I got to Harwood, the Sunday pot roast that was fodder to my fellow frosh was to me an exotic treat. But first they had to teach me how to cut and eat it. I had never eaten meat that had to be cut with a knife. Meat at home was always fork tender, like tongue, but nonetheless had to be chewed until liquefied. Once my Harwood pals discovered my 36 chews—and how could they not since what was for them a five-minute meal took me 30—they teased me mercilessly and effectively. They would count me down like the end of a football game—10, 9, 8, 7, 6, 5, 4, 3, 2, 1—SWALLOW! In self defense, I learned to bolt chunks of food without chewing at all, and learned so well that I later won a pie-eating contest at a spring carnival, gulping down a whole pie in under 60 seconds, doing my dormmates proud.

The one saving grace of our dorm food was dessert, not the dreadful packaged puddings—tapioca, rice, junket, colored white, brown, and yellow—nor the overbaked custard in little brown pots, nor the canned greengage plums which weren't half bad, but some munificent donor's gift of Betsy Ross ice cream with every meal and unlimited seconds. I bolted my casseroles to gain time for mushing ice cream. Those who like mushed ice cream will understand. Those who don't, won't. I liked best to mush together the red, green, and white layers of Neapolitan brick ice cream the way a painter would mix oils on a palette, melding strawberry, pistachio, and vanilla. Ice cream twice a day was heaven and the pearly gates, and I flapped my wings with every bowl until I fell to earth from excess baggage. I got so fat on ice cream that my pals—you can always count on your pals—called me the Crisco Kid because I was fat in the can. It was a '40s joke.

My freshman year was fraught with culinary events. Even today, when I eat a peanut butter and jelly sandwich I think of that April day we heard the news of President Roosevelt's death. In my house, Roosevelt was the anti-Christ (after the Pope), and even at Pomona the strong majority of those old enough to vote had supported Governor Dewey over our wartime Chief. Still, it was a moment like the assassination of President Kennedy 20 years later, a moment when everyone could remember exactly what he was doing when the news hit.

I was behind the Coop soda-fountain counter, where I worked part time to earn cash and eat free. What I ate, invariably, were chocolate milkshakes and peanut butter and jelly sandwiches. Skippy crunchy peanut butter and Welch's grape jelly on toasted white sandwich bread. A perfect food. I was about to crunch into the layered ooze when Doug Strehl burst through the doors. "Have you heard the news? The President's dead." The Coop radio was tuned, as always, to either Glenn Miller or Harry James. Doug fiddled with the dials and we listened, hushed. Even as a Deweyite I recognized history in the making, and I put down my sandwich uneaten. It would have been like eating in church.

That same college year which began with the Normandy invasion ended with the surrender of Germany in the spring and of Japan in the summer. Our days as 4-Fs and the food that went with them were numbered, as Spam, vets, and gasoline trickled back. Sophomore year was a traumatic initiation into wounds visible and invisible, into forbidden knowledge of legs blown off and minds blasted. It was our first unshuttered look at the reality of war, coincident, for me, with my first taste of real spaghetti and red wine.

The only spaghetti I had known previously came in sweet pink sauce, the color of the framed *Pinky* on my bedroom wall, in a can labeled Franco-American. Real, as opposed to canned, spaghetti was ostentatiously Italian and therefore anti-American, a subversive, fifth-column food. Real spaghetti, after all, had fattened Mussolini, not to mention the Pope. Real spaghetti that you twirled around a fork and hoped to slide into your mouth before it got away was never served in Harwood Court, home of gracious living, nor Frary Hall, when men were men.

For the real thing, you had to go out of town, heading east on Route 66 toward Upland, Cucamonga, and—Lucy's. Lucy's was a roadhouse that served ethnic Italian food *and* cheap jug wine, Gallo, by the gallon. At Lucy's, spaghetti sprawled full-length on the platter, wrapped in a dangerous blood red sauce that smelled of onions and unknown herbs. For a quarter extra you got a half loaf of toasted bread reeking of garlic and, for a dollar, a carafe of dago red. At Lucy's I fell forever from God and Calvin's grace by consuming papist bread and wine, debauched—as no doubt my grandfather would have believed, turning in his grave but 30 miles away—by the wickedness of vets returned from the dead three thousand, six thousand, miles away. From Anzio, Normandy, Berlin, Iwo Jima, Guadalcanal.

Return of the Vets

We were a culture shock to these scarred vets and they to us. They were as baffled by our cloistered innocence as we by their shell-shocked experience. Something was needed to bridge the gap and the handiest tool was liquor. Until the vets rolled in, lips that touched liquor had never—or seldom—touched mine. With drink as with food, I was a throwback, a disgrace to my pals. While I nursed a coke or a glass of milk, they ordered sophisticated things like Cuba libres, whiskey sours, rye old-fashioneds, and gin slings, "lady drinks" that looked smashing with blue smoke from carefully held cigarettes. The first vet I picked to go steady with was as teetotaling as I (Did he have an alcoholic father? A chemical imbalance? Was he nuts? I don't recall.), so my rite of passage was artificially delayed.

Soon, however, even those of us who'd floated on rivers of milk, now swam for dear life in floods of wine, beer, and gin. For week-nights most vets favored gin and juice, usually canned grapefruit be-cause it came in quart cans. But for weekends something other than mere volume was required. Weekends demanded a trip to Mr. Baldy Inn for hot buttered rums in front of a crackling fire. The cozier the fire, the more delicious the rum, the more hair-raising the hair-pin turns on the ride back down. Vets were used to putting their lives on the line. We were not.

By my junior year, even the most delayed pubescent among us was a veteran of the complicated warfare that accompanied these excursions. As 4-Fs, we'd devised strategies for handling trooploads of boys going overseas. Our civilian boot camps were USOs, where we were trained to welcome one kind of advance and discourage another, to read a fine line between the soft-focus romance we longed for and the hard sex we fled. We were skilled in establishing lines of defense and conducting trench warfare when it came to national borders like above the neck and below the neck. When those borders were breached, we drew new lines and manned new defenses—above the waist and below, some checkpoints nego-tiable, others not. Some vets laughed, others got mad, and some got violent. To GIs who'd been given a hero's welcome with all the perks and no holds barred in Paris and Tokyo and Rome, date rape in the Wash was an oxymoron.

Real men, my junior year, demanded real sex, but would settle for real food and drink if the setting were right. The right setting was the Sagehen, another den of iniquity on Route 66. You couldn't look or act your age at the Sagehen. You had to have fake I.D. to get served at the long, mirrored bar or in the black leather banquettes, where you ordered steak medium rare (a daring innovation) with salad and baked potato (lots of butter), and very dry, very large martinis (two olives please). This was romance. This was the real world not raping but seducing, our chastity guarded until the world was again safe for democracy and our boys could claim us as their just reward. That's what they were fighting, and what we were waiting, for.

By the end of junior year, half my friends were engaged or had married and dropped out. We had passed so many boxes of chocolates, our tribal way of announcing engagement, that our voices were hoarse from screaming and our fingers sticky with chocolate covered cherries. We were innocent of double-entendre but worried about biological clocks. If we weren't married by 21 with a baby the following year, would we be old maids, infertile, too old to have children? Our daughters, our granddaughters, laugh at us now, but we didn't laugh then. In the days when two-thirds of a high school class got married upon graduation, such fears were real.

In my senior year at Pomona, 4-F no longer meant unfit for service. It meant unfit for matrimony. Engaged or unengaged, we were all clucking like crazy to fly the coop. Many of us went to summer school to speed up graduation and get the hell out. Frustration, while we waited for our discharge papers, was alleviated by an unlikely R&R of food and drink. This was Lupe's, a Mexican beer joint that makes Taco Bell look like Rodeo Drive. Lupe's, like Lucy's, was the real thing. Behind the stained wooden bar where collegiates rubbed elbows with migrant workers and truck drivers, Lupe in her tiny kitchen cooked up *menudo* (tripe soup), steamed tamales in cornhusks, fried tacos with shredded chicken or pork, and served up cold Tecate beer along with a sympathetic ear and a word to the unwise. At Lupe's, we played Hemingway and dreamed of Pamplona. Lupe's was my window of escape from the prison camp of Fletcherizing Presbyters, parietal rules and cloisters, my prevision of Mexico, Spain, Europe, Abroad. Lupe's was a world away from Winnie's Waffle Shop in downtown Claremont, with its strawberry waffles and whipped cream. Lupe's was a plunge into fiery salsa and shots of tequila with lime and salt on the back of the hand.

We couldn't take the plunge fast enough or far enough. I graduated mid-year and hitched a ride to San Francisco to join the world as a raw recruit, trained for nothing but self-defense, but I could read and write and occasionally think and always argue. And I could eat. Now I could chew as fast as anybody and sip a martini with the best. I was 21. I was launched, with a $25 war bond in my purse and a peanut butter and jelly sandwich in my pocket. My purse in no way matched my appetite, but I knew what I wanted. San Francisco, 1948—linguine with clam sauce and a bottle of Grignolino. From now on, the world was my oyster. From now on, we were all 1-A.

Pomona College Today, 1993

The Artful Cafeteria

■

"I want you to know that I saw Hitler," she said.
"When—where?"
"In the cafeteria."

FOR MY CHILDREN and others of the McDonald's generation, the cafeteria means institutionalized grunge, a place where faces are gray, trays greasy, noise levels high and ceilings low. But for the older generation of Isaac Bashevis Singer, the cafeteria was a gathering place for the homeless. After the Second World War, Russian and Polish refugees became "cafeterianiks" in places like the Garden Cafeteria on upper Broadway in Manhattan because they could sit all day over a cup of coffee and recreate memories of another time and place. The cafeteria then was less a restaurant than a theater of the imagination. For Singer's heroine in his story "The Cafeteria," to see Hitler in the cafeteria was as probable as the coffee in her cup.

For my father, too, the cafeteria meant a place for migrants, but on another coast. Before the Second War, refugees from Iowa and Nebraska gathered at Clifton's Cafeteria on another Broadway, this one in downtown Los Angeles. At Clifton's Brookdale in the 1930s, thousands of Bible-Belt exiles to California gathered to see the Promised Land in the cafeteria.

Brookdale made that land literal long before Disneyland made movies concrete. As a child for whom movies were far more real than life, to go to Brookdale after church on Sunday was to pass from purgatory to Hollywood heaven. I carried my tray past a real waterfall, through a simulated redwood forest, where the Wurlitzer warbled and busboys sang. I paused in the Little Stone Chapel, threw a penny in the Old Tree Wishing Well and fetched my cone from the Ice-Cream Sherbet Mine. Other Clifton Cafeterias followed, even more baroque, like Pacific Seas in 1939, a Polynesian paradise of thatched bamboo huts, neon palms, live parrots, cement coral reefs and—in a grotto below—a life-sized Christ who prayed in the "authentic natural setting" of the Garden of Gethsemane.

For me and my family the cafeteria was a theater of hope as remote from the hungers of the Depression as Los Angeles was from Des Moines or Manhattan from Auschwitz. When my brother shipped out to Guadalcanal, I knew where he was going—to Pacific Seas. In the cafeteria everything was under control. "I like to take a tray with a tin knife, fork, spoon, and paper napkin," I.B. Singer writes, listing the props, "and to choose at the counter the food I enjoy." My father liked to take a tray in the cafeteria the way he liked to take a carriage in the supermarket, to assert power, for a moment, over the infinite goods at his command. In the cafeteria he was king, American style—a self-reliant, rugged, individualist. Here his ignorance of fancy restaurant rituals mattered as little as his ignorance of jungle warfare. Here he was freed from the fear of cowardice, humiliation, poverty or pollution from the sins of the drinking classes. For the cafeteria was first of all a family place, as decent, respectable, sanitary and safe as *The Saturday Evening Post*.

For me, the freedom to choose between Baked Custard and Chocolate Cream Pie was as intoxicating as gin. I liked to take a tray because it was the opening move in a game so simple an ignorant child or wordless immigrant could master it. The very word, "cafeteria," suggested that eating out was child's play, a form of fun. When H.L. Mencken identified the word as 1830s Cuban-Spanish for "a shop that sells coffee," he cited comic analogues like "shaveteria" and "casketeria" or, as we find today, "pizzeria" and "tortilleria." But "cafeteria" chiefly meant a *little* shop, without pretension, for the casual stroller.

Like the luncheonette, the cafeteria caught on because it suited the American style of self-deprecation, independence, nonchalance and improvisation. It jumbled times and places, classes and conditions, to make every man equal and mobile. Other casual eateries like drugstore counters, snack bars and fast-food joints evolved from America's compulsion to eat on the run. Other types of lunchrooms aspired to upwardly mobile gentility. But what made the cafeteria unique was that its very form dramatized the contradictions of democratic mobility. It provided mass feeding in the service of mass luxury, as historian Daniel Boorstin has said, but it did so in terms of modernist art by turning the whole dining scene into performance and process.

The cafeteria was a play in two acts. In the first act the eater was to reassemble the disassembled parts of a meal by means of a counter and tray. If the counter was modeled on the industrial assembly line, the tray was the flatcar he loaded while propelling it along the railway tracks. In the second act the eater had to select his place in the constantly shifting scene of the arrival platform. But the platform itself was a place of fantasy, plastered with symbols of art and culture of either the past or the streamlined future. The cafeteria was a trip, but arrival was illusory. For a nation of immigrants the cafeteria embodied a journey to a New World of placelessness.

* * *

It was the Old World, however, which gave the cafeteria its start at the beginning of the industrial age by keeping workers in their place. To improve worker efficiency, a Scottish mill owner in the early 1800s provided a room for workers in which they could make a hot beverage and be kept from the temptation of liquor. Despite its utility, the employee or factory cafeteria did not take hold until British military canteens of the First World War dramatized the efficiency of central commissaries and self-service lines.

Such mass production feederies were designed to control the diet of workers and soldiers, to provide maximal wholesomeness at minimal cost. At the opposite end of the scale were the posh feederies of the rich, the Restaurants Françaises of Delmonico's, Rector's, the Ritz, designed to provide maximal choice at maximal expense. With all of the changes in America after the Civil War—new wealth, new cities, new railroads, new working women—the country needed a new kind of eating place halfway between factory canteen and "lobster palace." It needed a place designed for the middle class.

New York businessmen solved the problem by founding the Exchange Buffet in Wall Street in 1885, to distinguish à la carte gentlemen from table d'hôte hoi polloi. The former selected their meal from a buffet froid modeled on the tables of Sherry's or Delmonico's. The latter fed on combinations like that of The Penny Restaurant in Grand Street, where a penny got you soup, corned beef, potatoes, cabbage, baked beans, and rice.

Midwestern working women solved the problem by founding Women's Exchanges and Lunch Clubs of their own. Chicago women opened the Ogontz Lunch Club in 1890; the Kansas Y.W.C.A. opened a self-service lunchroom in 1891; Evanston, Illinois, opened the Woman's Exchange Cafeteria in 1905 for students at Northwestern University.

Families had the problem solved for them by that extraordinary coupling of science and art in Chicago in 1893, The Columbia Exposition. The Fair advertised five acres of dining and refreshment rooms, where "the pilgrim to the great show can find within its gates such diet as suits his palate and purse." Choice in diet until after the Civil War, Daniel Boorstin points out, had belonged exclusively to the rich. Variety, balance and freshness were luxuries. Now the Fair was offering not only variety of refreshment, as in "the choicest products of the dairy" in the Dairy Building Lunchroom, but variety of refreshment room, many of them self-service "conscience joints" where you kept your own tab.

The Fair put mass feeding in a new context and dignified it by associating industrial science with the grandeur of Venice and Rome. The combination of choice, cleanliness, moderate cost and cultural artifacts spawned both the cafeteria and the restaurant chain. We know little about A.W. Dennet who, after Fred Harvey's "refreshment saloons," created the first national eating-house chain, but we do know that he trained two sets of brothers. One founded the first family cafeterias in the East, the other in the West.

In 1898, the Childs Brothers (Samuel and William), who had successfully combined white-tiled sanitation with crystal chandeliers in a chain of lunchrooms in Philadelphia, opened a branch on lower Broadway in New York with one singular innovation. "Before stepping into the passageway you notice a big pile of empty trays from which each guest takes one," the *Caterer's Monthly* explained. "Now as you pass along the lunch counter, you take off whatever you want and place it on your tray." The appeal of "guest" and "whatever you want" was underscored by the music of a five-piece orchestra as good as Victor Herbert's at Luchow's on Irving Place.

In 1906, the Boos Brothers (Horace, John, Cyrus, and Henry) provided counter and trays for their first cafeteria in Los Angeles, to the tune of Pryor Moore's orchestra and "an artistic water fountain" said to be Persian-Elizabethan-Gothic in style. Dennet and the Boos Brothers paced the way for the Clifton chain of my childhood.

In San Francisco, E.J. Clinton (the real family surname) was co-owner of a Dennet lunch chain before he left for China to become a missionary. On his return in 1907 he combined cleanliness with godliness in his Puritan Dining Rooms. In Los Angeles, his son Clifford bought a Boos Bros. Cafeteria in 1931 to take godliness in a new direction. At Clifton's he offered diners the ultimate privilege of choice. "Pay what you wish, dine free unless delighted." In his first three months 10,000 people chose to dine free. But his golden-rule policies paid off so well that he could construct Brookdale and Pacific Seas and put Christ, literally, in the cafeteria.

Of all types of self-service chains, the Automat was the most radical and the least middle-class. It turned the entire sequence of a meal—preparation and eating—into the comic abstractions of farce. It denied distinctions of time or place by dispensing with the assembly line and by reducing the disassembled parts of a meal to vertical geometry. All foods were separate but equal, all instantly available at all times, without human labor or pain. The Automat made eating a new kind of game of equivalence and risk, a slot machine game expressed by Paul Hervey Fox in "Automat":

> *Drop a nickel*
> *Get a pickle*
> *Or a cup of tea.*
> *You may risk it*

For a biscuit
Or a porker's knee.

The Automat was the great class leveler of the '20s and '30s in that it converted substance to style. In 1902 Joseph Horn and Frank Hardart imported the first wall-to-wall vending equipment from Germany to expand their baking business in Philadelphia. From the beginning, the response was less to mechanics than to décor. While a 1903 *Scientific Monthly* approved the mechanical accuracy of the dispensers for beer, Kümmel, Benedictine and "other fine liqueurs," they raved over the decoration: "Its electric lights, its dazzling mirrors, and its resplendent marble outshine everything on Broadway."

When Horn and Hardart brought the first Automat to Broadway and 13th Street in 1912, they brought the theater of public eating that New York, with its kaleidoscope of classes and styles, was born for. In the '20s the Automat at Broadway and 47th had more action than the stage. Here Walter Winchell kept a corner table to note Jean Harlow, Aimee Semple McPherson, and John D. Rockefeller rubbing elbows with bag ladies and bums. Cartoonists dined out on the class anomalies of a liveried chauffeur waiting in the Automat for Madame to put a nickel in the slot, or of a Helen Hopkinson matron opening an Automat window to say, "You are to be congratulated on your custard pie." In the '30s when the rich survived, instead of slummed, at the Automat, the comedy of the place was caught in movies like *Easy Living* with Jean Arthur and Ray Milland. The romance of the Automat was celebrated in musicals like *Face the Music*, with a nation humming Irving Berlin's lyric, "Let's have another cup of coffee, Let's have another piece of pie."

But in the 1960s and '70s Automats and cafeterias declined as cities declined. People abandoned cities for suburbs, feet for cars, and Childs for McDonald's. Today only a single Automat remains, on the corner of 42nd Street and Third Avenue, a relic of urban archeology, with its wall of nickel slots converted to quarters. In New York but a single public cafeteria remains—Dubrow's, at Seventh Avenue and 38th Street, in the garment district. (When a television network filmed Singer's "The Cafeteria" in 1983, they used Dubrow's because the Garden had just closed.) Dubrow's, too, is the last of its line, built in the '50s in the Art Deco classic-cafeteria style of the '30s. On its large wall mural, fashion models and Greek goddesses listen to Muzak beside the painted fountain, which is all that is left of the orchestras and fountains of yesteryear.

Only in the South and Southwest does the cafeteria thrive. From Florida to Oklahoma, the J.A. Morrison chain, begun in 1920 in Alabama, stretches now across sixteen states to provide "Southern Hospitality." Washington, D.C., remains the capital of America's cafeterias because they are built, literally, into the structure of government. Bureaucrats and visitors can still make the cafeteria journey by underground railway to stop at Longworth, Russell or the Senate Office Building. In the Southwest, a French chain, to complete the circle of prole to posh, has opened a number of Café Casinos, offering cafeteria customers "the ambiance of a Parisian sidewalk cafe" and a choice between Boeuf Bourgignon and Bouchée St Jacques. And in Los Angeles a fifth generation of the Clinton family has set its latest cafeteria in the former Brock Jewelry Store and called it "The Silver Spoon." Now diners can eat in the same bronze bank vault where Mary Pickford and Mabel Normand stashed their jewels.

"The uniqueness of America," Boorstin concludes, "is in denying uniqueness." By condensing food into cans, bottles, granules and pills, we have made food as portable as people in trains, cars, airplanes and spaceships. If spaceships deny the uniqueness of heaven and earth and TV dinners the uniqueness of gardens and seasons, still we demand the right to choose the food we enjoy, however restricted the choice. If choice is no more than the packs of seasonings and non-dairy products on the airline dinner tray, still I like to unwrap my plastic knife, fork and spoon from the paper napkin and assert my control.

I.B. Singer, musing over the past lives of his cafeterianiks at the Garden, thought of a herd of zebras attacked by a lion. "Do they have a choice?" he wondered. Whenever I visited my father in the long years of his second childhood, he would take me to a shopping-mall cafeteria, where he would take up his tray and linger over the quivering Jell-O and crusty rice pudding. He would not be hurried, even with death at his heels, in his choice.

Journal of Gastronomy, 1985

Class Action

∎

HOW GREEN IS my kitchen? In 2003, it's a question chefs ask. Over this past year, so many greening movements have run together that what once looked like counterculture now looks like mainstream. Once you add organic to sustainable to community-supported agriculture, layer on small-farm preservation, and top it off with environmental conservation and education, you've involved an impressive cross-section of Americans in a green food chain that connects farm to table. And in this chain, the most important link has now become the chef. Given new authority, chefs are transforming kitchens into learning centers and learning centers into farms and restaurants. One measure of how far the green tide has spread is that Alice Waters's Edible Schoolyard in Berkeley, California, has become her Sustainable Agricultural Project at Yale's Berkeley College in New Haven, Connecticut.

While the strategies for linking farm to table must vary widely from place to place, one of the most adventurous recent developments is the Stone Barns Center for Food and Agriculture in New York's Westchester County, scheduled to open early next spring. Just 45 minutes north of Manhattan, across from Tarrytown, Stone Barns is part of an enclave in the Pocantico Hills that has been preserved by six generations of Rockefellers. In 1910, John D. Rockefeller provided for that greatest of Eastern luxuries, open space, when he bought 3,500 acres here. Later, his family donated about half of those acres for a state park, and recently, his grandson David Rockefeller deeded 80 acres of his Hudson Pines Farm to the non-profit corporation of Stone Barns. Built by David Rockefeller's father in the 1930s of timber and stone, in an American version of French Norman translated by Italian stonemasons, the buildings themselves, enclosing a large courtyard, are magnificent in scale and craftsmanship. In memory of his father and of his own wife, Peggy, whose interest in sustainable farming led her to help found the American Farmland Trust, David Rockefeller and his daughter, Peggy Dulancy, decided to initiate at Stone Barns an educational program that would not only link farm to table, but would also link a non-profit center to a profit-making restaurant and chef.

After eating a meal at Blue Hill restaurant in New York City's Greenwich Village, David Rockefeller found his chef, Dan Barber. Barber had started with a catering business, which evolved into a family owned restaurant when he was joined by his brother, David, a businessman, and David's wife, Laureen, a graphic designer. The Barbers named Blue Hill after their grandmother's house in Great Barrington, Massachusetts, in the Berkshires, which had a showpiece garden that Dan Barber lovingly restored, adding vegetables to the flowers. Once the former cow barn at Stone Barns is transformed into a restaurant (named Blue Hill at Stone Barns), he will oversee both venues, his pastry chef, Pierre Roeble, will consult for both, and his current co-chef in the Village, Michael Anthony, will become the full-time chef at Blue Hill at Stone Barns.

Dan Barber's mission has always been to search out fresh, local, and seasonal ingredients, he says, in order to reveal the quality and integrity of their flavors. By teaming up with organic farmer Eliot

Coleman, of Four Season Farm in Brooksville, Maine, Barber can indulge a chef's fantasy of local produce in acreage surrounding the Barns. Coleman has been given 30,000 square feet on which to build the innovative greenhouses, which brought him worldwide fame when he proved he could grow delicate produce year-round in cold climates. In addition, Don Homer, the Rockefellers' personal gardener for 30 years, will continue to farm four acres of organic gardens that stretch beyond the new restaurant's outdoor terrace. Both gardens will supply both Blue Hills, as well as other restaurants and green markets, in addition to the Pocantico Day School that adjoins the estate, and hopefully other schools as the educational program grows.

This interior transformation of the Barns is the job of the Manhattan firm of Asfour-Guzy, which aims to preserve what's there by creating what Peter Guzy calls "a refined simplicity." To the right of the arched entry to the courtyard, a small café will serve snacks and sandwiches to accommodate hikers in the park. Next to it will be a bar with a big fireplace and quantities of books, then the long, open space of the dining room and kitchen beneath a vaulted ceiling webbed by steel trusses (1,000 square feet for the kitchen, with 290 seat capacity for the dining area), and beyond it, a gem of a private dining room that looks out onto an herb garden. Although this entire area totals 3,200 square feet, it is dwarfed by the size of the hay barn, which will house the Education Center on the ground floor and an event space on the second floor large enough to serve 200 diners from its own adjoining kitchen.

Although the Barns will be an architectural, educational, and culinary destination, what pleases Dan Barber most is the courtyard itself, which he envisions as a place of festal celebration, in which girls disperse apples, bands play, and banners fly. There are two families involved here, and both the Rockefellers and the Barbers are personally committed not only to preserving the ecology of the place but also to proving that high quality food, locally produced—food that tastes good and is healthy for people and the environment—can meet a growing demand in the marketplace and thereby make a profit. "We hope it will be a spotlight to raise the issues and get people involved," says David Barber.

"The natural world is well designed; we need to work with it," says Coleman.

But the most important voice in the greening of American kitchens is the chef's. In the words of Anthony, "What I've learned is to keep out of the way of the food, to do as little to it as possible."

If Stone Barns captures the essence of the settled East, Island-wood captures the wild West. This past October saw the opening in the Pacific Northwest of this radically different innovative center on Bainbridge Island, 35 minutes by ferry from downtown Seattle. Formerly called the Puget Sound Environmental Learning Center, this 255 acre ecological oasis is focused on a beautifully designed complex of buildings as "green" as the forests, marshes, ponds, and estuaries that surround it. Sunshine is converted by solar panels, wastewater is recycled in a unique "Living Machine" treatment system, building walls are made of hay bales, and interior building materials include recycled yogurt cartons, bluegrass roots, and glass bottle chips made into tiles. Even the kitchen is greened by using non-chlorine biodegradable cleaning materials, recycled barn boards for tables, and milled wood from the site for trim.

Islandwood is the dream child of Paul and Debbi Brainerd, who made money early in the dot-com game and decided to invest the rest of their lives in teaching ecological conservation and "community stewardship." They capped their environmental concerns by hiring noted chef/author Greg Atkinson, formerly of Canlis restaurant in Seattle, to create a culinary program for Islandwood. With Atkinson, they found a chef whose take on the seasonal and local in his own kitchens had moved him inevitably toward sustainable farming. "What made Canlis sensational in the 1950s was serving fresh asparagus and strawberries 365 days a year," he says. "Now Canlis serves asparagus only in the spring and something like kale in the wintertime, both raised organically on local farms."

It's not just luck that has brought to Islandwood a chef who is as passionate about teaching as he is about cooking. Islandwood benefits from an unusual educational mandate, by the state of Washington, that every child in fourth or fifth grade must have a four day outdoor experience. From lack of funds, however, many inner-city schoolkids had missed out. "Our goal from the very beginning was to create the best place in the world for children to learn about the environment," says Debbi Brainerd, and they targeted those kids who had never seen woods or a dark night lit only by stars. "It's the first time, even for some of their teachers, to see big trees growing, not in city parks, but in the forest," Atkinson adds. Partnered with the University of Washington's College of Education, Islandwood uses 16 graduate students who live on the premises to help teach the 7,000 students and their families who arrive each year. Sleeping lodges provide for overnight stays.

Because the cost of their ingredients is higher than commercial fare—wherever possible, they use organic products, including flour for pizzas and burritos, oats and bananas for granola, carrots for carrot cake—they must make everything from scratch, but they hold to the same budget as a conventional school. "I feed the kids for less than $5 a day per child, which is phenomenal," Atkinson says, "but we avoid all the multiple middlemen.

"We always knew we'd have to feed the kids," he continues, "but everyone was surprised when the culinary program for adults took off." People flocked to Islandwood for demos, cooking classes, and dinners with big-name guest chefs, all of which helps raise money to support the rest of the educational programs. Even Atkinson was surprised when his chef pals in Seattle jumped on the ferry to cook in his kitchen, pals like Jerry Traunfeld from The Herbfarm and Tom Douglas, a pioneer promoter of Northwest cuisine. "By going from a four-star restaurant to four-day sleepovers with kids, I thought I'd committed career suicide," Atkinson says now. "But I've had so much support from my colleagues—everybody wants to help."

Even family-run farms are turning into chef-driven learning centers. Typical of current trends is The Chef's Garden in Huron, Ohio, on the edge of Lake Erie near Cleveland. Here, the Jones family (father Bob and two sons, Lee and Bobby) lost their 1,500 acre commercial farm in 1980, but they were so determined to farm that they started over, from scratch, by growing vegetables for farmers' markets. "It was a hellish existence," Bob Jones admits, until local chefs began to make special requests for things then unheard-of in the States, like squash blossoms. Soon the Joneses were growing 30 different varieties of eggplant, then three-inch petite lettuces, and a global spectrum of unheard-of-miniatures to order. The word spread from local chefs to chefs like Charlie Trotter in Chicago, Thomas Keller in Napa Valley, and Alain Ducasse in New York City. On their thousand acres, the Joneses now grow more than 800 different crops, both heirloom varieties and experimental breeds.

Once the Jones family watched Trotter educating his own staff about their vegetables, they saw the possibilities of educating a larger public about the relationship between good farming and good eating. Last October, they opened the nonprofit Culinary Vegetable Institute (CVI), sometimes called Veggie U., on a hundred acres along the Huron River, in a handsome log and stone lodge with root cellar, culinary library, and state-of-the-art kitchen. Its advisory board is a who's who of the country's top chefs: Lidia Bastianich, Daniel Boulud, Ed Brown, Gale Gand, Christopher Hastings, Michael Lomonaco, Wayne Nish, Bradley Ogden, Douglas Rodriguez, Rick Tramonto, Norman Van Aken, Jean Georges Vongerichten, and Ducasse, Keller, and Trotter. This is surely the first "retreat and learning center" designed to lead chefs, food professionals, children, and adults down the pathway to vegetable knowledge under such pedagogical stars. Future plans, not surprisingly, involve television shows broadcast from the site to spread the word to elementary schools across the land. Chefs everywhere have already got the word: to color their kitchens green, begin with the vegetables.

Food Arts, 2003

Romancing the Stove

WRITERS ARE A hungry lot—hungry for fame, love, sex, money, and sometimes even food. "Man's *real* best friend," John Updike wrote in a poem called "Food," *is* food: "It never bites back; / it is already dead." How it died, or how we kill it and turn it into our own flesh and blood, is a transaction that matters intensely to certain writers—especially to those who know that food is a form of fiction and that fiction is a form of food.

Poets, such as Mark Strand in "Eating Poetry," know that when we eat we are eating images, that food is itself a language, compacted of metaphor and symbol, feeding and nourishing our minds while pleasuring our senses. I would rather eat poems, in fact, than follow the diets of those literal-minded nutritionists who reduce food and its consumption to chemistry and thermodynamics. In my book, it's not what we eat but how we imagine what we eat that counts.

Updike, for example, confesses that he dotes on "all dry, crunchy, salty things, not so much for the taste or the nutritional value as for the way they feel in the mouth, that first thrilling instant."

In his story "Survivor Type," Stephen King describes a shipwrecked doctor who must cannibalize his own body to survive and who, after noshing his left foot for a while, notes in his journal "I kept telling myself: Cold roast beef. Cold roast beef. Cold roast beef."

King got it right: In order to survive, writers cannibalize daily their own and other people's parts and use them to cook up good stories. But since I am a writer who is often concerned with actual recipes—with how to turn that left foot into a little something tasty by dint of root or berry—I want to know what actual writers actually eat. I want to know the precise menus of their cannibal lives. Let others snoop in writers' journals to find nasty secrets of sex and power. Food voyeurs know that food is more intimate than sex and far more revealing of what goes on in heart and head. If you want to know how a man is in bed, watch the way he eats. Does he wolf down his food without a word or linger voluptuously over each bite? By the same token, if you want to know how a writer writes, take a look at what he cannibalizes. And so I decide to investigate the secret food lives of writers in the interest of research.

When I ask Joyce Carol Oates about the title of her latest novel, *American Appetites*, she makes a metaphor overt: "My secret, or perhaps not so terribly secret, equation for a novel is: Food (an excess of, a fanaticism for) = (my) writing (which in its accumulation no sane person apart from my parents could deal with, or wish to)." But Oates's appetite is really only for words. "I have to eat at certain times, whether I'm hungry or not, or I'd probably never eat," she says. "But I don't want to eat. It's very boring." Nothing for breakfast but a pot of herbal tea before she feeds lives into her word processor and dishes up a feast of words. But surely she has a secret yen? What about that beer-batter recipe for zucchini blossoms in her short story "Night. Death. Sleep. The Stars"? "I give it as an example of how odd a character is," she says. "The second wife finds the recipe in a drawer and thinks how weird the first wife was."

Just my luck to begin a culinary survey with a writer for whom actual food is either boring or weird. I fare even worse with Philip

Roth. Despite the dictum of Roth's hero Zuckerman—"Your mouth is who you are"—Roth isn't talking. I'll never know what his real mouth devoirs, or what he cannibalized to create the cold roast beef—or rather, the unforgettable refrigerated liver—of Portnoy. I'll never know how Mother Portnoy, or Mother Roth, cooked that particular cold beef. With onions? A touch of flour?

Others are more forthcoming. Martin Amis for one, whose *Money* hero, John Self (note the sly name), euphorically satiates himself with "three Waistwatchers, two Seckburgers, an American Way, and a double order of Tuckleberry Pie." Amis is a master of gastroporn, but what does the author himself consume? When I catch him in his London flat, he is as innocent as his own infant son. "I find I eat the baby's food quite a bit right now," Amis says. "A bit of pasta or scrambled eggs or yogurt and mashed bananas—that sort of thing." I'm not about to let him off the hook that easily. Okay: He likes food to be dramatic, like a hot curry or maybe oysters—either "something icky or unbearably strong."

Amis warms to the subject. "I like my Bloody Marys hot, so that a moustache appears on your upper lip and tears come to your eyes. I'd say a nice cocktail is to be preferred to anything a cook can come up with." How would he survive on a desert island? "With this Bloody Mary thing, I think, I wouldn't care about the island. Any island would do. It'd be the Bloody Mary I'd be interested in."

Amis confirms a gender cliché I've heard—that men drink while women cook. I call a veteran of the drinking generation to check this out—a survivor of World War II cannibalism and booze, Bill Styron. Styron, however, doesn't want to talk about the meaning of bourbon and branch. He wants to talk about soft-shell crabs and fried chicken and crabmeat and Surrey County ham and homemade butter-pecan ice cream. For Styron food evokes the full world of his boyhood in Tidewater, Virginia, where every summer he'd collect crabs on the banks of the James River and sell them in little baskets filled with seaweed at two cents apiece; and where his family's cooks taught him how to make one of the world's most delicious dishes, Southern fried chicken.

Unexpectedly, I have found both an eater and a cook. "I make sure the fat is hot—the fat should come halfway up the sides of the chicken," Styron says. "Frying chicken—you have to hover over it, keep turning it to get that fine, crispy crust." Food for Styron is not only nostalgia but a mark of moral character. "I don't really trust people who don't like food," he says. "I think they must have some private sin, something somehow pinched and empty in them."

I attribute Styron's love of food to his southerness, but when I hunt up another transplanted Virginian, a favored cliché bites the dust. "My great passion in food is Arabic," Tom Wolfe says. He fell in love with Lebanese cooking during his first newspaper job in Springfield, Massachusetts, where he ate every night at a slum joint called El Morocco, and for 99 cents got the greatest meals ever prepared—baked kibbeh (lamb and cracked wheat), hummus, malfouf (stuffed cabbage). What really turns Wolfe on is what Middle Easterners do with vegetables like eggplant, cabbage, and okra, combining them with meat and strong spices. If Arabic food is an unlikely taste for this elegantly dapper man, so is his preference for an updated All-American Boy breakfast. "I just take Aspen cereal, wheat germ, 100 percent bran, a compote of dried apricots, prunes, and white raisins that has to be cooked first, and then I mix them all together in a bowl as big as a basketball."

If the men are coming on strong, where are the women eaters and cooks? I call Alison Lurie and learn that she survives on garden vegetables in Ithaca during the summer and flees to Key West during the winter, but not for food. "Conch?" she queries. "It's one of those local specialties you wouldn't eat for pleasure, only patriotism. Conch is like tofu. There are many things you can make it into, but the basic material is soap."

A good metaphor but austere eating. I need a female sensualist to even the score. Ann Beattie, a '60s survivor of urban cool relocated now in Charlottesville, Virginia, comes clean and admits to a passion for crunchy peanut butter. "I don't buy it, won't keep it in the house because I go straight through the jar with a spoon," she confesses. I know that as a cook Beattie has survived largely on improvised soups ("I have a secret soup base of cauliflower, chicken stock, and fennel"), but on request she improvises a Last Meal: lobster, broiled (with lots of butter), beefsteak tomatoes (really ripe), and endive (baked with cheese). Rather minimal, I think, until she explains, "You cut the endive in half, hollow out a few leaves, and fill them with triple cream cheese—that would be the first course. And then I'd end with some Manon chocolate or champagne truffles or Dove Bars, and listen to a little Mozart. I would *not*, as my critics would have it, make a meal of a glass of white wine and a Dove Bar and listen to the Hooters."

She would, however, set her table as she customarily does, with a world of miniature people, animals, houses, wind-up toys. "I like those tiny stamped and die-cut sitting figures. I place them in a long row, for a crazy centerpiece," she says, "and by the end of the dinner everyone has arranged them in little groups. When I clear the table I invariably find all the little people copulating."

This is more like it—real food with at least metaphoric sex. And by good luck, I run into Russell Banks, who tips the ante. Banks cannibalizes his own New England conscience to produce shellfish orgies. "I get really crazy at times for anything I have to break into—lobster, mussels, clams, crabs," he admits. "It's my Protestant work ethic. You have to work first to break them open, so I figure it's okay, but it gets me high. I lose track. Shellfish are a very sensual adventure—always wet, and you dip them in butter, also wet." He begins to open up the subject. "There's the contrast between the hard outer shell and the soft, tender insides, extremely satisfying." He moans a little. "I can tell quantity only by time, maybe four or five lobsters or three hours. It's a New Englander's kind of gluttony."

It also shows what a little Puritan imagination can do with a dozen on the half shell. Banks is the kind of eater I've been looking for; now I need the same kind of orgiastic passion in a writer who cooks. How was I to know that I'd find not one but a whole gang of cooks in Faulkner–Hemingway territory? Marlboro men who hunt and fish and drink and—when they really want to run wild—cook.

One of them: the late Raymond Carver, who once wrote a love poem called "Hominy and Rain." He liked to fish for salmon up in Ketchikan, Alaska, then smoke it and mix it with scrambled eggs or barbecue it with brown sugar and garlic and lots of butter. He and his wife, Tess, always kept smoked salmon in the freezer so they could give a piece out to friends—"a sort of blessing," he said.

Another such: Carver's onetime hunting and fishing pal Richard Ford, a Mississippian transplanted to a ranch in Montana. I know Ford's wife, Kristina, is a fine cook, but I've always thought of Ford primarily as a hunter-gatherer—until he acknowledges that he and his wife hunt and cook together. The best thing they make, he says, is Snow Goose Salmi, a wild-Western rerun of a great French classic. "We each clean what we kill and then make a sauce from the carcass with onions, garlic, and tomatoes. We roast the breast quickly so it's just warm at the heart of it, and then serve it on toast covered with pâté made from the liver." Before I can open my mouth, he is on to Coulibiac of Salmon, which they make once or twice a year, Richard cutting the fish design from puff pastry. Most of the year, however, they survive on simpler dishes, such as pheasant. "Most people I know who eat pheasant eat it like chicken—deep fried," he says. "Deep-fried pheasant breast, deep-fried snow goose—basically it's just a better hamburger."

When he can poach an invitation, Ford hunts over in Livingston, Montana, with his friend Tom McGuane. After reading McGuane's memorable scene in *The Bushwhacked Piano*, in which Doctor Proctor is accused of having transformed some surgically removed body parts of the novel's hero into a dish of pasta fazoula, I expect McGuane to talk about pasta. But he doesn't want to talk Italian, he wants to talk Szechuan. "I love to cook Szechuan," he says, "because I like the kind of frantic wok cooking it involves—just blasting things onto the wok and dumping them into a serving dish." Like Ants Climb a Tree, which McGuane learned from *Mrs. Chiang's Szechwan Cookbook* during the year he set out to cook everything in the book. Ants Climb a Tree is made of pork and cellophane noodles and garlic and peppers and ginger, and "looks like little ants crawling through something."

Another member of the up-country hunting-and-fishing gang is Jim Harrison, who hibernates half the year in the wilds of Lake Superior. From the author of *Farmer*, I expect talk of game and hearty American peasant fodder, but instead I get "truffles with shirred eggs, where you chop your truffles and let 'em sit in with the eggs for three hours before you put the eggs in the butter and cook 'em up slow, so they're very soft, and then put 'em in a little French pastry cup."

That was the first course of a meal he'd laid out recently for friends. "And after that, I got a 16th-century dish out of Ali Baba, where you braise some quail with leeks and garlic and fresh thyme and bake some potatoes and hollow 'em out, then put a quail in a potato shell with the mashed potatoes all around and bake it for another 20 minutes and people lift up the top of the potato and cry, "'Behold! A quail!'"

Harrison confesses that he took up cooking only when he got fed up with boozing. "It's an obsession I try to keep in check," he says, meaning cooking. But what he and a couple of hunting friends did with the 350 woodcocks they shot last fall was to rassle up a *terrine de bécasse* with the layers of woodcock, venison, grouse, wild duck, veal, apples, and Calvados. The food of excess is what it's all about, he admits, "but I crave the *gen-you-wine* . . . no dickying around with things like raspberry vinegar. Cuisine minceur," he adds, "is to me the moral equivalent of the fox-trot."

The ultimate cook turns out to be, of all people, Harry Crews. Crews has written a novel about eating a car—a Ford Maverick, to be exact. He grew up in Macon County, Georgia, as a sharecropper, and knows more links in the cannibalistic food chain than anyone I've heard of. But for Crews the process is the pleasure. Take tripe. "Most people don't like tripe because it's cross-grained, like a piece of plywood," he says. "You have to have a good set of teeth and you have to like to chew—but I want to chew, man, and I want to chew a long time, I want to fight with that sucker."

Other suckers he wants to fight with are pickled pigs' feet, backbone and rice, liver and lights, peanuts baked in cane syrup, prairie oysters with Jack Daniel's and Tabasco, rattlesnake steak, sea turtles, and 'gator tails. Crews was happy to pass on his recipe for 'gator tail, beginning with setting a brush hook on a limb to catch the 'gator, pulling him out and bashing him in the head and hacking off his tail to get "15 pounds of good, solid, edible, wonderful flesh," which he cuts into bite-size pieces, dips in egg-and-flour batter, and fries in deep fat. Basically—like Richard Ford's pheasant breast and snow goose—just a better hamburger.

If Crews really wants to pleasure himself in the morning, after some outrage the night before, this is what he does: "I take three ounces of Jack Daniel's Black Label and I suck a couple of eggs—but in a strange way: I punch a little hole in either end of the egg and then suck out about a quarter of the egg and then fill the shell with Tabasco sauce or Red Rooster. Then I suck that sucker down and drain off about half the Jack Daniel's and do the same with the other eggs, and I tell you, man, you're ready to eat nails."

When it comes to getting off on real food and actual stories, I'm about to give up on the ladies. They just don't go crazy the way the guys do. But I make one more call, a desperate one, since the writer is a naturalist who might well be a vegetarian or macrobiotic, for all I know. With Annie Dillard, however, a pilgrim at Wellfleet, I hit solid cannibalistic gold. "I love food, I love to eat, I love to think about food, I love to read about food." Dillard can hardly get the words out fast enough. When she married at 20, she didn't know how to make anything but popcorn, she says, but knew she could learn from books and did. I know she can cook from her rhapsody of a Last Meal of braised sweetbreads with tiny little pieces of bacon and onions and a creamed spinach soufflé with nutmeg and lemon juice squeezed right over the top, which would do it no harm at all. But the gold is still to come. "I dream at night that I'm at a buffet," she says breathlessly. "I have a nervous fear that I'm going to starve to death like a hummingbird." The naturalist explains that because hummingbirds have a very fast metabolism they must hibernate each night (they get very cold and their respiration rate falls) or they'll starve to death. Dillard fears that because she eats so often during the day, she may not stay alive at night. "This dream buffet changes, but it's always enormous," she says, "with maybe 120 dishes, all wonderful." Taking no chances, however, she stuffs herself with popcorn at night before she goes to sleep, as a kind of security blanket.

I want more details on that dream buffet, but she has to ring off. She is feeling peckish, and not even poets can survive on dreams alone. "Time for a little popcorn," she says—"buttered, of course."

Lear's, 1989

PEOPLE

Elizabeth David 1914–1992

∎

ELIZABETH DAVID BEGAN her writing career as something of a pornographer. To the England she returned to in 1947, words like apricots, olives and butter, rice and lemons, oil and almonds were "dirty words."

She wrote them in a fury, as she said later, starved for the hot sun and opulent flavors of the Mediterranean that had been her happy lot during the War, as the bride of a Welsh officer sent to Delhi. To survivors of England's wartime austerity, her first book, *Mediterranean Food*, was as shocking as *Lady Chatterly's Lover*—and as revolutionary.

David was the first to teach English ladies, for whom all foods and cooking were dirty words—one didn't do cooking, one had cooks for that—the sensuous pleasures not only of eating but of cooking itself, in one's own kitchen. The change was extraordinary. And it extended across the seas even to Yanks like myself, who had not inherited English cooks but had inherited English stodge. Before I ever set foot in France, I hungered for the unimaginable tables she set forth in *French Country Cooking*, just as I slavered for Italy reading her *Italian Food*. It was a fine way to first discover food, travel, Europe and pleasure, all at once, and all from an English lady's dirty books.

Shortly, I discovered through her *French Provincial Cooking* how far food could take my mind as well as my body, how much a person or a nation's history and culture depended on the wealth of meanings summoned by a simple phrase, like the title of her collected essays, *An Omelette and a Glass of Wine*. It was David who first took food scholarship all the way and devoted a 600-page book to the single subject of *English Bread and Yeast Cookery*, which took us from the querns of Ancient Egypt to oatcakes in the Outer Hebrides.

For readers, usually Americans, who expected cookbooks to be how-to manuals of specific exactitude, her recipes were maddenly vague. "But she gave you an understanding of a dish that you could not get from more explicit recipes," Nach Waxman, owner of Kitchen Arts and Letters, recently said. "She helped you understand where a dish came from and how it worked." And while she told you about it, she was witty and sharp, sensuous and opinionated, intensely personal and therefore memorable.

After three decades of writing and two of illness and seclusion, she died at 78 on May 22. I met her once, in London, but as is often the case with powerful writers, I remember her words better than her person. I remember her, like a first kiss, for my first passionate encounter with apricots, olives, lemons, almonds, and all those other dirty words.

News from the Beard House, 1992

The Prime of M.F.K. Fisher

■

AS I DROVE into the Valley of the Moon at the southeastern end of
Sonoma County in California's wine country, I was as apprehensive
as I was the day I drove along the coast of Naples to find the cave
of the Sibyl of Cumae. I have looked for moon goddesses in many
parts of the world, and the one I now sought had begun to work me
over from the moment I entered her valley. Although I'd been twice
before to the Bouverie Ranch, now, for the life of me, I couldn't
find it. When I paused at the crossroads of Glen Ellen to phone for
directions, a silver chain fell from my neck and with it the Peruvian
cross blessed by a Quechuan woman in Arequipa. I began to panic.
When I finally saw the little stuccoed Spanish house, shaded by live
oaks and warmed by a hot October sun, I fell on it with the joy that
Hansel and Gretel must have felt when they were lost in the forest
and came upon a house made of gingerbread and candy. That's the
kind of effect that Mary Frances Kennedy Fisher has on me, and
there's not a damn thing I can do about it.

She built her house near Glen Ellen 19 years ago. It has three
rooms—one for work and sleep, one for food and company, and a
dark red one between for luxurious ablutions—and all are heaped
with a totemic chaos of books and manuscripts, paintings and geraniums, Indian wall hangings and children's drawings, golden peppers, brass sculptures, ripe tomatoes and plums. In a shaft of sunlight

on the porch, by a bowl of orange nasturtiums, lies a sleeping cat. A Spanish arch frames a perfect backdrop of blue mountains that are haunted by the ghost of Jack London, who built his house near this place from red volcanic rock. It's all too perfect, this lair of M.F.K. Fisher—Scotch-Irish Celt adept at runes, fifth-generation word-smith, descendant of a great-grandmother she calls "part witch and part empress," and avatar—or so my fear tells me—of that awesome muse called by Robert Graves the White Goddess.

She greets me warmly from her wheelchair, skin and bones and frail from Parkinson's disease, hobbled despite an artificial hip, cursed with eyes so bad now that she can neither read nor type. "I was putting on earrings in your honor," she says in a whispery, little-girl voice that startles because it so contradicts her imperious brow, just as the snub nose contradicts her cool green eyes. She still pencils her eyebrows, '30s-style, and outlines her cupid's bow mouth in red. At the age of 81, in her person as in her prose, she defies time with bravado.

She has dressed with care and elegance—a hot-pink blouse and matching stockings, a black velvet pantsuit (the trousers covering the leg brace she hates), and multicolored combs to pin back her hair. At one moment she is baby-faced sophisticate, as glamorous as one of her Man Ray or Annie Liebovitz portraits. At the next she is an icon of Sister Age, a subject that haunted her from youth, until she decided she was too old to write about old age, and then did—compellingly. I am very glad to see her but I am afraid to tell her so.

She moves her wheelchair adroitly but impatiently, hating her dependence yet loving her attendants: her nephew Chris, visiting for a few weeks, and her frequent companion, Cathy, a young writer from Sonoma. Fisher insists that we go at once to see the old barn, transformed now into a center for the 400-acre Bouverie

Audubon preserve that protects her land—land that her friend David Playdell-Bouverie gave to her when she moved from St. Helena. She laughs as she tells how, to enlarge the preserve, she "conned some old boy, a monstrous old man," out of the land at the top of the ridge. Clearly she enjoyed the con as she enjoys the new life at the ranch, the bustle and stir of young botanists and docents, the busloads of schoolchildren, the tourists who stray from the path, get lost, and succumb to "wildwood panic." It's a fit place for a sorceress, this small, civilized enclosure in a wilderness that is still home to snakes and mountain lions, and boar that are "lean and mean on their dainty little hooves and put their noses down to root through a whole row of anything you have, snarfing it up." She's off and running with her stories, and I'm caught for good.

M.F.K. Fisher nailed me first in the 1960s in London, of all places, in a secondhand bookstore off Piccadilly, where I bought a bargain volume of five of her works in one called *The Art of Eating*. I was an instant captive to this Circe of the stove. That she could write so wittily, learnedly, and sexily about a subject as base as food shocked my Puritan upbringing and threatened my literary snobbery. But as I gobbled up her pages, I saw that food was merely the ruse of this libidinous oyster-eater, wolf-killer, gastronomical storyteller, kitchen allegorist, American humorist, metaphysical wit. She was an American original and a writer of the first order: a Mark Twain with Bloomsbury overtones, a cross between Emily Dickinson and Colette. I laughed aloud at her stories and regretted that I'd not heard of her sooner.

Later I learned how varied were her devotees (they included W. H. Auden and the Marx Brothers) and how effective were her disguises. Lucius Beebe fell madly in love with the M.F.K. he assumed was a "wispy young Oxford don," and he never forgave the "betrayal" of his assumption. Many who were smitten by her prose were hopelessly enslaved when they discovered that she talked, lived, and loved the way she wrote. They were enchanted by the pornographer who confessed to unspeakable rites involving catsup with mashed potatoes and mayonnaise with caviar. By the logician who frankly anatomized a recipe "To Drive a Woman Crazy" thus: "Ingredients: 1 or more nutmegs, ground; 1 left shoe, of 1 woman." Readers adored the healer who counseled women to regain the use of their senses "by touching an eggyolk, smelling a fresh lettuce leaf or berry, tasting . . . a fresh loaf of bread, or a fresh body."

I saw that her strategy was Circean, Little Red Riding Hood in reverse: Lure the wolf through that door, seduce him into the pot, and eat him up in a savory stew. Her erotic seductions masked steely powers of language, combining passion with precision to produce constant electric shocks. The way she could turn eating snails into a curiously pleasurable act of necrophilia: "Then there were snails, the best in the world, green and spitting in their little delicate coffins, each in its own hollow on the metal plates." The way she could turn homicide into Wildean wit: "She ran her kitchens with such skill that in spite of ordinary domestic troubles like flooded basements and soured cream, and even an occasional extraordinary thing like the double murder and hara-kiri committed by the head-boy one Good Friday, our meals were never late and never bad."

The way she could create ideal worlds under the guise of "factual" memoirs. With a twitch of her linguistic wand, she could evoke the "noisy personality" of places as distinct and diverse as Marseilles, Aix-en-Provence, Vevey, Dijon, Tahiti, Whittier. I had lived in Provence, but in a barren spot compared with the "home" she invented when she wrote of spending Christmas in a hotel room in Marseilles with her two girls, eating a strange breakfast of caviar on hot rolls and *café au lait*, toasting one another with three chocolate bars wrapped in foil, while she told them the story of Joseph of Arimathea and how he wandered to Glastonbury from Jerusalem to plant his dry hawthorn staff in the ground, where it burst into leaves in celebration of Christ's birth. "We felt safe and trusting—" she wrote, "*home.*"

Like her I was a westerner, born not far from her childhood home in Whittier, but my home and family were light years from the pastoral world she created in *Among Friends*. The eccentric characters of her family were far more real than my own—her handsome father Rex, her Anglomanic mother Edith, formidable Grandmother Holbrook, delicious Aunt Gwen, Miss Marrow the dope fiend, and "batty" Cousin Lizzy. In Fisher's pages they welcomed me to a 100-acre ranch where they grew oranges and blackberries, mirabelles and guavas, artichokes and dates. Where they kept a pig and a cow and a horse name Hi-Ho Silver. Where she and her three siblings spent Sundays in the print room of her father's newspaper. Where her Aunt Gwen made a ceremony of mashed bananas on toast and her father went hunting for antelope and wild kid while her mother read books and birthed babies. Where they celebrated the great summer canning festivals at nearby Valyermo and rode horseback on the cliffs above Laguna and held picnics on the beach and slept within a circle of horsehair lariats to ward off rattlesnakes at night. "It was," as she says of another time and place, "a good way to live."

It was also a good way to write. "I think the only good thing about me is that I stayed honest," she says now, adding, "because I'm the worst liar in the world." This paradox is why she's a great storyteller and a compulsive writer and reader. "With my own discovery of the printed word I came into focus," she once wrote, confessing that she read books "the way alcoholics drink, from dawn until Fall-down Time, and from left to right on the liquor shelf." The addiction to writing and reading was in her genes. "We were a very articulate family and we all read and wrote all the time and it was lots of fun," she says, recalling that she put out her own private little paper when she was 6, wrote a novel when she was 9, and went to work on her father's paper at 14. Now she is sorting through boxes and boxes of unpublished manuscripts, notes, and novels, and is working with Cathy on a new book about landladies. "I haven't said half what I wanted to, but I can't possibly do half of that," she says. "I'm a junkie about writing, I have to have it. That is my way of screaming primally."

Her primal scream has propelled me through all of the nearly 20 volumes she's published since 1937 on the art of living fully. "I believe in living fully," she once wrote, "as long as we seem to be meant to live at all." The Dickinsonian sting reminds us that the facts of life are based on the fact of death and that hunger is the common condition that links them. Even in her first book, *Serve It Forth*, written when she was not yet 30, she was wise to the "dark necessities" of nature—"we must grow old and we must eat." And we must die. From the very beginning, she compelled us to link our hungers to our fears in order to tame the brutes. "Central heating, French rubbergoods, and cookbooks," she wrote, "are three amazing proofs of man's ingenuity in transforming necessity into art."

Like any white witch, her art is the art of transformation. Her works are formulae for turning sensual pleasures and pains into acts of moral elegance, for turning all the acts of brute necessity into sacred ceremony. Auden understood her fully when he dedicated his poem "Tonight at Seven-thirty" to her. It details the perfect dinner party, with six perfect guests—"men / and women who enjoy the cloop of corks, appreciate / dapatical fare, yet can see in swallowing / a sign act of reverence . . . " Auden recognized that she had forged her own language to keep body and soul together and make them whole, a language of runes and charms like the tree-alphabet of the White Goddess who created order out of chaos by the word. For Fisher, writing is a talisman like the "assefeddity" ball worn in vain by a childhood friend, like the hired-girl's cure for a fever, which consisted of tea made from dried jackrabbit turds, like all the folk remedies she collected in *A Cordiall Water*.

Through her stories she has long taught us that the human need and the artist's need is the same—to civilize our innate savagery, to tame the wolf within. But I was slow to realize that this is also the root of her lifelong obsession with power, specifically the power of women and the division of power among women. Although she was "furious" with her first publishers when they required her to use her initials M.F.K. as a subterfuge, "because women, they said, don't write this way," she's always denied that she is a feminist. She was, she says, brought up to believe that men and women are equal. Yet she was happy to write a piece for *Newsweek* on "Why We Need a Women's Party" as a third party, "because the approach of the two sexes to religion, sex, love, art, money, and politics is completely different" and we stand in need of the "special inner language of the female mind to help clear up a few ever-present issues like war and peace, corruption and the price of beans."

Better than any American woman I know, she has written about women not as imitation men but armored in their nurturing and civilizing powers. In *The Gastronomical Me* she titled every other chapter "The Measure of My Powers," as if taking stock of her own place in the dynasty of "dominating, strong-willed women" into which she'd been born.

She measured her powers against her dowager-queen Grandmother Holbrook, who liked her son-in-law, she tells me, better than her own daughter. "Mother and she were at odds but they never, never quarreled," she says as we sit on the porch, she now in her empress guise, eyes hidden by enormous dark glasses, her throne a high-backed rattan chair. "You just didn't quarrel—even in private." Her Campbellite grandmother was the one who referred to the Catholic Church as "the Scarlet Woman of Rome," and who called Queen Victoria "that old hag in Windsor Castle." Possibly that is why her daughter Edith was such an Anglophile.

As the eldest of four, Fisher measured her height as well as her powers against her parents and siblings. At five feet eight inches she was the runt of the litter, overshadowed by a father of six foot seven, a baby brother of six foot six, and a mother and two sisters all six feet or over. From her sister Anne—"she was a real bitch," Fisher says with affection—she learned the strategies of the frail. "At Christmastime she'd put on such a scene! Two days before Christmas she'd have a terrible bilious attack and lie on the couch, this wan little fairy, and we'd put all her presents around her and open them for her—with her permission, of course. What a ham she was,"—and she pauses—"a beautiful, complex, fascinating woman . . . who died when she was 55. Like a dog."

When Fisher finally measured her powers against age, she wrote about an obscure woman, Ursula von Ott, whose portrait she had discovered in a junk shop in Zurich, painted on a piece of leather. From then on, Ursula's likeness hung over Fisher's bed—and when not her bed, her desk—as a symbol, half-eaten by silverfish but still potent as an image of someone "completely alive in a landscape of death . . . the enigmatic, simian gaze of a woman standing all alone." From Ursula she had wanted to learn the art of aging, and that is what I had come to learn from Fisher. For me, Fisher too is an image of a woman who supported her two girls by the small sums she made from writing, and who has lived single for nearly 40 years. And all this time she wrote well and lived fully.

Her specific against mortality is what it's always been and what forever links the spinner of tales to the nursery and the kitchen slaves on the Whittier ranch who "with their soapings and their knives and their hungers for hidden sweets . . . were all women trying to survive among savages." Through the power of the word she has not only survived but prevailed, despite the "damn brace," the sleepless nights, the eyes that can't read. Now, as before, she puts time in its place by ceremony. The simple ceremony of our lunch—the slices of ripe tomato from the garden of a friend, her sister Norah's good fresh butter, the whole-grain bread with sprouted wheat berries and the nice local white wine "that goes down easy at $2.98 a bottle"— is like a perfect dinner party for six, like the picnics at Laguna or the fairs and fetes in Provence. All are "ageless celebrations of life." So too is the ceremony of her conversation, her hunger to hold Cathy and me spellbound, to make us cry and make us laugh with stories about herself and others.

When I take my leave, she speeds me on my way with all the bottles of good $2.98 wine that I can carry. It's hard to thank her with the right words for the gift of herself. As I leave the Valley of the Moon, the shade is lengthening as the last light flames the leaves of the grapevines red and gold. I remember Fisher's words on our common mortality with the plants that give us food and drink— "first freshness, then flavor and ripeness, and then decay." But that is too autumnal. My ears buzz with the story she has just told about the cows that used to have the run of the ranch when it was still "a call-house for cattle." One day they began to lick the white calcium out of her stuccoed walls and would then throw it up, so that the house turned pink while the yard turned white. I hear her delight in imitating the cow sounds, linking man and beast, loving the absurdities, embellishing her effects. "Hearing the cows snuffing up, slosh, slosh, throwing up—*wuuuup, wuuuup*—I knew it was something I'd never forget," she says.

Nor will I; not a single blessed word. I laugh aloud and am no longer afraid.

Lear's, 1989

Great American Taste:
Claiborne, Child, Beard

■

Craig Claiborne Says Try Something New

In his 20 years of reporting and reviewing, Craig Claiborne has made food news the news of the world. And through food he has taken us around the world to become, with him, an international connoisseur.

Claiborne was the first to let Americans who had never been near New York City in on the secrets of famous chefs, to take us behind the scenes of restaurants we'd only dreamed of visiting, to tempt us into sampling exotic recipes that we could cook before we could pronounce the names. He became our surrogate palate and a king-maker, a man who could make or break the most obscure or the world's most renowned kitchen by rewarding or withholding stars. Through this unassuming man we tasted power.

What Claiborne liked to report was interesting people cooking interesting foods. He was the first to write in detail about exotic Szechuan, Vietnamese and Thai cooking and to document the cuisines with recipes. His recipes, a total of some 11,500 by now, are the blood and guts of his writing because they allow everyman to become his own armchair traveler by way of the stove. We, too, can sample the Sussex Pond Pudding cooked for Craig by Jane

Grigson in Swindon, England, or the Plantain Fritters served by Governor and Mrs. Romero in Puerto Rico. We, too, can search out the infinite variety of the American ethnic mix, eating at one time a Matzoh Meat Pie at a Sephardic-Ashkenazic Seder and at another the Hoppin' John from Mrs. Wilkes's Boarding House, in Savannah, Georgia. We, too, can play host to the world's greatest chefs and learn Chinese cooking from Virginia Lee, Italian from Marcella Hazan, Indian from Madhur Jaffrey, Mexican from Diana Kennedy. We can test out the latest and trendiest fancy French nouvelle cuisine and compare it with establishment French cooking, here and elsewhere, because for years Claiborne has described, translated and adapted the recipes of chefs such as Roger Fessaguet, René Verdon, Jean Vergnès, Gaston Lenôtre, Paul Bocuse, Jean Troisgros, and Michel Guérard, not to mention his long-time colleague, Pierre Franey. Claiborne is the medium through which we get the message.

He cheerfully shares our prejudices, listing his Loves and Loathes. Loves: breakfast, Kasanof's Jewish Caraway Rye Bread, picnics and covered-dish suppers, caviar, truffles, champagne, hamburgers, corn on the cob, chili con carne. Loathes: gluttony and excess, iceberg lettuce, tepid soup, cigars, maraschino cherries, dinner plates on laps, guests who use books for coasters, or who pour on soy sauce before tasting, or who "help" with the dishes.

Once a salt freak, he made salt-free meals a virtue after acute hypertension drove him to construct a Gourmet Diet. A snob about elegance, he deflates snobbery foods: "It's harder to make a good hamburger than it is to make an ordinary souffle."

Says Claiborne with his Huck Finn grin, "Eating is one of the greatest pleasures of my life." And by writing about his passion for food, he's added pleasure to our lives too.

Julia Child Says Have a Good Time

While holding an egg in front of the television cameras Julia Child explains the technique of egg poaching, "Swing the shells wide open and drop them in." She swings the shell open and drops the egg into vinegared water. "If you happen to live near a hen, you can have a fresh egg like this one instead of a nasty stale egg like this," she says, holding up another egg in a saucer. "The white is too relaxed and the yolk is practically naked."

"'If you happen to live near a hen'—did you hear that?" Her husband Paul laughs aloud. "I never heard her say that before."

Under the glare of spotlights and the ganglia of their cables, against a decorator wall of painted casseroles and plastic bouquets, Julia seems extraordinarily relaxed, yet totally in control. At six feet one inch, she towers over the kitchen counter, which conceals the surprising elegance of her long legs. As always, her crinkly blue-green eyes are lighted by a smile.

Beside her, Paul, ten years her senior and 36 her husband, plays straight man to her clown. "We decided from the beginning to be a couple," says the man who designs their kitchens, photographs their food, whispers the time at their lectures. "Julia does not have a good instinct for timing," he explains.

Her timing was right on one score, however. In 1962, when her television show premiered, America was hungry for just such a program. "There was a new interest in food, the Kennedys were in the White House, everyone was traveling to Europe. Food became chic."

But the clue to Julia's success is that she is anti-chic. "No fakery, no pretense, very free, natural, the same off-screen as on," Paul says admiringly. "We're middle-class Americans, we're not fancy," Julia explained to a visitor watching her at work in her Cambridge,

Massachusetts, kitchen. They felt free to break all the rules—and they did.

They shocked the fastidious by smoking between courses and drinking highballs before dinner. They shocked the meticulous by cooking up a storm rather than cleaning up the mess. When viewers accused Julia of being a sloppy cook, she replied, "I don't find it sloppy . . . they're just prissy people."

Julia Child is the cooking teacher we always hoped to find. She makes us laugh, involves us in her craft, encourages us to take our own direction. "A natural rightness rather than a pedantic correctness is my goal in cooking," she wrote in *Julia Child & Company*.

Good cooking "happened" to have begun in France, she says, so that the techniques of cooking are French in language and form, much as the techniques of music are German and Italian. Now that Americans have become far more sophisticated about food, French terminology and structures are less relevant. "I think we invented nouvelle cuisine before the French," she explains, "and now we're beginning to get confidence in ourselves as a cooking culture."

From the beginning, Julia and her French collaborators, Louisette Bertholle and Simone Beck, addressed their *Mastering the Art of French Cooking* to an ecumenical readership: "those who love to cook." They disclaimed French ingredients and French-movie atmosphere for the here and now of basic techniques that anyone could master, using the basic ingredients that can be found in almost any supermarket. They suggested, in fact, that "the book could well be titled *French Cooking From the American Supermarket*."

"A lot of us feel that America will end up being the food capital of the world, " says Julia, who through her television appearances is more responsible than anybody else for bringing home-cooking back into the American home. To live up to her prophecy, perhaps we should heed her advice: "Train yourself. Keep your knives sharp. Above all, have a good time."

James Beard Says Experiment

To discover America through its food is to discover James Beard, a man who has become larger than life, a genuine folk hero. As the father of American cookery in this century, he probably has done more than anyone else to reshape our country's palate.

Beard has taught cooking to amateurs and professionals for nearly 30 years, his students have become his extended family, many returning to his classes year after year.

"Get your hands into it," he tells a student folding egg whites with a spatula. "Get your hips into it," he tells a student rolling out pasta. At six feet four inches and reduced to a mere 260 pounds from his peak of 310 before a no-salt, low-fat diet, the 78-year-old Beard exudes authority. "Never skimp," the giant says to a student who asks, "How much cream?" "I've never had a cooking class," another student confesses, and the giant roars, "Me too."

To learn from Beard is to learn good cooking, whether its roots are French, Italian, Oriental, or down-home American. In his recipes and in his classes he teaches the virtues of simplicity. "Don't gussy up spareribs with all that gunk," he instructs. "Just sprinkle with plain salt and pepper and half an acre of garlic." His books are all basic teaching books. The first *James Beard Cookbook* begins with a chapter on how to boil water—to assure his readers that much of cooking is no more difficult than that. "Be bold," he tells us. "Taste for yourself," he commands. "Taste things half done,

done, and overdone, if that happens, mistakes are to learn from, not to pine over."

Beard's voice is definitely American as he insists that we improvise, experiment, shake up our ideas about menus to feature "whatever you want to star." A sense of theater explains such typical Beard products as his Forty-Garlic Chicken and the wild eclecticism of his melting-pot menus.

"What you cook is a reflection of you," he tells us. "Don't be afraid to try new combinations." It's the cook who unifies a meal, he explains, not a country or a culture.

"Put on a fine show!" Beard exhorts the readers of his book *Delights and Prejudices*. "Like the theater, offering food and hospitality to people is a matter of showmanship, and no matter how simple the performance, unless you do it well, with love and originality, you have a flop on your hands."

Redbook, 1983

James Beard, American Icon

IN 1954, THE *New York Times* dubbed Jim Beard the "Dean of American Cookery," but that's much too respectable. No academic or canonical dean would flaunt that bald head, big belly, and wide grin. He was a laughing Buddha with a bow tie and tiny moustache, looking far more like Oliver Hardy than Lewis Stone. A big country demands big people, and the first reason that Beard became the icon of modern American cookery is that, at 6' 4" and 300 pounds, he was a big man. His size was hyperbolic in the style of American comedy, with its love of Bunyanesque tall tales and Barnum & Bailey showmanship. Beard played "Big" to the hilt.

Even his imagination was grandiose—at one time grand opera was his goal—and he turned his small kitchens into prosceniums for large performances. When he pronounced, 30 years ago, that American cookery was "at a crossroads somewhere between technology and tradition," he was already straddling that intersection like a giant Keystone Kop, directing culinary traffic for Americans going all directions at once. I exaggerate, of course, but part of the power of the icon Beard became was that he was so outsize he could embrace opposite directions of technology and tradition, commerce and art, in his own person without looking crowded. For a culture of mobility moving at full speed, this requires a certain energy—the same energy that puts our stars into orbit.

His star loomed over the horizon at a fortuitous time. America came of age in the 1940s, during the Second World War, although it took the exploding prosperity of the 1950s for us to figure out that we were not only powerful, we were rich. Our appetite to spend money on travel, culture, and the good life burgeoned in the '50s, and Beard was there to equate our swelling appetite for the world's goods and the world's respect with food. American cookery has always hovered near the junction between the fast-food feed-eries of the masses and the hankering for haute of the upwardly mobile. So when the *Times* dubbed Beard "Dean of American Cookery," it shocked in two ways. Most of the world, including much of America, didn't think we had a cookery. Our icons were the Campbell Soup Kids, Aunt Jemima, Betty Crocker. Serious food meant elite food, which hailed from Europe and was promulgated by gurus with names like Lucius, Ludwig, Louis. But here was a guy called Jim, who rose as America's food consciousness rose in a slow upward curve, while we searched for the right words in which to declare food a symbol of liberation from our traditional Puritanism, provincialism, and cultural inferiority.

With his first cookbook, *Hors d'Oeuvre and Canapés*, in 1940, this guy called Jim spoke with a new voice for a new audience. Those who had chafed under the double prohibitionism of domestic science engineers and the Women's Christian Temperance Union embraced The Cocktail Party as both respectable and chic. Since American food had long been in the hands of women as real as Fannie Farmer and as fictive as Betty Crocker, a male voice in the kitchen rang with automatic authority and was a welcome change from the schoolmarm strictures of Home Ec class. *Cook it Outdoors*, in 1941, simply extended the territory of the male sex's natural affinity to fire, and liberated men from having to tote rod and gun as an excuse for campfire. The subtext of both books was that real men eat quiche and wear aprons, outdoors and in. They can make a mean canapé as well as a martini, and grill a steak as easily as a freshly caught trout.

Certainly Jim was skillful at riding the new trends he helped create, because he was open to every form of media, and usually those forms helped promote books. Television's very first cooking program, in 1946 (and think how early that was!), presented Borden Milk's Elsie the Cow. The format was comedic, like cow impersonations in vaudeville, and it was Elsie, our talking cow, who introduced James Beard in *I Love to Eat*. One comic icon midwifed another. But Beard was also a man to take seriously because he knew his stuff. He was America's favorite form of expert, the obsessed amateur, who would reappear two decades later on television in the guise of another serious comedian, Julia Child. But she cooked French. By the time of *The Fireside Cookbook*, in 1949, Beard was being called "America's foremost culinary authority," in part because he knew how to work the media in every form, from newspapers, magazines, books, and radio to the new guy on the block—television. But to his ear, "culinary authority" sounded pompous. So did the word "gourmet." He suggested that Americans instead use the word "epicure," because it denoted "the difference between a social climber and someone who has arrived."

In the 1950s, America had arrived. For the first time in the country's history, food aligned itself with the fashion industry and the travel industry, propelled by an explosion of media opportunities and advertising. America opened its mouth and swallowed the world in a feeding frenzy of consumerism. What better icon for this appetite than the man who, like Rabelais's mock-epic hero, Pantagruel, seemed to embody the food he ate? Beard's genial embrace of all the foods of America, from the coast of Oregon to the Eastern shore, from sea to shining sea, opened ever wider to include the foods of the Caribbean and Brazil, England and France. But he included them with typical American eclecticism, so that his first cooking school, in André Surmain's town house in 1956, featured a menu of Ham Cornucopia, Leg of Lamb Lucullus, and *Boules sur Chocolat*. It was an eclecticism that excluded nothing—not even the sorriest of processed or industrialized foods, from Kraft cheese to iceberg lettuce. In America, technology was always going head to head with tradition.

By 1954 his name got top billing on every one of his cookbooks, as in *Jim Beard's Complete Book of Barbecue and Rotisserie Cooking* or *James Beard's Fish Cookery*. As he became our primary food authority, Jim changed to James, and as the book branding became more intense, so did the plugs and endorsements. The Food Editors' Conference in New York City where his *Fish Cookery* was launched was sponsored by both Kool-Aid and Good Seasons Salad Dressing Mix. His endorsement of French cognac and Champagne was to be expected, as was his alliance with Green Giant's line of canned veggies and airborne Omaha steaks. More inventive, perhaps, was his recipe book for flamed dishes, produced for a blowtorch manufacturer. With the publication, in 1959 of his mass-market paperback *The James Beard Cookbook*, Beard became a household name because his publishers had located the right niche of the middle-class reading and cooking market, somewhere between the readers of the *Betty Crocker Cookbook* and those of *Gourmet*.

While he'd created a persona that became a Beard brand, a commodified image of the good life and all the fun and plenitude and generosity of spirit that went with it, it was an image everyone could aspire to because it was founded on American home cooking, not on fancy French or restaurant cuisine. The cover of his paperback displayed Beard grinning behind a table overloaded with tubs of sausages and mountains of sauerkraut, and the image said it all. He spelled out the same message in detail in his cooking classes: anything he could do, you could do too. Of course it was harder to knead bread dough with one hand, as he did, unless your hand was the giant bear paw his was, but never mind, the principles were the same for him as for you, and he explained principles clearly and simply. Before Julia, there was Jim, and Jim was the first national figure to create a "gastronomic democracy," as his biographer Robert Clark wrote, and to make cooking fun.

Julia Child acknowledged as much when she said, "In the beginning there was Beard." Soon after the beginning, there was also Beard the myth, in which publicity and persona melded with sometimes disastrous effects upon the man himself. While we Americans pursued the good life with abandon in the '50s and '60s, we were also just as frenetic in our appetite for self-improvement and self-help. We indulged ourselves in a consumerist economy of growth and expansion, but were horrified when those same qualities became visible at waist and hips. Diet books sold in even greater numbers than cookbooks, and often to the same buyers. If American cookery came of age in this period, so did American dietary schizophrenia, in a bulimic pattern of glut and purge. Beard himself suffered powerfully from the split between his lifelong desire to eat and his medical need to diet. "No spirits/No snacks/No fats/No seconds," became, by the mid-1970s, his doctor's ultimatum. "Diet or die." Beard did drop 50 pounds, but he was not the same man because he was not the same image, to himself or to others. In 1983, when the "King of Food" was crowned on the fold-out cover of the November issue of *Cuisine*, the Beard icon was such that he was instantly recognizable in the fold-out's double shot of his bald head, front and rear. No name needed, just the head. But it was a disembodied head, because reality had caught up with the myth, and the man was ill indeed.

At Beard's death in January of 1985, Craig Claiborne eulogized him as "a missionary in bringing the gospel of good cooking to the home table." He converted multitudes, and his heritage is touchingly embodied in the heraldic emblems of the Beard House—in plates, aprons, bow ties, semi-outdoor shower, bronze pig—as in the events of the Beard Foundation in showcasing a national standard of good cooking. But the legacy I like to remember is the personal one he memorialized in the story of his own family in *Delight and Prejudices*. There was the father who reached Portland by covered wagon, the mother who came by ship from England. There was the fat boy who grew up in a Portland hotel kitchen with Chinese chefs, and there was the man who became as symbolic of America as the Jolly Green Giant by singing hosannas to the love of good food, simply cooked. It's a very American story.

News from the Beard House, 2003

The Greening of Alice Waters

PAINFULLY NATURAL, IS she not? Oscar Wilde might have said of this American heroine, as he said of his own in *A Woman of No Importance*. Oscar, a *faux naïf* himself, would have seen through this child of nature at a glance. He would have sensed the art by which a diminutive five-foot-two, pale-skinned waif with a 24-carrot smile has become a woman of importance, named by a French magazine as one of the ten best chefs in the world. All the rest are French or Swiss— big guns like Paul Bocuse—and all the rest are men. Alice Waters is the Jeanne d'Arc of the food world, wielding salads instead of flambeaux. She's an American flower child who romps in pastoral gardens where all flowers are edible and 40 kinds of lettuce are always fresh.

It would take a Wildean paradox to explain how the founder of the legendary Chez Panisse conquered the world's culinary giants by cultivating—literally—her own garden. Even as a tot she was a garden girl. She appeared at a party as a vegetable queen, outfitted from her parents' victory garden in lettuce-leaf skirt, radish bracelets, and asparagus crown. But even Wilde might have trouble explaining how a girl from Chatham, New Jersey, could reinvent herself as a French gamine in the middle of a California university town she pretended was Marseilles—as invented by a French moviemaker. All of this, mind you, in the name of the true, the real, and the natural. Alice's Nature, as Wilde would say, is entirely a creation of Art.

In the actual world Alice is a plump 45, divorced and remarried, mother of a six-year-old child, and head of a thriving enterprise that includes restaurants, bestselling cookbooks and, soon, a big city market. For many her name spells California cuisine, but in the actual world Alice never saw California until her college days at UC Santa Barbara and Berkeley, after a migratory youth in which the Waters family (Alice is the second of four children— all girls) trailed from New Jersey to Chicago to Van Nuys. At Berkeley, actuality for Alice was the alienated, fractured world of the '60s created by Vietnam. She joined student protesters in the Free Speech Movement, ran a congressional campaign for a *Ramparts* editor, and majored in the French Revolution. "We all lived at a fever pitch," she says of those times. "We were so righteous, so sure we were right."

A junior year abroad in France added sensual passion to politics. "I fell hopelessly in love," she says, "with eating." She systematically devoured the countryside and, like other of our food prophets who found God in a French pot, returned to America inflamed by an evangelic mission. She didn't go to cooking schools or take cooking lessons. She read Elizabeth David and Richard Olney and *Larousse Gastronomique*, cover to cover. It was not technique but the communality of cooking and eating that turned her on—the vision of a better life, a heroine's dream.

That vision came to her full blown in the movie trilogy of Marcel Pagnol, made in the early '30s and named for the central characters—*Marius, Fanny, César*—who love, fight, eat, live and die in the bistro of this fictionalized Marseilles. Here was the Arcadia she sought when she made her Berkeley kitchen, shared first with graphic artist David Lance Goines, a gathering place for friends to talk art, love and politics. When the gatherings grew too large, she extended her kitchen into a restaurant, converting a small, two-story frame house in a working-class district into Chez Panisse, named for the fictional widower, *le bon dieu* of Pagnol's celluloid world. With that name she wanted to evoke, she says, "the sunny good feelings of another world that contained so much that was incomplete or missing in our own." As she told a recent interviewer, "They had that kind of community and caring . . . those ideal times back in the '30s and '20s that will never exist again. I was wild about those films. I still am."

What is crazy and Californian and Alice-Through-the-Looking-Glass is that she has made her version of that unreal world come true. Although she describes herself as "hopelessly lost in the past," this Alice is as willful as Lewis Carroll's in demanding and getting what she wants. Her starting point—"the *Idea*," as Alice says—was "to search out always the freshest and the best." The idea is ancient to the French and to the generation of Americans who discovered Europe in the bonanza travel years just after World War II. But it was still new to mass-marketed America in 1971, the year Alice founded her Wonderland at Chez Panisse and established total control over local sources of ingredients, so that the daily trip from garden-dairy-orchard to stove-table-mouth would seem as instantaneous as thought.

In actuality, it's a trip in which Nature must connive, a trip less possible in Vladivostok or Patagonia, say, than in the sunny climes of California or Provence. California sun had already produced vine-yards at Napa and Sonoma, organic vegetables at Tassajara, moun-tains of garlic at Gilroy and native celebrants as different as M.F.K. Fisher and Julia Child. What it needed was a center, and that's what it got. Like Joan of Lorraine, Alice of Berkeley surfaced at the right time and place, with a commune and a manifesto to translate all the natural bounty of California into a new American art form—the

Cal-Med restaurant—and to spawn American's first generation of sophisticated native chefs.

But in a genuine American style, which means casual "home cooking" instead of lah-dee-dah French. The prix-fix menu at Chez Panisse changed daily according to whim and to what was in the market. The staff? "Friends," says film producer Tom Luddy, who lived with Alice after her brief marriage to French filmmaker Jean-Pierre Gorin. There were friends, friends of friends, children of friends. When costs rose and the restaurant's fame spread, she added a Café on the second floor, with a pizza oven and no need for reservations—so friends could still come and talk.

Despite international acclaim and customers ranging from Huey Newton to Baryshnikov, only recently has the restaurant begun to turn a profit. "Spending money like Waters," her co-workers joke, in describing her exacting and costly standards when quality is at stake. In her ruthless search for quality at the source, she inspired an ever-widening network of cottage-industry subversives, who tend each baby lettuce or sugar-snap pea, make cheese from their own goats and raise their own free-range chickens or grass-fed lambs. Alice doesn't believe in money, says she'd pass it out if she could. She believes in value. Value and vision.

Her vision of simpler, summer days in old Marseilles led her to complete her restaurant trilogy with a painter and wine-merchant husband, Stephen Singer, and their daughter, Fanny, named of course for the heroine of Pagnol. That same vision drives her still, now that she has semi-retired from 15-hour workdays at the restaurant, to spend more time with her daughter, to write more books, and most of all to create in the middle of Oakland's downtown ghetto a huge public market where the freshest and best will be available to all as the center of a vibrant "social exchange."

If this dream comes true, she may even change the face of the American supermarket, that vast wasteland of the processed, the frozen and the canned. It takes her kind of faith to move that kind of mountain. "I have underlying faith that once having had good food put before them, [people] will choose the good," says Alice. "They just *will*."

What has made Alice a woman of real importance, now that she dresses in black with a period hat like a French matron of the '30s, is not simply a matter of style, of having invented California-Med or nouvelle Pacific or of having transformed vegetable worlds into art. Nor is it a matter of having created a new culinary culture, opening up taste and sensuality for ascetic health faddists and simplifying the palates of Frenchified foodies. Nor is it even a matter of food itself, for food is never simply its tangible, edible self. Alice is my heroine for her daring, for making food mean what she says it means, for transforming her person, her place and her commune of friends into a work of art that has changed us all. Alice is my Jeanne d'Arc for having put into action an impossible ideal. The rest, as they say in the food world, is gravy.

Savvy Woman, 1989

Grand Dame of Virginia Cooking: Edna Lewis

∎

YOU CAN'T MISS her in the farmer's market at New York City's Union Square. Tall, angular, in an African-style dress that sets off a chignon of white hair against dark skin, and with a smile that illuminates whatever she touches—blackberries, a country ham, people. She holds a Keiffer pear to feel if it's right for canning. She smells a quince that will go into a jam. She jokes with the farmer who sprays his cucumbers and buys hers from the farmer who does not. The market that links country to city is home for a woman who in her person and in her cooking links the farm country of Freetown, Virginia, to the city of New York.

So powerfully has she written in *The Taste of Country Cooking* (Alfred A. Knopf, 1976) of the joys of growing up in a Southern farming community founded by her grandfather and his friends just after their emancipation, that it comes as a shock to learn that she has spent most of her adult life in Manhattan. Born into a large family, she and a sister came by bus to the city as teenagers in the 1940s "to go someplace different." She dabbled in the then modish art of dipping blossoms in melted paraffin, "to preserve something you like," and she also did a bit of sewing for her friends in the fashion world. She remembers that after Richard Avedon photographed a Dior collection, his wife, Dorcas, asked her to copy a dress. "That's what I was doing when Johnny Nicholson called and said he was going to open up a restaurant and asked if any of us could cook."

She could cook, all right, everything she'd learned at home and everything she'd learned from a group of friends who'd cooked for fun on weekends during the war, when rationed gas, meat, and sugar challenged ingenuity and imagination. She cooked the same way in the under-equipped Café Nicholson when it opened in 1948 on 58th Street between First and Second Avenues. "I was too ignorant of the restaurant business to know better," she says. She started cooking lunch for 50 people a day on a stove with only two burners—omelets, with lettuce salad. She added cheese souf-flés after Johnny Nicholson bought an oven to sit over one of the burners. When they switched to dinner instead of lunch, they ran out of food at 5:30 the first night, at 6:00 the second. That's when they knew they had to buy a regular stove, and hire another person to make coffee, wash lettuce, and cut bread.

"It was always fun," she recalls. "All these chic people were coming, so it was like opening night every night." For the next five years she cooked pretty much the same menu, because people came to expect it: onion soup; broiled oysters on the half shell; mussels stuffed with tomatoes, saffron, and rice; roast chicken with herbs and a stuffing of carrots; filet mignon with sauce Béarnaise; and her signature dessert, individual chocolate souf-flés with lightly whipped vanilla-scented cream and dark choco-late sauce. Mostly the people came by word of mouth, until food writer Clementine Paddleford headlined them as SOMETHING NEW IN RESTAURANTS.

"I didn't realize it then," Lewis says, "but it was something dif-ferent." A limited menu where everyone brought their own wine. "We didn't think about a café style," she said. "We just wanted something that was good." They didn't think about it until someone opened a place down the street with similar café curtains, black-and-white walls, and gilt mirrors—and called it Serendipity 3. "That's when we became *classic* café."

After five years of fun and hard work, she married and left for Vineland, New Jersey, to start a pheasant farm. "It was real successful," she says, until one August morning when she found her 500 birds had collapsed. The health agent diagnosed sleeping sickness and ordered the birds destroyed. Edna left the farm and returned to Manhattan to cook dinners for private parties and to become a guest chef in restaurants around the country like Fearrington House in North Carolina, and Middleton Place in South Carolina.

As head chef of Peter Aschkenasy's Gage and Tollner (the 110-year-old landmark restaurant in Brooklyn), Lewis has been fussing over such Virginia specialties as Smithfield ham, pan-fried quail, and flounder in parchment since her menu was installed last Thanksgiving. Wise patrons save room for dessert because, with sous chef Tommy Jordon by her side, Lewis is making her own ice cream and watching over rafts of coconut layer cakes and Tyler pies baking in ovens on the premises.

What still illuminates her cooking are her country roots; she has kept country ways in her memory and on her table. Her memories are of an idyllic place, where the woods were full of wild berries and honey hidden in an oak hollow, where the men shot pheasants and slaughtered the hogs that turned into country hams or cracklings for corn bread; where the girls put up melon rinds and Aunt Jennie made hominy and her mother cracked corn. Cracked corn was for the chickens in little coops all over the hillside. When the chicks were small, her mother fed them chopped hard-boiled eggs with oatmeal and wild onion. "That was their medicine," she says. No wonder Edna Lewis looks for the organic farmers in the market at Union Square and, what's more, finds them.

Even in the Depression, "if you had a farm, you were well off in a certain way, because you had pigs and cows, and you grew corn and tomatoes, and what you bought was sugar and kerosene," she remembers. Where she lived in the piedmont plain, everybody had a farm. "When anyone started a house," she says, "they first planted grapevines and a variety of fruit trees, and a couple of people had a big orchard where you could go and pick apples." And she remembers the abundance of Sunday Revival picnic tables laden with hams and chickens and spiced Seckel pears and pork-flavored green beans and tender biscuits and Tyler pies and caramel layer cakes and watermelons and iced tea, "all served free to the visiting guests and relatives home on vacation."

When she came North, she took her roots with her, literally as well as figuratively. Her family kept her supplied with food from the farm. "Those were the days of refrigerated cars on a train," she says, "when you could send anything." She also found that fancy Italian markets in the city like Marolla's had the same good things they had at home, and some new ones too—like arugula, like olive oil. Back home they had salad only in the spring, and dressed it with sugar and salt and pepper and vinegar. The same tender little greens she now dresses with a classic vinaigrette. Back home they made a boiled salad dressing of eggs and oil. At Marolla's she discovered tons of tarragon, and turned her boiled dressing into sauce Béarnaise.

At a time when Middle America was captive to supermarket cans, refrigerator produce, and factory bread, and when herbs were as far-out as garlic and wine, sophisticated tastes were kin to country ones. As Edna Lewis says, "We just wanted something that was good." Something like turtle soup, for instance, that in the city was a costly luxury but in the country as common as branch water. Today Lewis buys frozen turtle meat at the Central Fish Market on Ninth Avenue, but when she describes the making of turtle soup back home, she recreates what for most of us is either a long-vanished world or a world that never was.

"After a thunderstorm when you had a big rain," she said, "the branch would overflow and a big fat turtle would wash up and start crawling toward the house. We had a huge barrel full of excess milk to feed the pigs, and we'd drop the turtle in there. Then they'd cut his head off and hang him up, and we'd dip him in boiling water to loosen the skin on the shell and belly—it was like the skin on a chicken's foot. After the shell dried, we'd use it for a soap dish. Turtle soup was delicious, and my aunt had a lot of soap dishes."

She invokes that world in her new book, *In Pursuit of Flavor* (Alfred A. Knopf, 1988), a pursuit that has led her deep into African roots. The red tomatoes-and-peppers rice that, mixed with meat or fish, is a staple around Charleston, her Nigerian friends call jollof rice and mix with leafy vegetables and crayfish. The cornmeal whipped with okra, introduced to her by a friend from Barbados, is an African dish called fou-fou. Sesame, or benne, seeds, still popular in Southern biscuits and breads, are like the beni seeds that slaves brought with them from Nigeria and planted "at the ends of crop rows and around their small cabins." Her "Saturday Night Yeast Bread" is not too far removed from the Ethiopian bread, flavored with caraway seeds and turmeric, taught her by Ethiopian friends, who call her "our mother in America."

In pursuit of flavor wherever she is, she follows the seasons. Late winter is a hard time "because it's so cold." But that is her time for good rich stews and root vegetables such as salsify, Jerusalem artichokes, green beans, and corn that she's canned during the summer—and hogs that have been killed and preserved in that glory of Southern country cooking, Virginia ham. To sense how sophisticated such country flavors can be, look at her recipes for eels and scallops or Vidalia onion pickles or steamed leek leaves or red currant pie.

Today, country pleasures are neither simple nor common. "I feel sad when I see so many farms foreclosed," she says. "When I was growing up, the farmer was the backbone of the nation, and now there's nobody. They have a machine that digs a hole and plants a seed in one operation and then sprays to kill the weeds—and poisons the food and the birds and everybody." Restaurants suffer, she believes, because modern, chemically treated food is unreliable. But some things don't change. "I love the country," she says, "and if you grow up in a certain culture and go away, you still stick to that." And so she does. If you don't believe that's possible in the city, just follow her around the farmer's market. She's the one you can't miss.

Food Arts, 1989

Breaking Bread with Africa:
Marcus Samuelsson

■

THE ETHIOPIAN CHEF Kassahun Tzegei (pronounced kassa-HOON tse-GUY) is no stranger to globalism. He is better known by his Swedish name, Marcus Samuelsson, and he has become one of America's most innovative chefs, recognized for his transnational riffs on traditional cuisines. A decade ago he reinvigorated classic Swedish cuisine at New York City's Aquavit. In November 2003 he linked Sweden to Japan in his new Big Apple restaurant named Riingo (Japanese for apple), where he remapped the territories of fishy, salty, and pickled foods. Now he's linking America to Africa in a cookbook, *The Soul of a New Cuisine*, due out this fall, that will explore the cultures and cuisines of that yet undiscovered continent. As a culinary globe trotter, Samuelsson embodies a new breed.

At a youthful 35, he's already touched down on every continent but Antarctica. True, he got a head start by being orphaned in Ethiopia at age 3 and adopted by a Swedish couple in Göteborg. But he had no memories of Ethiopia. "I woke up in Sweden," he says, "so I never had to deconstruct anything." He learned to speak Swedish as quickly as he learned to cook Swedish in his grandmother Helga's kitchen. Training at the Göteborg Culinary Institute was but the first step of his culinary journey from classic European training in Switzerland, Austria, and France to sailing around the globe, courtesy of a job on the Seabourn Cruise line.

The one place he hadn't visited, until 1998, was the country of his birth. Only then did he make his first trip to Ethiopia, where he discovered not only his roots but his culinary heartland. "Food is very central to the culture. The family is very central," he says. "There's a friendliness, a great sense of humanity, of spirituality, whether you're Jewish, Muslim, or Christian." Ethiopia has been half-Muslin, half-Christian for countless centuries, so perhaps it's his birthright that drives Samuelsson to unite opposites, both in his own life and in his kitchens.

His culinary innovations have less to do with fusion, where too often different elements are melted into the same pot, than with juxtaposition, where dramatically different elements retain their identity in the mix. At Riingo, for example, he tops a cake of sushi with rice with foie gras and ties it with a nori ribbon. At Aquavit, he serves Western smoked salmon with the spiced Ethiopian butter called *niter kibbeh*, which is clarified butter flavored and preserved with Eastern spices like ginger, cardamom, and turmeric.

His subsequent trips to Ethiopia have only reinforced his penchant for dramatic juxtapositions because the land teems with them. Addis Ababa slams the sleek modernity of the Sheraton Addis hotel, the grandest in Africa, against the chaos of the city's ancient open-air market—compare the size of Central Park to Manhattan—and one of the largest in Africa, where humongous bags of teff (one of the most ancient and miniscule grains) jostle baskets of pomegranates, figs, lemons, and custard apples. Honking cars clog traffic next to a wedding procession of caterers carrying their platters under traditional umbrella canopies of red and green. "Half of Addis is very modern, and the other half is people on donkeys," says Samuelsson.

Wherever he looked in Ethiopia, he found startling disjunctures of ancient and modern. As the birthplace of coffee 800 years ago,

Ethiopia combines its elaborated coffee ceremonies with vintage Italian espresso machines, which arrived in the 1930s when Italian troops attempted to conquer the only country in Africa that has never been colonized. For this reason, Ethiopian culture has remained relatively pure, which is astonishing given its antiquity. Not only coffee began here, so did our own ancestors. Lucy, the world's oldest hominid, was discovered here in 1974, but not without a weird temporal twist. She was named by the diggers who found her bones after *Lucy in the Sky with Diamonds*. The year before Lucy was found, Emperor Haile Salassie was deposed, but not before he'd lent his birth name, Ras Tafari Makonnen, to an expression of black nationalism in Jamaica. Any country that can link the first modern human three million years ago to the last of a dynasty that began with Solomon and Sheba—and link both of those to the Beatles and Bob Marley—is bound to be full of surprises.

The biggest surprise for Samuelsson was his discovery five years ago that his birth father was still alive, working a small subsistence farm in Ethiopia with a new family of eight children. Samuelsson's birth mother had died in a tuberculosis epidemic, leaving his father unable to care for Marcus and his five-year-old sister. Samuelsson had thought his father was dead until he learned that his grief was such that he'd studied to become a Coptic priest for a decade before starting a new family in a village remote from Addis. As a farmer now, he raises chile peppers, corn, and teff, in a system of communal farming that sends anything left over to the market. Because the Ethiopian government has never set up a method of saving, Samuelsson explains, farmers are at the mercy of the elements. There are two rainy periods, one in the spring and one in the summer, and if the rains don't come, drought and famine follow. This is the picture of Ethiopia that Samuelsson had, in common with most of the world, until he experienced the country firsthand.

Where a family may have to subsist on a dollar a day, Samuelsson says, "The true meaning of food becomes something different." And because it is sacred, food is intimately linked with ritual and ceremony. The Coptic calendar, for example, is based on more than 200 fasting days a year, so that legumes, vegetables, and fish become primary elements. Samuelsson is especially fond of a legume dish named *shiro,* a puree of yellow split peas, which at Riingo he mixes with mashed potatoes and the essential Ethiopian spice mixture, *berbere.* For him the three building blocks of Ethiopian food are *berbere, niter, kebbeb* (the spiced butter), and *injera,* the pancake-like bread that is made of finely ground teff, fermented like sourdough, then poured as a batter onto a hot griddle and cooked on one side only.

Ethiopia is a place where the literal meaning of breaking bread together overtakes the symbolic, for the bread is served as an edible tablecloth spread on a low round table, around which family members and guests sit on stools. A hand-washing ceremony begins each meal because every eater uses his right hand to tear off a small piece of bread and roll within it a portion of one of the stews, or *wats,* that have been dished onto the bread in front of each place. Traditionally the host or hostess feeds each guest his first mouthful of food by hand. Drink may be *taj,* an amber-colored honey wine, served in small individual gourd-shaped vessels, or the homemade beer called *tella.* Restaurants in Ethiopia always have music and dancing because that's part of the communal meaning of food, of gathering together to eat and drink.

"It's a whole new world of flavors and food uses," says Samuelsson, and obviously some are more transportable than others. "It's a far stretch to get Americans to break off bread with their hands, but we can use our own techniques to incorporate Ethiopian flavors into, say, steak tartare or smoked salmon." The chef is thinking of Ethiopia's own form of tartare, in which diners dip large chunks of minced raw beef, *kitfo*, in butter and in mixed spices. At Aquavit he's already incorporated *lab*, an Ethiopian cheese which he makes with fresh curds, seasons with chives, and adds to dishes that are hot and spicy for its cooling effect. Since translation is key, he tends to moderate the heat of the spices in *kebbeb* or the *berbere* mix to suit palates less accustomed to what has been called the hottest, most peppery food in all of Africa.

The first trip to Ethiopia was the catalyst, he says, for his wanting to go deeper and broader, to investigate all of Africa because it's the only continent left for American chefs like himself to explore. First they looked to France, then Italy, Japan, Southeast Asia, and South America. "There are 3,000 books about Tuscan food," he says, "and only two about African food." In his new book on Africa, he touches on 30 countries, without being able to visit all of them. But he's also interviewed lots of ordinary people in New York who've come from Libya, Ghana, Liberia—all over—who've sent him to family and friends in their native countries. "I speak to people who are expert and let their stories speak for themselves," he says. "In America when you cook, I want you to have Africa on your mind."

It is America, he believes, that has allowed him to be fully both Ethiopian and Swedish. In Sweden you can only be Swedish, he says. You must learn to speak the language without an accent. In New York, on the other hand, the smartest people in the world have an accent. Or, as he puts it, "In Sweden, Einstein would have been a dishwasher." For him Ethiopia evokes warmth, people, friendliness; Sweden evokes Nordic light and the smell of salt.

Putting the warm and the cool together is like putting a spicy dish together with fresh cheese.

His new television show, which debuted this past fall on the Discovery Home channel, is designed to do just that in ordinary American kitchens. Called *The Inner Chef*, the show brings Samuelsson and a construction team into someone's house in order to first renovate the kitchen and then show the person how to cook a meal, whether it's a mother with four kids or a guy who wants to do barbecue for his Harley Davidson gang. "It's about each person finding his inner chef," he says, which is what Samuelsson finds in whatever part of the world he explores.

Food Arts, 2006

The Count of Cuisine:
Jean-Georges Vongerichten

■

IN A PRETEND-ITALIAN hotel called Bellagio, I look across a fake lake called Como to a faux tower called Eiffel and feel lucky that the steak on my plate is real. In the virtual geography of Las Vegas, food may be the only real thing left—except for money and the giant numbers game that sucks it up. And yet there's some conjuring going on here, too: the creator of this seemingly down-to-earth American steak house, called Prime, is one of New York's finest French chefs, and his Las Vegas debut is typical of his skill as a gamester who keeps diners on their toes.

"I love blackjack; that's my game," Jean-Georges Vongerichten says, when I ask him whether he gambles when he flies to Vegas— which he does for four days every two months, to check on his tables. It's a world Vongerichten understands because it's about numbers, and he's addicted to numbers. I am not surprised when Vongerichten tells me that geomancy, divination through numbers, is an essential part of his private life. He depends on geomancer Jerome Brasset, "the crystal-ball guy," as he calls him. "Right away I connect. I go to him for everything," His Prime menu is a study in numbers: seven types of red meat, five sauces, six flavored mustards, eleven potato sides, six salads, six desserts. (As a footnote, he also offers chicken, lobster, and dover sole.)

Other well-known chefs have installed more predictable versions of their best-known brands in Vegas: Sirio Maccioni replicated both Le Cirque and Osteria del Circo restaurants from New York, Todd English transported Olives from Boston, Wolfgang Puck brought Spago from L.A. But when Vongerichten's partners, the advertising team of Bob Giraldi and Phil Suarez, asked him how he would like to fill one of the dozen restaurant spaces in the megalopolitan Bellagio, he surprised them. "Steak house," he said.

"It was brilliant," says Giraldo. "Gamblers. Guys. Broads. Hotels. Money. Steak." And in the high adrenaline atmosphere of the casino, Vongerichten is onto a sure thing. I was told that Prime is the biggest cash cow of the restaurants in his empire and that sales swelled to $14 million in 1999. (Note: Jean-Georges and his partners refuse to release any more-recent figures on this or his other enterprises.)

Vongerichten is young, he's hip, and he likes motorcycles, Prada shoes, the Knicks, jet airplanes. He's airborne one week out of four and has plotted unique game plans for each of his restaurants, five in New York and six more around the globe. And, like others of the world's finest chefs, he is in the business of fine cuisine. While Americans in particular cling to a *nostalgie de la vie pastorale* in which the master chef lives above his studio and daily turns out masterpieces for a favored few, 40-odd years of wanderings by France's celebrity chefs—Bocuse, Vergé, Ducasse—should have exploded the myth that an haute kitchen demands the constant presence of the master. "Maintain quality" is the mantra of Vongerichten's Rat Pack, the key staff members who travel with a batterie de cuisine that includes cell phones, computers, digital cameras, and archived databases. Given the speed of technology and a global economy, regionalism and authenticity are rapidly being replaced by *la cuisine sans frontiers*, whose lingua franca is English—American English—and whose pilot is arguably Vongerichten, who has changed the rules of the game in a very American way.

When I first met Jean-Georges Vongerichten in 1986, he was the executive chef of Lafayette, the restaurant in Manhattan's Drake hotel. The menu had been conceived by Louis Outhier of L'Oasis, at the time a three-star restaurant on the Côte d'Azur, and even though Lafayette's menu was haute French—foie gras, salmon, lobster, caviar—it contained enough surprises to quicken the pulse. In every dish was discovery: the sea urchin roe was puréed and molded under a ginger vinaigrette; the sea bass was wrapped in zucchini flowers; the brie sprouted black truffles. When Vongerichten emerged from the kitchen, I was surprised not by how young he was (29, looking 20) but by how French he seemed, his accent so clipped he was hard to understand. His food was too much fun, too exuberant, to be French; he'd transmitted his passion for food onto the plate directly, or so it seemed, without pomp or circumstance.

By the time of my next visit to Lafayette, after the crash of '87 had ended Wall Street's party, Vongerichten had changed the menu entirely. Instead of the traditional three courses, he now offered four "building blocks" of equal weight and importance—Bouillons, Vinaigrettes, Huiles Parfumées, and Jus de Légumes—that could be arranged in any order. Juxtaposition was more important than sequence; instead of a narrative, he offered a painting. And the food itself had changed, too. Juices—of carrot, zucchini, fennel, and any other vegetable or fruit whose liquid could be extracted—came to the fore. But Vongerichten did not invent liquid cuisine. In France, a new generation of nouvelle chefs had progressed from *cuisine du terroir* to *cuisine de l'eau*, and Jean-Georges inhaled such ideas easily and instinctively, then exhaled them, in translation, for American palates. It's less that Vongerichten "invented" a fashionable style than that he radically restructured the nature of the meal to reveal the essence of flavors displayed in different contexts. He imparted a sense of risk and adventure and freedom to experiment with flavors and textures that broke open the mold of classical French culinary thinking and felt American to the core.

Jean-Georges Vongerichten is as hybrid as his moniker. His first name joins his mother's Jeannine to his father's Georges; his surname, too, represents a grafting—like the half-German, half-French history of his native Alsace. He looks like a Frenchman, but sculpted by a German woodcarver, with symmetrical black eyebrows, precisely carved mouth, long, indented upper lip. He was born in 1957 in the village of Illkirch-Graffenstaden, on the outskirts of Strasbourg. The River Ill, which named his village, also christened Auberge de l'Ill, the three-star restaurant where he began his apprenticeship, at 16, under the discipline of chef Paul Haeberlin.

As the second of four children and the eldest son of a coal merchant, Vongerichten was expected to take over the family business, but even as a boy he was fanatically tidy and avoided coal in favor of the kitchen. Watching his mother and grandmother prepare lunch for 40 employees each noon, Jo Jo, as the family called him, became so obsessed with food that they nicknamed him "The Palate." His other obsession was clothes. "At night he always folded his little pants, his little socks, and if the band of the socks or pants was not exactly right in the morning, he would not get dressed or go to kindergarten," his mother recounts. "He would stay in the corner and sulk." Yet Vongerichten remembers that he was a wild kid, getting into trouble, hating everything in school except the two things he was good at, numbers and geography. He believes that the strict regime of Haeberlin saved his life. "Otherwise I might have ended up a gangster or who knows what," he says.

He showed talent from the outset, Paul Haeberlin remembers, and earned his professional certificate. At 19 he went into the navy, fulfilling his mandatory military service; afterward, he headed to L'Oasis, where he met Outhier's style of improvisation. "At Outhier's there was nothing on the stove, nothing in the kitchen," he recalls. "You came in, and then you cut the fish, made your sauce from scratch, sprinkled on some herbs—it was spontaneous." He'd found his métier.

After two years Vongerichten left to continue his apprenticeship, first under Paul Bocuse in Collonges-au-Mont-d'Or and then with Eckart Witzigmann in Munich, but he was forced back to prepping and quickly grew restless with restraint. When Outhier called him and asked whether he'd go to Bangkok to the Oriental hotel, Vongerichten replied, "I'm your guy." Romance blossomed as well as career: his girlfriend, Muriel Prévost, a hairdresser he'd met in the L'Oasis hometown of La Napoule, came to visit, and when she became pregnant, they got married and eventually had two children. (They divorced after a decade, and Muriel moved with the children to live on the Côte d'Azur.) After two years of cooking in Thailand, Jean-Georges left to execute Outhier's French menu in six-month and yearlong stints at restaurants in Singapore, Hong Kong, Lisbon, Geneva, London, Boston, and, finally, New York City—where he finally encountered an energy to match his own.

When he left Lafayette to open his own place, in 1991, he surprised everyone by abandoning the four-star game for a bistro, Jo Jo, in a pocket-size town house on East 64th Street that felt like a grown-up's playhouse—with tiled floors, mirrored walls, and a menu laid out like a child's primer: Soup, Salad, Pork, Salmon, Chicken, Chocolate. Of course the Salad was composed of fresh asparagus with morels and dressed with both hollandaise and a soy vinaigrette, the Pork was in a clay pot with potatoes and Riesling, and the Chocolate was his fun cake, the individual kind that leaks molten chocolate when you poke it with a fork.

Vong was Vongerichten's next venture. Designer David Rockwell fabricated a scene at 200 East 54th Street that looked like a collage of old Siam—full of glittering mosaics, gold-leaf walls, louvered shutters behind orchids and palms. Vongerichten's combinations of Eastern and Western flavors and ingredients defied geography and needed to be explained as well as tasted in order to be understood. The waiters would instruct the diners, bite by bite: Dip the lobster daikon roll into the rosemary ginger sauce, the prawn satay into the fresh-oyster sauce, the crab spring roll into the tamarind.

Something else was interesting about Vong, too: it could be replicated. "With a computer you can have a Vong anyplace because it's a very precise cuisine, more than 150 spices," Vongerichten points out. Every recipe is carefully formulated so that the spices, the sauces, will produce exactly the same flavors in London that they do in New York. In 1995 he and his partners opened a Vong in the Berkeley hotel in London, in 1997 in the Mandarin Oriental in Hong Kong, in 1999 in downtown Chicago. The world was Vongerichten's oyster, with a full range of dipping sauces.

If Vong is a game based on multiplication, the restaurant Jean Georges (without the hyphen), which he opened in the Trump International Hotel and Tower on New York's Columbus Circle, is a subtler and more complicated game of division. Here Vongerichten ingeniously solved the problem of how to combine 24-hour room service with a four-star restaurant. He laid out two separate spaces—restaurant

Jean Georges and Nougatine café—and connected them with a theatrical show kitchen, all of it designed by Adam Tihany to make a cool understatement as geometric and urbane as a martini glass. The nitty-gritty working kitchen, which would also handle room service, went into the basement. Vongerichten's tasting menu is like an edible autobiography. Here are Outhier-inspired dishes like turbot sauced by the sweet yellowish vin de paille of Château-Chalon. Here are later innovations like orange dust for the langoustine, made by pulverizing sugared and dried orange zest. Here are Vong-ish desserts—six crèmes caramel with flavors like green tea and ginseng.

On Sunday, his day off, Vongerichten stays home in his apartment on the 11th floor of Tribeca's historic Textile Building with his fiancée, Maria, and their year-old baby, Chloë, and collapses, as he says, like "a soft vegetable." He's never cooked a meal there, he admits, and grabs breakfast at a local Starbucks. Any vacations he takes he spends exploring new flavors in new topographies: in 1998, he went with Mark Bittman, co-author of his third cookbook, *Simple to Spectacular*, to Vietnam to research an Asian cookbook based on Vong's recipes, which he hopes will be published in the winter of 2002.

Personal earnings of $3 million in 2000 placed Vongerichten third on *Forbes* magazine's list of millionaire chefs, after Wolfgang Puck and Emeril Lagasse. Despite the boom in business, he's kept standards high, maintaining, as he puts it, his own "flavor." "What you want in a restaurant is consistency with your flavor," he says. "When you put your recipes in the hands of somebody else, you've already lost 20 percent of yourself; then if that person adds his own 20 percent, you're down 40 percent. If your key workers are trained by you and have been with you for 16 years, you'll close that gap."

As the chef's empire grows, the question becomes, At what point does it expand so much that the cooking no longer has his own "flavor"? Already he considers restaurant Jean Georges a one shot— "it's too demanding." He worries that the inevitably rising costs of four-star dining may mean that no one in the future can afford to produce it. His solution has been to invest in real estate—he bought a building on Perry Street in Greenwich Village and constructed 28 apartments within it—and aims to open a hotel one day. Hotels are cheaper to run than restaurants and require less personal energy, he figures. Of course, he can put in a small restaurant, he says, perhaps one that does only vegetables. That would be a predictably unpredictable next move.

Saveur, 2001

PLACES

The Beautiful Birds of Bresse

THERE WAS NOTHING on our plates but boiled chicken in a little broth, with a carrot slice and a bit of salt on the side. Was this the touted *poularde de Bresse*, the most famous kind of chicken in all of France? We had driven miles to achieve it at the hand of Mère Brazier, the "last of the authentic *mère lyonnaises*." For sixty years now Mère Brazier, as white and plump to bursting as the chicken she serves, has been turning out *la volaille demi-deuil* ("chicken in half-mourning") in the restaurant of her name on top of Col-de-la-Luère outside Lyon. She learned her art from Mère Filloux, who built her reputation on the dish at the turn of the century. We had come therefore to Mère Brazier's because we knew that nowhere else in France would we find the *poularde* served with such classic simplicity.

But the bird on our plates looked so unutterably dull. Then we bit into it: meat as thick as a fist, white as milk, and juicy as melon. *Formidable*. With truffle slices slipped beneath its skin, the bird had been wrapped in muslin and poached in bouillon. Simple as boiling water. But the secret, according to Elizabeth David, "The secret, they say, is to cook fifteen chickens at a time—at least."

Now that we'd met the bird in its virginal state, we sought a less innocent encounter. Of course we could have found it in Paris in a posh restaurant such as Lasserre or in a bistro like Aux Lyonnais, but we went to Lyon because *poularde de Bresse* is to Lyon what steak is to Texas. It heaps the platters of the city's best restaurants—Léon de Lyon, La Mère Brazier, La Mère Guy, La Voûte—as well as the country inns, where traditional home cooking is still maintained by a unique dynasty of female chefs.

Three generations of Mère Blancs have cooked at Vonnas in the heart of the Bresse district. Chicken every Sunday is what the first Mère Blanc cooked for her family. When her farmhouse evolved into a restaurant, her chicken evolved into *la volaille à la crème*, a dish appropriate to a chef named "Blanc," for the chicken's whiteness is intensified by an ivory sauce of egg yolks and *double crème*—a perfect white on white.

After sampling this version, we were hooked. We now lusted after ever more elaborate renditions. A baroque version was rendered by Paul Bocuse, whose *auberge* at Collonges-au-Mont-d'Or purveys much of the excitement once generated by La Pyramide in Vienne. Bocuse learned from a Lyonnais colleague, Gérard Nandron, to stuff the bird with vegetables, poach it in a pig's bladder soaked in cognac, and serve it with *sauce supreme.*

"A beautiful bird for such a dish," says Bocuse, "must weigh at least three to four pounds; she must have a frame that states clearly, 'when you eat me you eat a woman, not a chick.'" Even with the entire output of Bresse to choose from for his auberge, Bocuse spent nearly a year locating "chicken which really tastes like chicken." To Americans, who consume about seven billion pounds of poultry a year, much of it frozen and nearly all raised in hatcheries on commercial feed, a chicken of the quality of *poularde de Bresse* seems as anachronistic as the horseshoe crab or Princess Grace. How has the Bresse bird managed to survive into the computer age? We determined to track the beast to its lair.

We heard that one of the best producers of the birds of Bresse was a M. Cyrille Poncet, president of the Club des Laureats (motto: *Beauté et qualité*), of Saint-Etiénne-du-Bois. Saint-Etiénne is one of many small villages in the rolling farmland of Bresse, which lies in the Saône valley in the modern department of Ain. Bresse, the birthplace not only of the finest chicken in France but also of her most famous gastronome, has slumbered virtually unchanged since Brillat-Savarin praised his native fowl a century and a half ago.

Poncet's farm was not easy to find among the ancient buildings scattered like chicken feed across the valley. At one such house, where great bunches of maize hung from the eaves, I peered into an open door and met blackness. Gradually I made out a *genre* scene that Millet might have painted—an old woman in a black felt hat sitting at a table and an old man in a black felt hat sitting apart in a rocker eating silently from a bowl in his lap. I had uncovered the lair.

A man in his eightieth year, with a greyhound's lean face, Poncet put on spectacles to riffle through the vast memorabilia heaped on his desk and to explain the passion of his life—the *volaille de Bresse*. The farmhouse, he said, had been built by his grandfather, who competed in the first *concours*, or exhibition, of the birds organized at Bourg-en-Bresse in 1862 in honor of Napoleon III. When Cyrille's father took over the business, he won the *prix d'honneur* six times between 1900 and 1914, a record. Cyrille increased the honors of the house in the half century following but he's now decided to retire in favor of his son. "As you see," says Poncet. "I am no spring chicken."

Since 1862, Bourg has canceled its annual exhibition only once—in 1939 at the beginning of the war. At the outbreak of war in 1914, the mayor of Bourg held the *concours* anyway, and gave the prize-winning birds to the King of Belgium for his bravery. In the same year, Poncet's father took the grand prize at the Verdun exhibition with five capons, each weighing ten pounds. Poncet reached for a photo. "In those days they were fattened down to the claws," he continued, "for that was the time when fathers and grandfathers made *la gloire* of the *volaille de Bresse* and with the prize money bought land on which to raise their birds."

The turn of the century was *la belle époque* for these birds, but the breed had been known since the 16th century and had been praised ever since for its "table properties": rich in flesh and meager in bone. Because of an unusually long breast bone, the Bresse fowl can increase its weight by solid meat rather than fat and may reach fourteen pounds. The bones are negligible in the bird's weight because of their porous structure, said to be caused by the local limestone.

To preserve the purity of the breed has been the crusade of Poncet's life. "It is the race Bresselange which has always existed; these farms have never changed. They tell us that we *must* change, but in our house—never, no, because all would be lost. We keep always what is most beautiful and then they are unbeatable. *Imbattable!*"

The first official decree to protect the breed was issued by the Civil Tribunal of Bourg in 1936, and it was for that, says Poncet, "that I fought for three years, me, without stopping." There were then two areas besides Bourg where the bird was raised—Louhans and Solons—but the decree limited legitimate production to Bourg. The French government made the Bourg decree national law in 1957 and thereby awarded the *volaille de Bresse* with the distinction of being the only poultry in France with a formally guaranteed quality.

The law prescribes not only the standards of the breed and the area in which it may be raised but also the exact conditions of its care, feeding, and marketing. Each bird wears a numbered ring on its leg to indicate the man who raised it, another ring on its neck to indicate the man who killed it, and yet a third ring to indicate its exact quality. "I believe this is why there are no trickeries," says Chef Bocuse, "for the *volaille de Bresse*, like wine, is a controlled product."

Before government control, there were trickeries. The unscrupulous might attach the Bresse label to a bird that was merely raised in Bresse, though not of the Bresse race.

Birds of the pure breed are blue bloods in more ways than one; they have blue legs, blue wattles and blue combs. Bresse producers will warn buyers to "Demand the Standard—the Bird with the Steel-Blue Legs."

One purist, a French agricultural engineer, distinguishes even between shades of blue and wants to create *crus* of Bresse on that basis. He claims that the finest birds are to be found only in a special wooded area called "*le grand perimeter*," and that these birds have legs of *clair-blue*. "They are to the race of Bresse," says our designer, "what the *cru* of Pommard is to the wines of Burgundy."

Poncet remounted the fight for purity in 1964, this time against the *poularde du Mans*, the Bresse's heaviest contender, when Mans producers also sought a government-controlled label. "Without question," admits Poncet, "the *poulardes du Mans* are stronger, larger, but they do not have that boldness of eye, that fineness of structure; they are not so *degagé*, the crest is not so pronounced. The *colaille de Bresse* has a little crest thin as a leaf of paper, by which you know already the quality; you know that this beast is fine *throughout*." Again Poncet won his battle.

A purebred, the Bresse chicken is also well bred, under conditions which are pastoral in every sense. The law demands a minimum of three to four months for fattening (but they may be fattened for ten), and demands that the birds be raised "at liberty in the open air" for a third of that time. "While they are in the field," Poncet rhapsodizes, "they are really pretty, look you. They live in the shadow of the trees, upon the fresh grass, free to fly where they will." Free also to eat what they find: insects provided by nature, and bran, wheat, and barley provided by the farmer.

Like true Frenchmen, the birds fatten on liberty, but like Americans they fatten on corn. During a bird's final stretch, which may last two months or more, it pays for its former liberty by imprisonment in a dark cell, its gullet crammed by the farmer's wife with a paste of corn and skimmed milk as it awaits the guillotine. Poncet ascribes the glory of the *volaille de Bresse* to the farmer's wife, for traditionally hers is the delicate task of getting baby to eat his spinach. "Like gourmands, they demand something good on the plate," says Poncet, "and so you make them a special cuisine. And you must be a specialist to administer it, for you must not give them too much and yet you want them to eat until the Very Last Day."

To the farmer's wife, again, goes the job of caponizing, a process as old as the Romans, who first brought the art to France. According to a Bresse legend, the Gallic natives of the area induced the occupying Roman legions to depart by bribing them with a dozen fat capons.

"The operation of caponizing is not very pretty," Poncet admits, "but after the bird's crest is cut and he's had a couple of days rest, he is turned loose again—if all goes well. If not, *ma foi*, the bird will run and peck but he won't get fat; his flesh will not have the same fineness." Actually the French generally prefer the spayed female, the *poularde*, to the capon, as a bird of finer texture and flavor.

Once fattened, the birds are marketed from October through March, a period coinciding nicely with the seasons of Christmas, the New Year and Epiphany. Fernand Point found the season for birds of "character" to be even shorter; he found them somewhat "insipid" after February.

At the *concours*, the displayer reserves his finest fattest birds for the competitive exhibition; the rest he sells to whoever wants to buy, for his own table or for gifts. "Nowadays in Paris," says Poncet, "you present sixty birds and they are gone the first day because everyone knows they won't come on the market again for a long time. Even the newspaper sellers want one, even members of the Chamber of Deputies—because the birds are unique, *quoi?*"

A bird fattened on natural goodies and for months longer than his artificially raised compatriot must necessarily command a fat price. When an ordinary chicken costs seventy cents wholesale, a *volaille de Bresse* will cost two dollars and up. No surprise then that the French Ministry of Agriculture, anxious to compete in the Common Market, has pushed the production of battery-raised poultry to new levels of "progress." What *is* surprising is that the government also supports with honors and cash the "unprogres-sive" pampered birds of Bresse. Among Poncet's hodge-podge of photographs is one showing President de Gaulle himself awarding Poncet the *prix d'honneur* in Paris.

One reason for Poncet's awards is his skill in preparing the birds for exhibition, an art in itself. "We are artists who do it," says Poncet. "Your technicians build batteries, but I am invincible with my beautiful birds, naturally raised, even against the scientifically superior Americans." A sign of his invincibility lies in Poncet's trick of making the bird's legs and wings disappear. Instead of trussing the bird with thread as a U.S. housewife would do it, Poncet pushes wings and legs in under the skin of the bird's body in a process called "enveloping" or "rolling." The bird is then displayed back up, its head, with feathers unplucked, dangling below. "You see no bone when they are rolled," he explains, "neither wing nor leg: only white flesh from neck to tail. They are impeccable."

For Poncet there are only three ways to cook the *volaille*, all of them simple: *poulet gros sel, poulet à la crème* and *poulet rôti*. But the chef must know his bird. Even in "a great restaurant in Paris," for which Poncet had furnished forty pullets at a banquet of *les Grands Vins de France*, the chef had let the birds dry out. A disaster. "Just think, Madame, all the great *crus* of France, thirty kinds of wine and forty beautiful birds—if there had only been a chef from Bresse."

Poncet increased in vigor as the afternoon wore on. Like the Ancient Mariner, a *volaille de Bresse* his albatross, he raised a bony finger to hiss, "I tell you this and I would say it before no matter who. It is not a question of producing 36,000 birds. It is enough to make twenty, entirely beautiful and one of the first quality. Like the wines of Burgundy, it is on the palate that one appreciates them. The rest is words in the air."

He insisted on serving me a glass of wine, "for your trouble in coming to see me." I insisted on a photograph. Madame changed her black wooden shoes for carpet slippers, her hat for a white kerchief. Monsieur changed his duster for a braided jacket, but the hat worn indoors and out remained fixed. They posed very formally beneath the bunches of maize, he holding a splendid white cock with blue wattles, and she a splendid white hen.

Holiday, 1969

Rich, Robust,
and Rewarding Normandy

■

THE NORMANS ARE good fighters and big eaters—they can dish it out both ways. This crossing of military with gastronomic prowess I attribute to the crossing of Viking with Gaul when the Vikings hit the Normandy invasion beaches a thousand years ago. An abundance of food from land and sea turned Nordic warriors into French farmers on the spot. To reap the fruits, they had only to tether their cows, plant their orchards, and spread their nets.

Milk, apples, and fish—an unlikely combination—became the basis, nevertheless, of the Norman cuisine that has been flourishing ever since William the Bastard turned Conqueror.

From one of the most productive dairy regions in the world has developed one of the richest cuisines—rich in butter, cream, and cholesterol. Normandy cooking means pools of butter and rivers of cream drowning every variety of local fish and fowl—*langouste* (rock lobster) from Cherbourg, sole from Dieppe, chicken from the Auge valley, duck from Rouen. It takes a strong constitution—a Norman constitution—to survive it all.

I do not have a Norman constitution. But simple *hubris* and a temperamental inclination toward "Everything in Excess" led me to believe (wrongly) that I could eat my way from Dieppe on the north to Mont-Saint-Michel on the south without irreparable damage.

There were plenty of warnings. Here, for example, were a people who traditionally began the day with a bowl of tripe, a plate of oysters, and a shot of calvados. Here was the tradition of *le trou normand*, a joke phrase for a glass of calvados knocked back between courses. The *trou* creates a "hole" in two ways: a refreshing pause in the meal and room for more in the stomach.

Curnonsky has described the typical Norman pre-war menu, its essential structure unchanged today. "We begin," he writes, "with *bouillon* and *pot-au-feu*, after which a glass of wine is taken—then tripe, then leg of mutton. At this point a halt is called for *le trou normand*. We fall to again with roast veal, then fowl, then the desserts, coffee, and again calvados."

Here, even the cows are sturdy hedonists. *La race normande* is, in fact, a cross between Viking cows and indigenous breeds, such as Jerseys. Bred for both meat and milk, they graze out-of-doors for ten months of the year. It is this rich pasturage that gives their milk its high fat content and delicious taste. Thick cream produces golden butter—unctuous, aromatic, and nutty in taste. In Norman restaurants no piddling, wispy butter curls appear on the table, but a two-pound wooden tub of solid gold, labeled "*un très grand cru.*"

Perhaps because they have no local wines, the Normans speak of both butter and cheese in terms of *crus*. The Auge Valley is the heartland of their produce, and the three great Norman cheeses are made along this route of the *grand crus des fromages,* Camembert, Pont l'Évêque, Livarot—you should eat them in that order, say the Normans, from mild to strong.

Something labeled "Camembert" is produced all over the world, but only Normandy makes the real thing, by traditional methods and with unpasteurized milk. America has paid tribute to genuine Camembert in a curious way. In the village square of Vimoutiers stands a statue of Marie Harel, who, around 1760, sprayed a local cheese with the mold *Penicillium candidum* and thus "created" Camembert. Or so the legend, hotly disputed, goes. The present statue replaces one that Americans bombed during the war; it was the gift of four hundred residents of Van Wert, Ohio, the home of American Camembert,

Pont l'Évêque, though known since the 13th century, is not so universally imitated. Most of it is made in the area between the village of its name and nearby Lisieux. The most purely Norman cheese, however, is Livarot—powerful and enduring. The Michelin green guide warns that its "strong smell alarms the uninitiated." And though I find Livarot wonderfully tasty, packing some in a suitcase to take home was perhaps a mistake, as skeptical glances from fellow tourists seemed to indicate.

The Auge Valley also produces the second staple of Norman cooking—apples, and their happy derivatives, cider and calvados. Apple trees cover the landscape: in May umbrellas of apple blossoms shield the chewing cows, and in September falling apples bombard them.

Small wonder that apples abound in the cooking. And what makes them special is the way that Normans slice them thin and sauté them gently in butter. Sometimes they are piled two inches high in tart shells and blanketed in cream; sometimes they accompany duck, chicken, or even sweetbreads—for they go beautifully with cream sauces.

From apples, cider. *Cidre bouché*, or the bubbly kind, is as remote from the kiddies' Hallowe'en liquid we swallow as it is close to a medium-dry champagne. "More salutary than water, wine, and beer," wrote a 16th-century Norman doctor, "cider is a specific against all melancholy vapors." Norman monks first cultivated cider in the 12th century, not only to cure melancholy but to prevent an immoderate consumption of wine. Today's Norman, however, scorns to drink cider *instead* of wine: he tosses off a bottle or two between meals and then downs both cider and wine with his meal.

As cheese absorbs the taste of milk, so calvados absorbs the taste of apples. For centuries Norman farmers had made an *eau-de-vie* from pears and from cider, but Gilles de Gouberville was the first to register his distillation in 1553. The name *calvados*, so curiously un-French, is said to derive from a Spanish ship, *El Salvador*, wrecked off the coast of the Auge Valley after the defeat of the Armada in 1588.

Aging is essential to calvados. The spirit should mature for at least fifteen years in oaken casks, with a few hazelnuts added. Like sherry, calvados is blended, with each year's distillation added to the older casks. Consequently, there are no vintages—but, roughly speaking, the older the better. A pre-1900 bottle of calvados is now as rare, as costly—and certainly as magnificent—as a fine armagnac.

As a matter of fact, I prefer it. I spent a most pleasant, albeit increasingly fuzzy, afternoon "inspecting" a calvados distillery on the grounds of a 16th-century country estate, the Château du Breuil. Here M. Bizouard, the owner, has installed his copper alembics in an abandoned chocolate factory. But he has placed his finest, his oldest casks to sleep peacefully in the stalls of the former castle stables.

Calvados puts a period to the end of each meal as a matter of course; but, more important, the liqueur provides a kind of unifying undertaste throughout. Calvados flames fish, fowl, and meat; simmers (together with cider) tripes *à la mode de Caen*; flavors cream sauces; and dominates desserts. Especially lovely is an outright *soufflé au calvados*, where calvados replaces the more usual Grand Marnier or Benedictine, the latter also a Norman product.

Fish are as plentiful in Norman seas as are apple trees on Norman land. Each coast town has its specialty, but Dieppe, as the central commercial fishing port, has everything. The rebuilt beach front is a sad reminder of the disastrous Canadian raid of 1942, but the ports in back are full of life—the smell of tar, diesel fumes, and fish; the noise of bars and cafés dispensing Pernod with fish and chips.

In the fish market are mountains of tiny sweet mussels, laced with parsley, and kept black and shiny by water hoses. About the size of a thumbnail and sweet as a hazelnut, mussels are eaten in every possible way—raw, steamed, and served cold with tartar sauce; grilled and served hot with garlic butter; baked in a *quiche*-like tart; poached in a *sauce dieppoise*.

A proper fresh seafood platter will display on its bed of ice and seaweed a handful each of mussels, whelks, cockles (to be picked out of their shells with a straight pin), clams, oysters, and the shrimpiest of shrimps called *crevettes*.

At Honfleur, where the Seine meets the sea, you eat mounds of these tiny creatures served hot—*les crevettes chaudes d'Honfleur*, the Normans say, as if reciting a half-line from Racine. So tiny are they that you eat them, shell, multiple legs, and all (except for head and tail), in quantities limited only by finger fatigue.

Their larger sisters, *langoustes*, come from the Cherbourg peninsula and were called "*les demoiselles de Cherbourg*" long before Cherbourg became associated with either umbrellas or landing beaches. Of course, you eat *langouste* everywhere in France, but not in the superb cream sauces of, for example, M. Nauwelaerts at his restaurant Beauséjour in Léry.

The mustard cream sauce in which M. Nauwelaerts composes his skate is excellent, but his *civet de langouste à la crème* is a masterwork. His restaurant consists of two rooms in a small house fronting a weedy churchyard and a Romanesque church. Léry is a nearly invisible village not far from Rouen and requires the kind of map study that gives teeth to the Michelin red guide's directive "worth a detour."

Between Honfleur and Cherbourg lie the oyster beds of Courseulles, which were here for fattening up Breton and Portuguese varieties as far back as 1855. The present owner of the beds, M. Benoist, is an impresario who depicts the romance of the oyster in *son et lumière* in his Oyster Diorama. He is also a restaurateur who encourages the *degustation* of the oyster on the terraces of his Pleasure Island. (Local record for degustating oysters is five hundred in one sitting.) An oyster enthusiast of the first water, M. Benoist feeds his passion with facts: "The protein in a dozen oysters equals that in a liter of milk. Good for a hangover."

The classic seafood dish with a Normandy label—*sole à la normande*—is not Norman at all, but Parisian. And its origin and ingredients are as controversial as those of *homard à l'amoricain*, or is it *à l'américaine*? The sole dish appears in Carême's great cookbook of 1835, but a contemporary Paris chef named Langlais usually gets the credit. In his restaurant Rocher de Cancale, Langlais dished it up to such grateful gourmets and good publicists as Victor Hugo and Honoré de Balzac.

Matelote à la normande, on the other hand, is genuinely regional and the probable base of Carême's more citified version. Elizabeth David cites a simple recipe for sole stewed in cider with lots of mussels; Waverley Root adds conger eel and other local fish served in cream sauce with mussels, and shrimp or crayfish, oysters, and mushrooms. Strictly speaking, a cream sauce for fish garnished with mussels and shrimp is called *à la dieppoise*; with the addition of oysters and mushrooms, it becomes *à la normande*.

But Norman specialties are far more diverse than fish dishes. The salt marshes of Mont-Saint-Michel, like those of Brittany, furnish the finest lamb of all, that which appears on menus as *gigot de pré-salé*. The banks of the Seine supply the ducks of Rouen and Duclair, which are larger and gamier than the equally famous ducks of Nantes.

On the old market square of Rouen, the Hôtel de la Couronne has been flaming ducks from the time of Joan of Arc. Today, the Couronne serves a *caneton à la rouennaise au sang* as fine as that of the Paris Tour d'Argent, and at a fraction of the price. Couronne's chef wittily presents each duck in two ways: after roasting the duck, he flames the breast slices in calvados and covers them in blood sauce; from thighs, shoulders, and wings, he creates four "drumsticks" that are wrapped in fat, crumbed, and grilled very crisp. Delicious.

The *triperies* of Vire furnish what are probably the most distinctively regional of all Norman dishes: *tripes à la mode de Caen* and *andouille de Vire*. Nobody makes tripes-in-the-Caen-way at home any more; the housewife buys them in a jellied mold from *charcutier* or *tripier* and reheats them at home. Competition among tripe makers is fierce: at Longny-au-Perche the knights of the Fellowship of the Dish of Tripe stage an annual contest for the best dish of tripe in France; at Caen the April Tripe Fair determines the champion tripe maker in the world.

One of Vire's most distinguished citizens is M. Ruault, world champion in 1966 and present chief judge at Caen Fair. Another is M. Danjou, the best *andouille* maker in Vire, and, therefore, in the world. *Andouille* is made from several yards of pork innards; they are washed interminably, cut into strips, stuffed into a natural casing, soaked in brine, and finally smoked very slowly for several weeks. Hung from hooks in the smokehouse, like uniform black stalactites, the *andouilles* will keep almost indefinitely. To ready them for eating, M. Danjou cooks them in boiling water in an enormous caldron, which desalts and softens them. Sliced thin and served cold, they have the pungent taste of a smoked Virginia ham.

In spite of sampling the local products between meals, in spite of consuming meals of six courses twice daily, in spite of *le trou normand*, I was still alive at the end of a week of Norman living. But at the restaurant Au Caneton in Orbec, I tasted defeat.

It was a Sunday dinner at high noon. The menu offered all the Norman products in successive courses. But as I dipped into the butter tub, I knew that even with my survival kit—an expandable belt and a bag of Vichy digestive mints—I was finished. Empty-plated, I watched my husband conquer a serving of whelks, a *timbale de langouste au porto*, a caneton *"ma pomme"* (duck roasted, calvadosed, creamed, and appled), a *soufflé au calvados*, and a glass of calvados straight.

Capillaries burst, liver shot, I knew I was due for home leave.

Holiday, 1971

Umbrian Truffles and Game

∎

BURIED IN THE center of Italy, without seacoast or foreign border, Umbria is as shaded as its name and as deeply rooted as the treasure it conceals—the black truffle. Its mountains, pastures and plains are made green by rivers and lakes and are shaded by forests of pine, chestnut, cypress, olive, fig and, above all, the umbrageous truffle-breeding oak. Removed from the tourist traffic of Tuscany to the west and the Marches to the east, Umbria is a place set apart from the modern world and urban sprawl. It is Italy's secret garden, guarded by a chain of medieval hill towns as picturesque as their castles—Gubin, Assisi, Spello, Spoleto, Todi, Orvieto, Perugia. And the fruits of that wild garden are as ancient as those Umbrian tribes who ate their truffles on the hoof by hunting the wild boar that hunted the truffle, making Umbrian boar the first of the world's gastronomes.

"Sow-bred" is what the Romans called this staple meal of pigs both wild and domesticated before human gastronomes determined not to cast black pearls before swine. Taking no chances, Umbrians today train dogs to hunt truffles and truffle-hunting is very much a regional sport. While Umbria does produce some white truffles in the Appenines near Gubbio, the center of the black-truffle country is in the southeast corner, between Spoleto and Norcia. Here the family of Carlo Urbani has turned the village of Scheggino into the world's major producer of the finest and most prolific black truffle, the *tartufi neri de Norcia*. On their 10-mile estate, the Urbanis employ some 10,000 truffle hunters in season to reap a crop so abundant that Norcia distills some of its leavings into a truffle liqueur, *Amaro al Tartufo*. (Truffle mavens, determined to track truffles to their source, can stay in guest rooms on the Urbani estate, but in season [Sept–March] you need to book two or three months ahead.)

The same shady woods that breed truffles breed other products of the wild—mushrooms such as porcini, chantarelles, the royal agaric (or *cèpes*). Woods and pastures are full of wild fennel, rosemary, sage and thyme, wild greens such as chicory and an edible thistle that Perugians batter-fry as *cardi alla perugina*. There is wild aspar-agus, *aspariagi di bosco*, not to mention chestnuts and pignoli, black berries and wild currants. Not only wild boar thrive in the under-brush, but also mountain sheep and goats, deer and hare, pigeon, quail, pheasant and thrush. Lakes and streams jump with trout, eel, pike (or *luccio*), salmon trout called *coregoni*, a type of perch called *persici*, of smelt called *lattarino*, and of carp called *lasca*, the gem of Lake Trasimeno, sent for centuries to the Pope for Lent.

Umbrians have always celebrated the good food of their land by feasting, even after death. Today outside Perugia, which was an Etruscan city-state as early as 700 BC, you can visit a vast under-ground tomb, the Hypogeum, where a ruling Etruscan family, the Volumnii, feast forever on the banquet couches of their sarcophagi. Feasts of the later kind are memorialized on the portal of the Duomo at Assisi, where a stone lion dines on a Christian and doubtless finds him tasty.

Umbrian foods are simple, earthy foods cooked homestyle, *alla casalinga*. Umbrians are country folk who grill their meats over coals, *alla brace*, or roast them on open hearths, *girarrosto*. While most

Americans have only recently discovered the virtues of charred fish and meats through regional Cajun cooking, Umbrians, for centuries, have charred fish over hot flames to make *pescati carbonaretti*, or "carbonized" fish. So too they have charred lamb to make *agnello all'arrabbiata*, or "angry lamb," sprinkled with salt, pepper and vinegar as an American Southerner might sprinkle his barbecue.

The barbecue connection is apt, for Umbrians love their spit-roast highly seasoned *porchetta* as avidly and as disputatiously as Southerners their barbecued pork. At every country or city market, the *porchetta* vender chops pieces of crackling and the succulent flesh of his herb-stuffed peppery-hot suckling pig to slap them between thick slices of Italian bread. In Umbria he will add wild fennel to his garlic, rosemary and sage to make *porchettini umbri ar girarrosto*.

Pigs that feed on chestnut and acorn, as they once fed on truffles, will naturally make the tastiest pork, as Romans discovered at the time of the Tarquinian kings. From that time on, the men of Norcia were so famous for the pork they turned into sausages and hams that even today pork butchers all over Italy are known as *norcini*. Many of Italy's best "sausage factories," or *salumificii*, are scattered across Umbria. Factory, however, is hardly the word for these family cottage industries. Take the *salumificio* of the Renzini family in Montecastelli just outside Umbertide. If you are on the trail of boar sausages, their specialty, you will have to hunt for an airy shed hidden in fields of wheat and corn. Here Tina and Dante Renzini coddle and fatten the pigs they will roast for *Porchetta* or grind for *salami Perugino* and the somewhat softer *salucce*, or cure for the full array of *panchetta, prosciutto, cacciatori, culaiello* and *capocollo umbro*, or mix with boar for *salami* and *salace di cinghiale*.

In Umbria butchers not only raise their own pigs but hunt their own boar. Go to Orvieto to find Erminio and Philippo Batalocco, the brothers of Dai Fratelli, whose delicatessen is jammed with great fur-covered hams and the heads of boar they have hunted in the woods around their home in nearby Civitelli di Lago. They will tell you how to make *prosciutto di cinghiale* by marinating the hams in brine, washing them in wine seasoned with peppers and garlic and drying them in a cold north wind to make the meat shrink faster. They will tell you how to make a milder cure for *filetto di cinghiale*, sliced thin as a leaf for antipasto.

If you fancy game, linger in Orvieto in Ristorante Il Morino to eat boar steaks in season or roasted mountain goat, served in a mustard sauced with grilled vegetables and washed down with one of the fine dry Orvietos from Il Morino's vast wine case. Or move on to Torgiana, just south of Perugia, to sample a boar salami, marinated in wild herbs, or a pheasant stuffed with truffles in the village of Le Tre Vaselle. Here you can browse in Lungarotti's Wine Museum celebrating the history of Umbrian wines and its current DOC Robesco Riservata and Torre di Giano from Torgiana's increasingly famous vineyards.

For tamer game, go to Gubbio and search the cobble-stoned alleys twisting through the walls of its ducal palaces for Taverna del Lupo, named for the wolf who cried when St. Francis rebuked him for eating the good people of Gubbio and who promised to eat rabbit instead: At the Taverna you can eat rabbit stuffed and roasted like *porchetta*, and called *coniglio al porchetta*, served with fried batter bread or grilled polenta.

Go to Assisi, rising like a ship's prow above the plains of wheat and corn, grapes and tobacco. After watching Giotto's St. Francis preach to the birds in the Basilica of San Francesco, sit in the deep shade of the vine-covered terrace of the Hotel Umbra and feast on fennel-flavored olives, *spaghetti norcina*, black with truffles and roasted pigeons, *piccione*, dripping their juices into pâté-spread canapés.

Wheat and corn are transmuted into breads, pasta and polenta, just as Umbrian olives are transmuted into green oil and the milk of Umbrian lambs into pecorino cheeses. If polenta is the traditional accompaniment for game, wheat, oil and prosciutto, or the sweet and peppery dry-cured pork *capacollo*, mingle in many of the rustic hearth breads that are a meal unto themselves. In Umbria you can still find breads like *tarta al testo*, named for a sandstone wheel that is spread with the bread dough and covered with hot ashes in the hearth. Perugia, too, still makes its traditional egg and oil Christmas bread called *torcolo* and an Easter cheese bread as finely crumbed as brioche.

As befits an ancient capital, Perugia, spiraling high above the Tiber valley, is the center of Umbria's most sophisticated foods, namely its sweets. Here truffles are made of Perugina chocolate, the finest in Italy, and here the hazelnuts of the woods are wrapped in bittersweet chocolate bites called *Baci*. Less well known are the regional delights of the local *pasticerrias* crammed with pastries like *attoria* of almonds and candied fruit, with the sweet egg and pinenut tarts *pinocchiate*, the paper-thin wafers *cialde*, the cookies shaped like a dead man's bones, *stinchetti di morto*, and little almond cakes shaped like fava beans in memory of the votive offerings found in Etruscan tombs and called locally *fave dei morti*.

So unspoiled is Umbria that you have to work hard to eat poorly. You expect to eat well in Perugia after feasting your eyes on the Peruginos and Pintoricchios in the Palazzo del Priori and you will, in the garden of La Rosetta, savoring ravioli filled with ricotta and spinach and sauced with cream thickened with ground hazelnuts. More surprising is the feast to be had in a little wayside inn such as Il Ruscichello, just north of Umbertide, where Fortuna Antonia prides herself on an 8-course gastronomic turn, or *Giro Gastronomico dell'Umbra*, with a new wine for each course.

Even if you run out of gas in Umbria, as I did outside Spoleto on a backroad to Todi, do not despair. Just head for the local albergo and ask for the lunch of the day. At the Albergo Trattoria "San Giovanni" of Sorini Teresa, lunch proved to be cannelonni, followed by chicken with peppers, olives and lemon, followed by a salad of radicchio and tomato, followed by a slice of ripe melon, followed by a zuppa inglese strongly laced with liqueur, and concluded—despite my protests—with a brandy sniffer filled to the brim with amaretti.

A place like this is the kind of secret I wouldn't divulge in any territory other than Umbria. But in Umbria such secrets are safe. A land that has kept its identity through more than 2,000 years of Etruscan and Roman empire builders, of Renaissance and Napoleonic dukes, of modern military and industrial princes is surely proof against tourism and the fumes of the combustion engine. My most treasured memory of Umbria, in fact, is of driving at dusk toward Umbertide, the smell of wild flowers strong in the air, when my headlights caught the unmistakable bristled hump of a boar, hoofing it lightly across the road to get to the truffles on the other side.

Vintage Magazine, 1986

Festival of
the Flowering Almond

■

WHEN THE SNOW hits heaviest is when hope for spring hits hardest. Because the almond is the first tree to blossom in Mediterranean climes, it was anciently a harbinger of spring and symbol of hope. To this day Greek bridal couples dispense white-frosted almonds for luck the way we dispense cake. At the beginning of February, when we in northern climes are ankle- or thigh-deep in snow, spring comes to Sicily in a carpet of wildflowers spread beneath canopies of snow-white sweet and blush-pink bitter almond blossoms. From February to May Sicily is synonymous with spring.

The promise of spring is what took me to Agrigento the second week of February to celebrate their annual almond flowering festival, *sagra del mandorlo in fiore,* when the loveliest cluster of Greek temples in existence rise like Persephone from a sea of blossoms. Not only billowing almonds but waves of red poppies, white alyssum, indigo rosemary, yellow *acetosello,* purple mandrake, scarlet cacti. Captioned photos can convey the look but you've got to be there to feel the light and smell the fragrance. You've got to be there to fondle lemons the size of melons, drown in Sicilian cartloads of blood oranges, savor freshly pressed virgin-green olive oil and test local wines from bubbling *spumantis* to sweet *moscatis* that wash down almond pastries and confections. For even moderate sensualists, February is the time and Agrigento the place for days of wine and almonds.

When Cretan Greeks in the fifth century BC built Akragas (the Romans named it Agrigentum) into a city of 200,000 inhabitants of fabulous wealth, they built monuments to hope in the form of temples. Not in marble, like the Parthenon, but in limestone the color of honey, honey from the combs that Daedalus is said to have offered Aphrodite when he fled here from Crete. If his hope was for the immortality of art, his offering succeeded, for the ruins of a dozen major temples in Agrigento are dominated by the best-preserved Greek temple in the world, the Temple of Concordia, a fit symbol of the endurance and harmony of Sicily's crossroads civilization.

Inside Concordia's classic Doric columns stand Byzantine walls and arches erected by San Gregorio delle Rape ("St. Gregory of the Turnips") in the 6th century AD. Everywhere are visual reminders that Sicily was and remains a crossroads between Asia Minor and the African mainland to which it was once, in the mists of geologic time, attached. Carthaginian slaves who built these temples took revenge on their Greet masters in the 4th century when Carthage besieged and conquered the town. If art is long, power is short. After the Romans laid out their own geometry, early Christians dug catacombs, Normans built chapels, Spaniards cathedrals, and French Bourbons a Cistercian convent where the nuns still make excellent couscous cookies and almond and pistachio pastries. Although the modern town above the Valley of the Temples is a backwater in comparison to the glories below, yet its twisting cobblestone streets, its plazas, pizzerias and discos, its tree-lined esplanade looking beyond the temples to the sea, all belong to Sicily's anomalous mix of past and present.

Especially at festival time, when folk dancers from round the world gather here to dance in the temples and parade in the streets. The first sight of costumed "Incas" from Colombia snaking past espresso bars, followed by drum majorettes from Holland and sword-waving Turks, can give one pause until Sicily works its traditional absorbent powers and makes them part of the landscape, part of its cultural collage. For a week (February 11 through 15) bands play and dancers dance nightly in a large Moorish tent at the foot of the town, but the best moment is the final Sunday when Sicilian families come from around the island to picnic in the flowers and watch their own groups dance among the columns to the sound of tambourine, drum, bagpipe, and flute.

Sicily still has strong folk traditions because, as the largest island in the Mediterranean, it remains a place set apart, a pastoral island made fertile by ash from the highest active volcano in Europe, Mt. Etna. Its black earth attracted first the Phoenicians, then Trojan and Mycenean Greeks who planted olives and grapes and called the island for its triangular shape, Trinacria. Arabs planted orange trees and almonds and called it Paradise. Because of its inexhaustible fertility the island belongs to Persephone, who was abducted into the Underworld through black Lake Pergusa in the island's center, and to kindred goddesses whose temples and shrines punctuate the headlands. At Erice, the temple of Venus Erycina, at Selinunte the Sanctuary of Demeter, at Cefalu the Temple of Diana and at Tyndari the Byzantine Black Madonna.

In every town of Sicily legend and history crowd the present. Both Empedocles and Pirandello were born in Agrigento, the one incinerated in Mt. Etna, the other buried on a seaside cliff near the 18th-century Porto Empedocle built from remains of the Temple of Zeus. Up the coast from Agrigento a Greek theater, Eraclea Minoa, is named for legendary King Minos who, pursuing Daedelus, was killed in his bath by the daughters of King Cocalos. Further along the coast the limestone rocks of a seaside spa, Sciacca, offer both ancient mineral baths in its grottoes and a bizarre piece of modern folk art known as the Enchanted Castle, where a peasant, Filippo Bentivegna, carved every rock surface into a thousand human faces.

Inland from Agrigento the towering hilltown of Caltabelotta built by Arabs, rebuilt by Normans, recalls the legend of San Pellegrino, who subdued a child-eating dragon in a cave that is now an abandoned monastery. Caltabelotta also boasts an exemplary local taverna, named for the saint, where I ate green olives steeped in wild fennel, crackling peasant bread, crisp fried ricotta, and hearth-grilled sausages and lamb, all furnished by the Prinzivalli family who retired here from the New York Bronx.

If Sicilian history is a richly jumbled stew, so is Sicilian food. Tuna, swordfish, sea perch, squid, sardines, shellfish abound, but so do delicate pasture-fed veal and herb-scented lamb. So do local cheeses like tangy pecorino and fresh ricotta draining in a reed basket, made creamy by a bath of warm sheep's milk and fragrant with a sprinkling of sugar and cocoa. Typical of Sicilian pasta is pasta con le sarde, which combines fresh sardines, wild fennel, hot and sweet peppers, capers, pine nuts, and sultana raisins. You can hear Arab echoes here and everywhere: in panelli, a preparation of chickpea flour, boiled and fried, to eat on festal days; in pasta mixed with saffron, raisins, and the green cauliflower they call broccoletti; in a saddle of lamb roasted with rosemary and sage on a bed of couscous.

Sicily blossoms most in its desserts and here the almond reigns, from cassata cakes with ricotta and delicately candied fruits and nuts, to burnt-almond praline ice creams and the witty marzipan shapes they call *frutta alla Martorana*, made to look like figs, cacti, ears of corn, even plates of spaghetti, bars of soap, and baskets of confetti. Sweet almond liqueurs like Licor de Mandorlo, Amaro Averna, and Almond Marsala are desserts in themselves. And the hundreds of good local wines, white and red, seem to take on almond fragrance by osmosis.

My first visit to Sicily nearly thirty years ago was to a land darkened by the war, the Mafia, and what seemed to be incurable poverty. Today even a town as black as Palermo once was is shot with light, its architectural gems spotlit to glow in the dark. Both blessed and cursed by volcanic fruitfulness, Sicily is an island renewed by a budding prosperity hard won by those who work its earth and seas but who know the fulfillment of hope each spring in the almond blossoms of Persephone.

Diversion, 1990

Tracking Cortés in Mexico

■

WHEN HERNANDO CORTÉS first met the food-bearing em-
issaries of Montezuma on the Gulf of Mexico coast of Veracruz in
1519, he spoke like a sly apothecary, "My men suffer from a disease
of the heart," said the Spanish conquistador, "which can only be
assuaged by gold."

If Cortés's medicine was gold, mine was food, when I met up
with Rick Bayless (Frontera Grill and Topolobampo, Chicago) and
met Marilyn Tausend in Mexico City last year to explore the prov-
ince of Veracruz. The aim of Tausend's Culinary Adventures, joined
sometimes by the author of Mexican cookbooks Diana Kennedy,
other times by Bayless, and always by Mexican chef/author Ricardo
Muñoz Zurita, is "to open the door to the flavors of Mexico." That
means opening the door to the past, because in Mexico, history is
as old, as visible, and as tangible as the pyramids of Egypt. Unlike
the bifurcated history of the United States—before and after the
Pilgrims—history in Mexico is layered, like the 23 layers of the Pyramid of the Niches at Tajin or the layered ingredients of a tortilla
or tamale.

Savoring the flavors of Veracruz would mean savoring in our
imaginations the first great Olmec center near Acayucan, which
began around 1200 BC on a plateau above the fertile flood plains of
the coast. A couple of millennia later, these lowlands were supplying

Montezuma at Tenochtitlan with the same staples of cacao, vanilla, avocados, crayfish, prawns, and cacti that today supply the markets of Mexico City, the megalopolis built on the ruins of Tenochtitlan. Just as the Aztec capital gathered tribute from its conquered regions, so Mexico City today reverberates with regional produce from everywhere. That's why the best way to begin any journey into Mexico's culinary past, I found, was to begin in the city itself.

Many things have not changed. In Mexican cuisine, the methods are simple because the tools are ancient: a grinder (*metatze* or *molcajete*), a clay pot (*olla*), and a clay griddle (*comal*). Houses still have open fires, inside and outside. Cooking is still hearth centered, domestic, a *cocina des madres*, since it is women who are the chief preservers of Mexico's ancient culture. Today, many of Mexico's best restaurant chefs are women, with cookbook author/culinary ambassador Patricia Quintana at Restaurant Izote de Patricia Quintana a most prominent example.

As with methods, so with ingredients. Mexican cuisine consists of elaborate flavor variations on a basically simple vegetal theme, with corn as both food and drink, paired most often with beans and flavored most often with chiles. What astonishes an American is that ancient practices of foraging are still everywhere evident in the daily use of flavorful herbs, grasses, seeds, bulbs, algae, snails, maguey worms, honey ants, and grasshoppers.

"We eat everything and always have," says anthropologist and chef/restaurateur Alicia Gironella De Angeli, who created a Veracruz style dinner for our group at her restaurant Los Naranjos. Mexicans simply layer on new products as they come along. De Anjeli's signature dish, in fact, is a tortilla made of epazote-flavored dough, topped with pork cracklings. The herb-flavored dough is as ancient as corn, cracklings were added when the Spanish introduced pigs. Other typical layerings are the addition of post-Columbian cinnamon to the drink called *pinole,* made during ancient times of toasted finely ground corn and ground cacao. More complexly, tamale dough itself is a fusion of native and Spanish elements— corn dough enriched with well-beaten lard (*buena batida*)—as symbolic as the Virgin of Guadalupe, who fuses the most ancient of corn and moon goddesses with Our Lady of Christ.

To speed us on to Veracruz, De Angeli grilled palm flowers (*choches*), sauced with roasted wild tomatoes (*tomachiles*); wrapped chicken tamales in Veracruz's wild leaves (*hoja santa*); layered tortillas with chayote; and flavored beans with *xonequi,* a Veracruz green related to the morning glory plant. Even breakfast the next day was full of specialties prepared by Veracruz-born Carmen Ramirez Degollado, whose restaurant El Bejio has been a favorite of those searching for country cooking: fresh mandarin and guayaba juices; corn turnovers (*molates*) with three sauces—*verde, roja,* and *negra* (green, red, and black, respectively); poached eggs on herb-flavored corn cakes; and drinks of pineapple atole or hot chocolate (*champurrado*).

Once out of the city, passing under the brows of the smoking volcanoes Popocatépetl and Iztaccihuatl, I realized we were following the historical trail of Cortés in reverse. He had landed on the coast just north of the present city of Veracruz and worked his way over the formidable Sierra Madre Oriental to the Valley of Mexico, conquering Tenochtitlan at last in 1521. He must have tasted, as we soon did in a little village a couple of hours east of the city, indigenous amaranth. The family of Donato Garcia, working in the courtyard of their adobe house, showed us how they popped the cereal grains, then poured on boiling sugar syrup and quickly molded the mixture into rectangular blocks to make the snack called *alegria.* An Aztec family would have used corn syrup or honey for their "glue," but otherwise the process was as unchanged as the wood-smoked and grilled blue corn/chile tacos that concluded our lesson.

By the time we reached Cacatxla, a ninth-century site of Putún Maya and once an important trade route for cacao (one of the brilliant murals at Cacaxtla depicts a Mayan merchant god next to a cacao tree), we were hot on the heels of Cortés. At the neighboring town of Tlaxcala, Cortés regrouped his men after their horrific defeat at Tenochtitlan on the Night of Sadness in 1520, to build a fleet of boats that they carried in sections over the mountains to attack Tenochtitlan by water.

Tlaxcala today is a 16th-century jewel, its plaza recently restored to former glory by glowing colors and gleaming tiles. In her beamed colonial kitchen, Yolanda Ramos Galicia, another anthropologist/chef, explained the ancient process of making corn dough: first by boiling dried corn kernels with calcium hydroxide (slaked lime from limestone, or *cal*) for only three minutes, if making tamales instead of tortillas (the corn is more coarsely ground for tamales); then by letting the kernels soak in the same water for two days to loosen their skins. For seasoning and leavening, the Aztecs would have added *tequesquite*, a mineral from the dried marshlands of Tenochtitlan compounded of sodium chloride and sodium carbonate. Boiling the husks of tomatillos provided an acidulated water which, when added to the powdered *tequesquite*, had the same effect as modern baking powder (which combines an acid and alkali). Since the tamale was a sacred bread offered to the gods, it was usually enriched with other ingredients, listed in copious detail by that astonishing Spanish chronicler, Bernardino de Sahagún: turkey meat and eggs, maize flowers and kernels, squash (flowers, seeds, and flesh), chiles, fish, frogs, tadpoles, mushrooms, tuna cacti, rabbits, pocket gophers, fruit, beans, honey, and bees.

Under Bayless' direction, we tried our hand at making little oval-shaped corn cakes with black bean filling (*tlacoyas*), typical of the town as the name implies, with a salsa of roasted tomatillos and Serrano chiles. Spanish garnishes furnished toppings of crumbled cheese, chopped onion, chorizo, and radish. An entrée of pumpkin seed sauce for chicken (*pepian verde de pollo*) was a colonial variation on a pre-Columbia theme. While the base of the sauce was native—pepita seeds, tomatillos, green chiles, epazote, chayote, and *calabasita* or zucchini (all squashes but the marrow originated in the New World)—Spaniards layered on white onion, garlic, marjoram, bay leaf, thyme, and cilantro. Today, these latter flavorings are as typical of Mexican cuisine as of European, but here they were added to native wild roots and herbs, just as the Spaniards' chickens were added to native wild fowl and their eggs.

Like Cortés, we traveled across highlands into the rugged Sierra, but in the opposite direction, to reach the tiny village of Pahautlan, deep in a valley, on the eve of its celebration of a battle with the French in 1862. We'd celebrated earlier with an outdoor *barbacua* at the hacienda of a family of artisan *pulque* makers and, believe me, *pulque* never tasted so good. Like any home brew, the quality of *pulque* depends entirely on its freshness and on the skill of the maker. We examined from start to finish how the sweet sap (*aguamiel*, or honey water) is extracted from the heart of the agave (maguey cactus) with a gourd (*acocote*) that acts as a siphon. The liquid is then fermented traditionally with the aid of an herb called *cipactli*, or "*pulque* remedy," during which the liquid turns white. At the hacienda we drank pitchers of *pulque* flavored with pineapple or tangerine juice and most deliciously with a froth of ground pine nuts. Unlike the Aztecs, who were abstemious in using *pulque* and might punish drunkenness with death, Cortés adapted the juice to

European palates by increasing its potency, distilling it into clear alcohol to make the first tequila.

In this same valley Cortés might have seen many villages engaged in making bark paper (*amate*), for the written accordion-folded books (codices) of the Aztecs, from the *cordes* tree. We watched the process at the nearby village of San Pablito. Villagers boiled strips of bark in huge iron pots with wood ash or slaked lime until the bark softened into long ropes. Some they bleached, others they dyed with vegetal colorings, before a worker would lay out a grid of strands on a flat table and pound them vigorously with a stone to make the fibers spread into a single sheet. Next, they hung the sheets in the sun to dry.

When we reached the coast near Villa Rica, where Cortés founded his first Spanish settlement, we visited the Totonac center known now as El Tajin, which Cortés did not see. Built from 600 to 900, the site lay undiscovered until the late 18th century, but today its reconstructed plazas and pyramids, mainly the Pyramid of the Niches, record in stone the sacred astronomical calendar that governed New World rituals. One of them is performed daily for tourists by costumed *Valadores*, in a rite well described as "a slow-motion quadruple bungee jump" from the top of a very tall pole, where a fifth man on a platform the size of a large dinner plate dances, whistles, and drums while his four companions spin upside down, in 13 revolutions to total 52—corresponding to their calendar of 52 solar years—before they hit the ground.

Today's Costa Esmeralda furnishes lush shade for vanilla and coffee plantations. The Totonacs were the first to plant and then trade the pods of the wild orchid we call vanilla, which provided a major flavoring for cacao and corn drinks before the Spanish brought in coffee.

In this region, while Cortés's men might have been offered *pulque* (or *octli*, as it was called by the Aztecs), Cortés himself would have been offered chocolate, perhaps sweetened with honey, and most certainly formed by pouring the liquid from cup to cup. Chocolate, after all, was the drink of the elite of Montezuma's court, and, unfortunately, the ruler and his courtiers mistook Cortés for a reincarnation of their disappeared god, Quetzalcoatl.

In the town of Coatepec, a magnificent former coffee plantation turned hotel, Posada Coatepec, became our luxurious headquarters for exploring two inland sites Cortés had passed through on his way to Mexico City. Today, Xico, founded by the Nahuas in 1313, is a tiny dazzler of ochre, blue, and green colonial arcades. Xalapa, now the bustling capital of Veracruz, is home to the Museo de Antropologia, remarkable for its superb collection of Olmec sculptures. At Xico, we dined at El Mesón Xiqueno, a restaurant created within the century-old house and tropical garden of the Peredo family, headed now by Peredo Dominguez. To the chatter of parrots, we sampled such local specialties as a frothy bean soup flavored with *xonequi* (a native green) and garnished with blue corn dumplings. To the rhythm of tequila shots, interspersed with shots of chile-spiced tomato juice (*sangrita*) and of lime juice, we nibbled on "little witches" (*brujitos*), such as corn and bean cakes flavored with avocado leaves. But the main dish was chicken in black mole, since the village is famed for moles that symbolically fuse pre- and post-Columbian elements: native cacao, tomato, plantain, peanuts, and three chiles—mulatto, pasilla, and chipotle—with Spanish garlic, hazelnuts, almonds, allspice, black pepper, cumin, and thyme.

At Xalapa, we met Raquel Torres Cerda, an art collector and anthropologist, chef and restaurateur, who had added a new restaurant to her popular Churreria del Recuerdo by converting a handsome 19th-century house into La Criolla. Our focus was on a ritual dish of the Aztecs, a giant communal tamale called *xaca-huil*, which reminded me of the church supper tamale pie of my childhood. The corn dough, textured with fresh corn kernels and flavored with ancho chiles, epazote, *hoja santo*, and oregano, originally formed the base for enclosing and baking the human hearts of victims sacrificed to the sun god. Today, however, the dough is layered thickly with slabs of pork and chicken, enclosed in banana leaves, and baked for 22 hours in a slow oven.

Returned to the coconut palms of the coast, we hit another Cortés destination at Zempoala, where the Totonacs had once built ceremonial stone platforms, pyramids, and temples. One of these lodged Cortés and his men in 1519, when they found in the Totonacs their first allies among groups who chafed under Aztec rule. When Cortés returned to Zempoala the following year, he defeated his Spanish rival, Panfilo de Narvaez, who had been sent from Cuba to arrest him, at this spot. If Narvaez had won, perhaps history would have been different, but not the native culinary base of that history, which is still a coast of tropical fruit by a sea full of fish.

Upon reaching the old port city of Veracruz, we fell upon fish as if we were starving explorers. Seated at one long table at Café Prendes in the central square, jammed with open-air seafood restaurants, mariachi and brass bands, hawkers of all kinds, cigar smokers, and *el damson* dancers of all ages, we dove into platter after platter of pink shrimp in the shell (*camarones en pilar*) and bowl after bowl of Veracruz bouillabaisse (*caldo de largo*) made of fish from the market—grouper, red snapper, pompano, king mackerel, sergeant fish, and striped mullet.

The next day, after a long drive through pineapple plantations to the end of a marshy estuary to reach Alvorado (named for Cortés's second-in-command), we pretended to watch the annual Festival of the Virgin of Candelaria—brass bands, jugglers, and the statue of the Virgin carried in procession to the sea—but we were distracted by more platters of shrimp, which were appetizers for a final fish hash at Restaurant Villa Rica. Here, the specialty was a chile-crab soup (*chilapatebole de jaiba*), a crab fumet colored deep red by chipotle chiles and flavored with onion and garlic. But who could forego an order of red snapper (*huachimango del golfo*) in a Veracruz sauce of capers, tomatoes, onions, and olives, or in a deep green sauce of *baja santo*?

When Cortés, despite breeding children by Malinche and living it up in Mexico City, sailed for the last time to Spain, he did not die a happy man. He never got enough medicine for his heart disease, and he died in 1547, bitter and impoverished. We, on the other hand, flew to Mexico City with stomachs stuffed with complexly flavored corn and beans and heads heavy with history. True, we could have died from overeating, but that is one sure way to die happy.

Food Arts, 2003

Bahia Black and White

∎

AS A PAIR of historians, black and white, Bahia was the logical place for us to go. Jessica Harris, as an Afro-American, has written extensively about the continuity of black cultures on both sides of the Atlantic, from her own backyard in America to the Caribbean, Brazil, and, most recently, the entire continent of Africa. Betty Fussell, as a Scottish-Irish-American, has explored through the lens of corn the culture clash between Native Americans and colonial settlers in the New World. Where better to continue our mutual adventures in black and white cultures than in fabled Bahia—particularly since we're both mad for carnivals?

Bahia looks the way it sounds: African drumbeats, black women in white turbans, blouses, and hoopskirts. Baroque churches in rainbow colors. Bean fritters and shots of fermented sugarcane.

That's the way it is in Salvador, Bahia's capital today and four centuries ago the Portuguese capital of Brazil. Salvador is the mouth of Brazil, surrounding the country's largest bay, Bahia de Todos os Santos, just beneath the "nose" of the Brazilian profile, 1,000 miles north of Rio.

Here, food is so intimately allied with topography that if you drive along Coconut Highway to the Dendè Coast, you can't sit on a beach without someone rushing from a thatch-roofed *harracha* to bring you a white-lightning Caipirinha (made of distilled sugarcane—*cachaça*—flavored with lime and sugar or passion fruit, pineapple, coconut, whatever you want) to wash down platters of fresh-out-of-the-boat seafood such as deep fried whitebait, needlefish, crayfish, crab, and shrimp, accompanied always by *farofa* (manioc flour) and hot salsa.

If you drive inland through the cane and tobacco plantations of Cachoeira to the dry cattle country of Sertão, you will eat sun-dried beef jerky, roasted cheese, fried sweet cassava, and grilled steaks the size of dishpans. And everywhere tropical fruits are so abundant that most of the time you drink them as juice: passion fruit, mango, guava, tamarind, cashew.

In this surf-and-turf landscape, the mix of African and Portuguese cultures and cuisines comes to a boil in Salvador, where every carnival, every festival, every restaurant celebrates the two faces of the city, black and white. In this city, the spires of Portugal's Catholic churches—365 of them, with a saint and a festival for each day of the year—stand next to the temples of Africa's Yorubian religion called Candomblé. In this city African *dendè* (palm oil) and okra meet Portuguese beef and *bacalhau* and mate with native manioc, peanuts, coconuts, and chiles.

This is the only place to eat Brazil's culturally sumptuous stew of black beans and white rice—*feijoada*—enriched with dark smoked pork and lightly toasted manioc flour, because here all food is symbolic and ritualized. In Salvador, all food is party food, in the best sense of the word.

We hit the high end of the *feijoada* party at the five-star Hotel Tropical de Bahia, where at noon the chef lines a buffet table with a row of black iron pots filled with sausages, smoked tongue, smoked pork chops, jerked beef, pig's ears, trotters, and tails to mix with beans and rice before garnishing with plain or fluffy manioc (cooked in palm oil), deep-fried squares of fat back, plantain fritters, collard greens, and hot salsa made with red and green chiles and tomatoes. To heap your plate is to reenact the five-century history of Brazil's double culture in its trans-Atlantic exchange.

But *feijoada* is also a communion dish sacred to the Yorubian religion of this most-African of Latin American cities (80 percent of the population is black) in the ceremonies of Candomblé. Because Jessica is an initiate of the oldest and most revered Candomblé temple (*terreiro*), named the White House (*Casa Blanca*), we were able to eat homemade *feijoada* at the house of Kuto, a daughter of *Casa Blanca*. In the context of whitewashed walls lined with green palm branches, covered by a ceiling of floating blue paper and supported by a central pillar that symbolically connects earth to sky, the harvest of beans and rice and manioc, enriched with meat was shared as a gift with the *orixà*, ancestral spirits manifested as gods.

The power of the sisterhood of Candomblé is felt everywhere in what has been called the City of Women, but nowhere more than in its sisterhood of chefs and the restaurants named for them. This is a city where women run the culinary show, whether it's street food, carnival food, religious feasts, or intimate cafes and public restaurants. We remembered that the mythical Dona Flor of Jorge Amado's novel and wildly popular Brazilian film, *Dona Flor and Her Two Husbands*, ran the Cooking School of Savor and Art and treasured her recipe for Turtle Stew ("a dish served to the gods at the Candomblé") as it was given to her by the teacher of sauces and seasonings, Dona Carmen Dias.

In fact, all the restaurants we ate in, with the exception of hotels, embodied the tradition of *cuisine de mères*, as the French would say, or as Americans would say, Mom's good home cooking. Restaurant food in Bahia is largely an extension of the elemental mixtures, highly flavored and richly oiled, sold by Bahians on the street or out the kitchen door. Typically, to make *acarafé*, a Baiana purees a mortar full of black-eyed peas on the spot, forms the puree into cakes to deep-fry, then slits them open and fills them with a little chile salsa or the peanut/coconut paste called *vatapa*. For a variation, she may make an *abarà*, mixing the puree with pounded dried shrimp, pimiento, and hot peppers to steam in banana leaves. Or she may wrap white fermented cornmeal in banana leaves to make *acaçai*, a Bahian tamale.

One of the most popular spots in town is the tiny restaurant of Dona Alaide, known as the "Queen of Beans," who began by serving take-out pots of beans (*marmitas*) to taxi drivers on the run and now serves a huge communal pot of oxtail stew with beans in her big open kitchen where black politicians gather daily for lunch. Another is the restaurant of Dona Dadá, who began in much the same way by selling *marmitas* from her kitchen into the backyard of hanging laundry and scratching chickens. When house and yard became her restaurant, one reviewer wrote, "Between the chickens and the underwear, you will find good food." Surrounded by brightly colored Bahian murals and paintings, we found good shredded crab, seasoned with green peppers, onion, and tomatoes (*casquinha de siri*), zapped with lime and chile salsa. We also found codfish fritters (*bolinbas de bacalhau*) and roasted red snapper served whole with mashed potatoes thick with butter and cheese. And as always, there were table garnishes of *vatapà*, lime, cilantro, and two kinds of manioc.

In the heart of the Pelourinho, named for the whipping post where slaves were auctioned as late as 1888, flanked now by the Jorge Amado Museum and the stunning facades of 17th- and 18th-century churches, we found the modest powder-blue house of Dona Celina, whose restaurant has expanded across the cobbled street, which serves as a terrace for drinks, to the house opposite. Trained first by her mother, then by hotel restaurants, Dona Celina serves a classic Bahian menu of quality ingredients prepared by the precepts of Savor and Art. Here we savored *moqueca*, a traditional stew of coconut milk and palm oil to flavor a mixture of fish, shrimp, or other seafood and vegetables. The table was lined with garnishes: *vatapà*; an okra puree mixed with dried shrimp, palm oil, and ginger called *caruru*; a pinto bean puree mixed with coconut milk called *feijao de leite*. Along with the stew came a roasted and deep-fried whole red snapper and a black-peppered beef fillet called simply *mal asado*, meaning "rare." Appropriately, a large native painting on the wall behind us depicted the feast of the Last Supper.

Slightly more upscale in restaurant style is the nearby Restaurant Uaua, run by Dona Juana, and named for a little inland country town. Here, doors are outlined with willow sticks and gourds, walls are lined with faux rustic clay and wreaths and hung with old-fashioned farm tools and animal skins. Huge wicker lampshades dominate the bar and illuminate bins of green coconuts and similar plantation produce. And here we sample fried goat cheese, grilled chicken with vegetables, and the sun-dried salted beef typical of the altiplano of cattle ranches begun by the Portuguese in the early 16th century and now so large that the cows are herded by helicopter.

But we have neither time nor appetite to savor Dona Juana's full menu because it is Tuesday night in the Pelourinho, when every street corner booms with the drumming bands (called *blocos afros* and *afoxès*) that practice all year round for the explosion of rhythm, music, and dance that is Carnival in Bahia in February or March. Jessica has been to Carnival many times and danced samba reggae to the Olodum, the most famous of the *blocos afros* who are playing tonight, but Betty has never seen full-out deep-knee bending drummers who dance; the crowds dancing with them are so tightly packed that all she can do is wiggle her hips in her head and hope to come back in February to see the streets turned into rivers of blue and white, the colors of the original *afoxé*, a group of dock-workers who paraded 50 years ago as the Sons of Ghandi (Os Filhos de Ghandi) and now 5,000 strong, still parade through the streets.

Away from the old town, a grand colonial house offers respite from the chaos and crowds. Casa de Gamboa, its rooms furnished with antiques and tall windows overlooking the Bay of All Saints, offers a glimpse of what it would have been like to live on a cacao and cattle plantation of an earlier era, a rich *fazenda* such as the one in southern Bahia where Dona Conçeicão grew up as a child. A handsome, ebullient hostess, she moved to Salvador nearly 30 years ago but was homesick for the country of her youth and so turned the downstairs of her townhouse into a restaurant to serve country foods. She had learned to cook by watching the women who worked in the plantation kitchen, and she is now called the mother of "nouvelle Bahian cuisine," for her dishes are lighter and more delicately seasoned than most.

For appetizers, we eat cheese pastries the size of cashew nuts and shredded crab in a tiny crab shell. A thick fish soup seasoned with lime juice is followed by a *moqueta* in which olive oil has replaced much of the palm oil. Desserts are Portuguese translated to Brazil: a circle of thickened boiled milk with egg yolks and coconut, and a minimold of cassava with sugar and egg. If we come for a week and cook in her kitchen, Dona Conçeicão promises us, we will know everything we want to know about Bahian food, black and white and technicolored. We hope the offer stands because we can hear those drums right now beating out Carnival time.

Food Arts, 1999

Turning 60 at the Top of the World

■

WHEN I LEARNED about Peru's legendary Chosen Women of Machu Picchu, virgins who tended the altars of the Sun God and brewed his sacred beer, I too felt chosen, or at least damn lucky. Here I was, 60 and single, with children grown, husband remarried, parents dead, and my feet eager to carry me up Andean cliffs or down jungle paths. This year would be a turning point in my life.

Peru was perfect, a country that puts decades in the context of millennia and puts my time in its place. I had been there the year before; now I wanted another dip in the "energies," as a long-haired barefooted girl I met at Machu Picchu had called them. She had called herself a witch woman, a healer, and had come that day, June 21, the winter solstice in Peru, to transmit them. "It is up to women, the life givers," she said. "Each of us must absorb and radiate the rays."

The rays? OK. Without some kind of rays how did I make it to the top of Huayna Picchu, the awesome mountain rearing above the ruins? I am neither climber nor aerobic dancer, and I don't know what possessed me to haul myself up a sheer rock face for two hours. Even youthful climbers have trouble at Huayna Picchu, but for anyone over 50 the rule is, never look down, never look back. When I collapsed at the top, giddy with disbelief and lack of oxygen, I was almost literally on top of the world. I wasn't even deflated when a scrawny Englishwoman in her 70s scampered into view and said, "Bit of a trot, what?"

Looking down, I had seen, far below, hundreds of tiny white-robed figures moving through the central greensward of the ruins. They were carrying scarlet banners toward the great stone altar, the Intihuatana, where five centuries ago, at each winter solstice, the sun's rays were "harnessed" to the stone.

Every 12 years these sun-worshipers travel to Machu Picchu from all over the world. "We come to pay our respects to Mother Earth and Father Sun, here at the center of the earth, where all the forces converge," an East Indian had explained to me later. Speaking in delightfully singsong English, he described the coming golden age, when all would live "in piss and hominy."

This year I wanted to celebrate the peace and harmony of *my* golden age. So I crossed the Andes twice, once to enter the jungle of Madre de Dios, in the southeast corner of Peru, and once to reach the highest navigable lake in the world, Lake Titicaca, near the southern tip of Peru.

In the seedy jungle airport at Puerto Maldonado, a Belgian schoolteacher said of a small, raggedy boy who asked to polish her Reeboks, "That's what you get in these poor countries. We don't have that in Belgium." They also don't have emerald rain forests full of giant otters, macaws, jaguars, and spider monkeys, such as the one that clung to our guide's wife as we boarded a pair of motorized long boats, called *peci-pecis*, for a four-hour trip upstream.

Twenty-five Belgians, two Israelis, and I were headed for an inn at the heart of Tambopata Reserve, one of the richest and least ex-plored of all the Amazon jungles. We arrived in time for the sunset and the "blue light" cast by shadows of the distant Andes, giving the illusion of searchlights in the darkening sky. That night, under a black dome lit by the Southern Cross, we used our peci-pecis to hunt with spotlights for caiman, an Amazon alligator. Jeff, a young English zoologist, transfixed with his light what looked to be a five-foot sea serpent, red-eyed and dragon-tailed. Nina, a Spanish biologist, spotted a jaguar stretched arrogantly on a mud bank, indifferent to the roar of motors and the chattering of Belgians.

What impressed me at Machu Picchu was the silence. What struck me in the jungle was the noise. In fierce competition for light and air, every square centimeter of earth is gridlocked with loud life. Birds honk like taxicabs, insects natter and buzz, leaves sputter with unseen armadillos, tapirs, even cheetahs. Jungle harmony, I discovered, is war: fig vines strangle trees; butterflies sit on the heads of turtles to suck their tear ducts dry. A magnificent double-petaled orange flower attracts birds by the bright blue berries in its "mouth." Nora named it lover's lips, and indeed the lips of jungle love are voracious, compounding sex and violence with an intensity that puts mere human love to shame.

From jungle depths I flew to Andean heights at Titicaca, 12,507 feet above sea level, where the air is thin and bitterly cold. Here my guide, Jorges, hustled me into a boat with a Chilean TV crew to visit the weaving center of Titicaca on the island of Taquilla. The island's village sprawls across a terraced bluff. To reach it requires a 30-minute vertical climb. Even with Huayna Picchu behind me, I needed more than the rays this time because I'd been hit by *soroche*, or altitude sickness. "Slow, we'll go very slow," said Jorges, pointing to the heavy equipment lugged by the TV crew, who looked positively green. I was feeling smug, having reached the top alive, until I learned that Jorges and the Chileans were half dead from hangovers after celebrating Jorges's 29th birthday with Peruvian boilermakers of beer and Pisco (a tequilalike drink made from grapes).

Back on the mainland, Jorges drove me across a golden plain to one of Peru's great ancient monuments, the giant funerary towers of Sillustani. Each mammoth stone tower has a small doorway at ground level facing east so the sun can enter at the winter solstice. As I watched, the sun set behind pasted layers of pale blue mountains above a midnight-blue lagoon. I thought of how the same sun had guided the builders of these awesome tombs, lighted the Chosen Women at the altars of Machu Picchu, and given life to me, under the sign of Leo, in a desert in Southern California.

This was where I came in. Looking forward but walking backward, I ended my journey where all journeys should end, at the refreshed center of yourself.

Lear's, 1988

The Surviving Galápagos

■

WHEN CHARLES DARWIN landed on an island of black lava on Sept. 15, 1835, in his fourth year aboard the HMS Beagle, he found the scene so weird that he thought he'd arrived on "some other planet." He complained of the infernal heat, the nauseous smell, the hideous ugliness of the flora and fauna in this "little world within itself."

He was in the Galápagos Islands, a volcanic archipelago of 19 islands and numerous islets lying on the Equator, in the Pacific Ocean, about 600 miles west of Ecuador (which owns them). When I landed on these same islands more than a century and a half later, aboard a creaking tub named Darwin, the scene was still weird—but in ways that the great English naturalist could not have imagined.

The isolation of this "world within itself" provided Darwin with a laboratory in which to study the biological change we now call evolution. But what was an evolutionary lab for Darwin is today an ecological lab, where the issue is not whether, or how, adaptive change takes place, but how fast and how irrevocably.

Darwin's concept of the "struggle for survival," as elaborated in his *On the Origin of Species by Means of Natural Selection* (1859), was generated by his observations of the unique flora and fauna of the Galápagos. Today the islands themselves are struggling to survive an onslaught of humankind. Since the first tour operator began offering organized visits to the islands in 1970, the number of tourists has grown from about 4,000 a year to more than 60,000. Today, 90 cruise boats (larger cruise ships were recently banned) serve the islands and there are 35 hotels—and the once sparsely populated archipelago now has at least 14,000 permanent residents. Anyone who wants to see the little world that Darwin saw here, with a minimum of human overlay, had better hurry.

I went to the Galápagos myself not long ago with my grown daughter, who was keen on snorkeling and hiking around the islands. I intended to laze about with camera and notebook. After a short flight from Quito, the capital of Ecuador, to the island of San Cristóbal (the easternmost of the Galápagos), I got a look at the "economy motor vessel" that was to be home for the next seven days—and that ended my fantasies of restful observation. On board the Darwin, we found a band of 10 thrift-minded athletic youths— one Australian, two English, two German, five Dutch—and a crew of five Ecuadoreans, including a guide my age, a captain half my age and a cook and boat boys young enough to be my grandchildren. Just boarding the vessel had required a certain agility, and it was clear that if I couldn't swim, I'd sink.

Charles Darwin survived five years on the poop deck of the Beagle, where he was a "martyr to seasickness." Our bunks were stacked in the stern in a closet next to the engine and below a porthole boarded shut. One whiff of the diesel fuel and I downed the Dramamine given to us by a kind traveler who'd warned, "If you're on a small boat, you'll need it." Our boat was not only small, it also listed heavily to starboard for reasons that were never explained. Never explained either were the chronic failure of the motor in heavy seas or the frequency with which we took in water, occasioning frantic bailing by the boat boys. During the long hauls between islands (we stopped at eight), only the crew escaped seasickness. But if Darwin could take it, reading Milton's *Paradise Lost* in his hammock "for comfort," so could we, reading Darwin's *Voyage of the Beagle*.

In his diary, Darwin expressed surprise that the islands had not changed more than they had since their discovery in 1535, for they had been "frequently visited by buccaneers and whalers," not to mention sailors hunting tortoises and, on their way, taking "delight in knocking down the little birds."

As early as the 1700s, the island's famous giant land tortoises were being taken by the thousands to Europe and Asia, where they were prized for their oil as well as their meat. Because they could survive for as long as a year aboard ship, they provided fresh meat for the sailors along the way. Because they could store large quantities of water internally, they were also sometimes killed by islanders, who, when "overcome with thirst," Darwin observed, would slaughter one to drink the contents of its bladder.

Today, the Charles Darwin Research Station at Puerto Ayora, on the major island of Santa Cruz, is the chief conservator of the land tortoise in the Galápagos, numbering eggs and nurturing hatchlings. Here tortoises are so tame that we were astonished to see them stretch their necks and beg to be scratched, almost like dogs. To see a tortoise close its eyes in ecstasy at your touch, then sink back into its shell with a sigh, is in itself worth a week of *mal de mer*.

Darwin is memorialized here in contradictory ways, though. Charles Darwin Avenue, Puerto Ayora's main drag, numbers tourists instead of tortoises and nurtures them with pizzerias, souvenir shops, seedy discothèques and sad concrete hotels. Worse, the inevitable symbiosis between tourists (at least half of whom are Ecuadorean) and developers—drawn here by the chance to collect quick tourist bucks—is adversely affecting the environment. Divers have ruined the black coral reefs, cutting pieces for souvenirs. Fishermen, overharvesting lobsters and sea cucumbers (for the aphrodisiac markets of Asia), are upsetting the delicate ecology of marine life on which local sea birds depend. All over the islands, water resources have diminished and pollution has increased.

The Ecuadorean government has attempted to control tourism in the Galápagos by banning larger cruise ships, which probably does some good, but not enough. Tourists are reminded to "Take only photographs, leave only footprints"—and though this rule is hard to enforce, most visitors do seem to stick to the marked trails and conscientiously clean up after themselves and others. Even the well-meaning, however, unwittingly transfer pollen, insects and bacteria from the mainland to the archipelago and from island to island— ultimately as threatening to the local ecology as the mainland goats and pigs imported in Darwin's time to help feed residents of island penal colonies.

In the extraordinary formations of lava on the Galápagos, Darwin saw "a sea petrified in one of its more boisterous moments." To me, the earth looked as if it had spilled its guts, in intestinal coils of black and red, hardening in ropy strands, fans, globules, braids, pools shiny as molasses. Sometimes the volcanic rock seemed to breathe, when a tidal sea-surge sprayed through a hole and subsided with a groan.

Except in the rain forests of the highlands, most of these islands are so hostile to vegetation that Darwin complained he could collect but a few "wretched-looking little weeds." What we saw mostly were huge cacti, like the bark-trunked prickly pear, or strange scalesia trees, which shed feathery strings of foliage that litter the ground like dandruff.

Everywhere were reminders that life here is tough. We came in October, a hard time of year in the reverse seasons of the Southern Hemisphere, for it marks the end of winter and the beginning of spring. On the Galápagos, this is the season of birth and of starvation and drought. The beaches were packed with baby sea lions nuzzling their mothers, and the seas were full of them somersaulting, diving, playing tag with snorkelers. But we also saw numerous dead sea pups and learned that each mother births but one a year. If the mother dies, so does the pup, because no other mother will nurse it.

We learned that the islands' clown, the blue-footed booby, lays three eggs on the ground in a nest she encircles with guapo. Should a chick fall or be pushed from the circle, neither parent will feed it, and it will die.

We watched a starving young pelican try to snatch a piece of fish from a nesting adult. The adult attacked fiercely, grabbing the younger bird's neck in its enormous beak and biting it until the bird flopped away and collapsed in a heap of wing and beak.

Even the birds' mating rituals seemed hostile. On Seymour Island, where the magnificent frigate birds nest, males whooshing their wings and puffing their throats into huge scarlet balloons (to attract the attention of a passing female) appeared ominous against an amazing sunset striped red and black. On Española Island (also called Hood Island), the ritual dance of a pair of boobies, webbed feet thumping, necks thrusting, wings hunching, beaks clacking together between whistles and honks, seemed more like a lovers' quarrel than a courtship.

The comical waved albatross, about 12,000 pairs of which nest on Española Island in the world's last colony of the birds, seemed doomed to extinction by their own goofiness. Chicks stand immobilized for hours, like oiled and feathered beach balls, waiting with their absurdly long necks and beaks to be fed quarts of fish oil regurgitated from their parents' digestive systems. But the adult birds are so heavy, they can scarcely take off to hunt for fish. We watched one galumph toward the cliff three times and flop in failure before he finally caught a wind current to carry him aloft.

In one mangrove swamp in Black Turtle Cove on the north coast of Santa Cruz, we saw white-finned sharks feed and sea turtles mate with equal frenzy. Our guide rowed us silently at dusk, beneath branches so low they scraped the tops of our heads, to peer into shallows clotted with sharks, swerving back and forth in relentless pursuit of food. In the adjoining lagoon we watched sea turtles, some weighing 100 pounds or more, clamber over each other to mount in succession a single female, who treaded water below the surface, occasionally surfacing for air or, clinging with her flipper to a mangrove root, pausing for a breather between bouts.

While Darwin's scientific interest lay largely in the birds unique to each island—especially the 13 species of finch that had adapted to different habitats—he was most fascinated and repelled by the iguanas. "Disgusting clumsy lizards," he called them, "hideous looking . . . of a dirty black colour, stupid and sluggish in [their] movements." The land iguanas ate cactus, he observed, while their marine cousins fed on seaweed. They were so torpid and so dumb, he reported, that he laughed aloud when he picked them up by their tails.

Of all the islands' fauna, though, the hideous iguana seems the most thoroughly adapted to its environment. We saw heaps of marine iguanas (found only in the Galápagos) spread-eagled on rocks to catch the sun, their scaly backs encrusted with salt. One day, we climbed for two or three hours up scrabble rock on the volcanic cone on Santa Fe Island to see crowds of land iguanas, even more sluggish than usual now because they were waiting for the cacti to bloom, having stripped the plants of all the pads they could reach. In the shade they looked like blobs of clay. In bright sunlight, they were transformed into op-art designs of black and tan, their faces a parody of reptilian ugliness, with wraparound mouths and hot pink tongues.

After five years on the Beagle, Darwin longed for his billiards table, an English garden, his family—all far distant from "that mystery of mysteries" he'd discovered in the Galápagos. After a week of such mysteries, our group could sympathize. One of my fellow passengers, an Englishman, expressed best what we all felt when we celebrated our impending departure with a final meal ashore. The restaurant had run out of chocolate cake, and while the Germans had offered a bar of chocolate to him, he was not consoled. "Chocolate cake's different, isn't it?" he asked rhetorically. "It's sort of wet and creamy, you know what I mean?" We knew what he meant. He meant home.

Los Angeles Times Magazine, 1994

China Solo

◼

STANDING IN A drizzle of cold rain at the rail station in Xi'an, with a heap of bags at my feet and neither transport, guide, hotel, nor a word of Chinese but *shay, shay*, I knew I had made a serious mistake in coming to China alone. *Shay, shay*, or "thank you, thank you," I'd learned from Willard Scott when the *Today* show visited China last fall. Otherwise, the only China I knew came from *Terry and the Pirates* and a montage of movies like the Charlie Chan mysteries, *The Good Earth*, and *The Bitter Tea of General Yen*. What madness had possessed me to set out for this fictional land on my own?

It was less madness than stubbornness. For years I had resisted the traditional group tour of China because, as a lover of Chinese food, I was damned if I was going to eat tourist hotel fodder in a country that had produced one of the world's most magnificent cuisines. An American friend, who'd been spending a lot of time in China to help a Chinese woman write her life story, whetted my appetite with tales of hairy-crab festivals and osmanthus-blossom tea. When he suggested that I hop over to Beijing for the midautumn festival, I leapt on a plane. With his Chinese connection—a lady of impeccable background, excellent English, and relatives as numerous as sand pebbles—what could go wrong?

Everything. My pal neglected to tell me that he had fallen in love with China because he had fallen in love with the lady. Nothing had prepared me for his romance. Nothing had prepared the Chinese lady for me, particularly not lengthy explanations from my pal of our platonic friendship. One look and she flash-froze me with her smile while politely offering a moon cake.

That she had survived both Mao and the Red Guards—though her position, family, property, and husband had not—was testimony to her toughness. That she, an intellectual aristocrat, managed to pass for a plebeian-comrade was ample testimony to her wits. She was Chinese history condensed, and as a traveler I should have been grateful. But after a week of deep freeze in Beijing, I plotted my escape to Xi'an. That's when I discovered the literal cost of traveling in China alone.

Every foreign devil in China knows there are two sets of everything: Chinese money and tourist money, Chinese prices and tourist prices. There are also two sets of tourist prices for everything; group prices and individual prices, extending even to restaurants where the same dish for one person may cost ten times as much as for a group. That's how I discovered that the Chinese simply have no understanding of *single* or *solo* or *alone*, and waiters will either ignore you because they assume you are waiting for your group, or they will cluster about you, concerned that you are the victim of some catastrophe.

Among the 50,000 characters of the Chinese language, Fox Butterfield tells us in *China: Alive in the Bitter Sea*, there is no word for intimacy or even for privacy. The Chinese have no concept of the individual. The more than one billion people who now inhabit China live, think, and feel in groups: immediate family, extended family, neighborhood, village, community, commune. By traveling solo I discovered that the communes of the People's Republic are glued together by *guan-xi*, or backdoor connections. With *guan-xi*, at the railroad counters, airplane offices, and hotel desks, everything is negotiable. If Chan sent you, and he is a cousin twice removed, maybe you can wangle 50 percent off; if Yang, and he is a first cousin, maybe 70 percent. Without *guan-xi* I was going nowhere, because as an individual I did not exist.

My solution lay in the youth of China. Seventy percent of China's population is under the age of 35, and 90 percent of this group, particularly the gaggles of teenagers employed by hotels, will do anything to learn English. To get *guan-xi*, I would have to barter phrases that could help them communicate with English-speaking guests, as in this exchange:

"Will you wait in line for hours to buy me a train ticket for Xi'an?"

"Yes, madame, gladly. Do you wish a soft seat or a hard seat?"

"A soft seat, *please.*"

A soft seat means a compartment with four bunks and a Western toilet at the end of the car. A hard seat means a bench in a cattle car with a squat toilet for as many bodies as can be crammed into the car. In the lobby of the Shangri-la Hotel, I found a promising English student in Chen, who after four hours secured me a soft seat for Xi'an the next day, despite official assurance that none were to be had.

I was snacking on sweetened bean paste and preserved garlic cloves in my soft-seat compartment when my bunkmates arrived for the 26-hour trip to Xi'an. They were a pair of Swedish boys, on their way to Australia via the trans-Siberian railway and now mainland China, and Irma from Bavaria, a 75-year-old widowed grandmother who had never been sick a day in her life or lost a night's sleep as she traveled about the world visiting her own *guan-xi*. In Beijing she had ridden a bicycle everywhere because, she told us, "to know a country you must do what they do, to get *inside* the people, *ja?*"

Chinese incomprehension of privacy became clear when it was time to sleep. After a few postprandial games of gin rummy, kibitzed by Irma, the boys stripped to their shorts and retired with their Sony Walkmans to the upper bunks. Irma and I stripped to our underwear and, true to her word, Irma instantly fell asleep. I woke often during the night to the blast of platform loudspeakers and the roar of the crowds rushing for hard seats. One of the Swedes had looked in earlier at the hard-seat car to our rear and reported, "Hell to our heaven." I took his word for it.

When we detrained at Xi'an, a taxi driver held up ten fingers twice. I laughed derisively and held up five. Outraged, he held up ten. I nodded, he laughed and packed me and my bags into a dilapidated van to deposit me at the Golden Flower Hotel. This was a Western mirage of golden glass walls, bronze beams, and burbling fountains. But although a single room at the Golden Flower began at $80 a day, there were no beds to be had at any price. A youth at the desk, however, had enough *guan-xi* to get me a room in a hotel near the airport.

The Hotel Concord was a cement block that had hardened yesterday and would crack tomorrow but meantime supplied beds for tourist groups from Bulgaria and Uzbekistan, and for singles like me.

My first job in Xi'an was to make sure I could leave. A gangling bellboy named Yang, wishing to improve his English, claimed that his Muslim friend Lin had good *guan-xi* at the rail station. It was not good enough, however, to get a ticket for Shanghai, though by the time we discovered this I'd already gifted him with an hour of my "practical" English.

His *guan-xi* at the airport was better, and at the Muslim restaurant that evening, where Yang appeared with a clutch of teenage pals, Lin produced a scrap of paper purporting to be a ticket for an unscheduled flight, costing three times the usual tourist price. Only time would tell if the ticket was real. There was no question of the reality of teenage appetites, on the other hand, as the boys dove into our communal Mongolian hot pot after polishing off deep-fried sausage, vegetables topped with quail eggs, a sweet-and-sour whole fish, and several quart bottles of beer.

I had not come to Xi'an for the food, however, but for the terra cotta warriors of Emperor Qin Shihuang, who in 221 BC set 700,000 workers the 36-year task of molding more than 7,000 warriors, horses, and chariots that he might conquer the netherworld as he had China. At his death, thousands of the craftsmen were buried alive with their handiwork lest their emperor journey alone.

Looking at the vast excavation, I could see no hosts of warriors because of the host of Chinese tourists jostling for vantage points in the crush against the railings. But I soon saw that mobs were the point—mobs of spectators mirrored by mobs of mud soldiers, not unlike the mirroring of the living and the dead reflected on the surface of the Vietnam Veterans Memorial in our nation's capital. It was not the individual detail of these clay soldiers that gave them power but their uniformity, their community of purpose, standing in rows in the tunneled earth, facing forward with grave, dignified faces, each with a mustache and topknot, men and horses squarely planted, stock still and silent.

So many bodies gone, so many bodies present, gave me pause. "Earth to earth," my ancestors would have sermonized, quoting the Preacher: "Vanity of vanities, all is vanity."

But I was not in the land of Christian prophets. I was in the land of Confucius, where individuals are not saved by faith but are civilized by rules of etiquette; where conformity is not an evil of totalitarianism but an ideal of Confucian compromise; where sincerity is not a personal truth but a social mask, one of the "eight faces polished like jade" that enable a man or woman to be all things to all people.

My ticket for Shanghai turned out to be real, and once in Shanghai I headed straight for the Peace Hotel, formerly the Cathay, where Noël Coward wrote *Private Lives*. I had always loved the play as farce. Now I understood it as British fantasy, provoked by city streets so clotted with human flesh that Shanghai made New York look deserted.

In the end I was grateful to the Chinese lady. She made my fictional China real in ways I could not have imagined. At the same time, she seared me forever with the knowledge of who I was and where I came from and what I stood for, on my own two feet, solidly and gladly—alone.

Lear's, 1988

FAMILY

The Eyes Have It

ALL FAMILIES HAVE their totems and my family had two, side by side on the parlor table. One was the family Bible and the other the family photo album. They were strangely alike. Into one I pasted Sunday School pictures of the Holy Family and into the other snapshots of my family. To one who conflated God the Father with her grandfather, the connection of images seemed as natural as glue. The album told our genesis and exodus, our numbers and denteronomy. To us Scotch-Presbyterians, the act of posing for the camera unto the third and fourth generations—sainted elders behind, blessed babes to the front—was as much a family ritual and as urgent a family need as prayer.

For migrants like us, whose forebears had crossed oceans and then prairies without benefit of camera, the Eastman Kodak was an agent of salvation akin to the Ford V-8. Eastman's accordion-pleated roll-film camera enabled us to document our passage across the American wilderness, as we re-enacted the wandering of the tribes of Israel in search of the Promised Land. The camera, now as mobile as ourselves, could record the very tracks of our Firestone tires across Kansas, the Rockies, and Mohave Desert. And when we reached paradise at last, we took pictures to prove it, comparing the desert palms of California with those of Canaan.

The camera commemorated the union of our personal destinies with those of country and of God. The camera was our exegete, the album our epiphany—in short, a book of revelation. Here my Grandmother Harper in her aproned skirt and high-buttoned shoes stands on her horse Minnie at the farm in Edgerton. Here my new-lywed parents picnic with their parents on top of Pike's Peak. And here my mother cradles in her arms beneath an orange tree in Los Angeles a tiny babe, no bigger than the one in Mary's manger.

In photos of my mother, the halos of the Holy Family glowed most bright because, like them, she had died and gone to Heaven. Unlike them, she left photographs behind. They were a godsend. From the time I was a baby, when she died, I was said to look much like her. Studying her photographs, I saw that I did. Such witnessed testimony I took for granted, not realizing the fortuitous collisions of mechanical and natural births. My mother was born the same year, 1892, that George Eastman determined he would put a camera in every hand the way Henry Ford would put a Model T in every garage. For the first time in history, ordinary people would be re-corded, in graven images, in their passage from cradle to grave. For the first time, children would track their genetic past and future, stage by stage, by the visible evolution of their ancestors. For the first time, children would anticipate how they might look as par-ents from how their parents had looked as kids. The camera forever altered family relations, as historians liked to say, because "Photog-raphy could keep the dead around forever."

Through photographs I could see, as I grew from butterball tod-dler to bony teenager, my ghostly mother grow in me. The camera reflected our copycat changes and continuities better than a mirror. A mirror compared only living faces, while the album compared the living and the dead, not only dead bodies but dead selves, dead dreams, lost innocence. Here my mother looks out in lace collar and giant hairbow, here in Gibson Girl blouse, here in schoolmarm spectacles, and here—allowing for period styles of dress and gesture—she looks again in me, at age five, fifteen, twenty-five. The album and I were living proof of the message the Bible conveyed, now by camera as well as words, that there is life after death. The album told me so.

My mother lived on in me so completely that I endured years at the piano, despite no talent, because my mother had been a pianist and therefore so was I. If I didn't inherit her piano hands, I did inherit her "nervous temperament," as they called it then, and was warned constantly to "calm down" lest St. Vitus dance do me in. I studied my mother's photos for clues to the nervous breakdowns that did her in. The photos that fixed my identity securely within the family, within God's family, were also a source of deep anxiety. Keeping the dead around forever could serve as a daily reminder that what had happened to them might happen to me.

But there were other powerful images to shape my destiny. Growing up in the heyday of the photo magazine and the picture paper, I saw the world through the adventurous camera eyes of *The National Geographic*, *Look*, and *Life*. Beneath the star of Bethlehem, I shaped my identity by the stars of Hollywood. My high-school pompadour and Revlon lips owed everything to Betty Grable's. Her famous pin-ups determined not just my war-time looks but my war-time beliefs. "I guess what you would call us girls is kind of their inspiration," Betty had said of pin-up girls and fighting boys. It was, as Betty said, "a grave responsibility."

Newspaper photos, which for most of the war censored the dead bodies of American boys, sustained the cheerleader optimism of us homefront girls and prepared us not at all for those first shots of the mushroom cloud at Hiroshima or the living skeletons at Dachau. My eyes were opened by the unleashing of photographs at the end of the war—the war of Betty Grable, Betty Hinton, Bette Davis, and me—photographs which exploded my naïve belief that photos couldn't lie and that all things worked together for good. Within our family circle, my brother's snapshots of the war exploded the innocence and sanctity of the family album. Here Bob was with his grinning Marine buddies at Tarawa and Guadalcanal, holding up the decapitated heads of Japs. Here he was with me in the album, he in knickers and me in bloomers, holding up our little Easter baskets. Freckled boy and grinning Marine—there was danger in revelation.

If public photos had lied about the war, so private photos had lied about the family. The photos in the album hadn't changed, of course, but my brother and I had. Today if I look at a photo of myself at eight, an unfocused dreaming girl in pink silk dress and large bow topping Shirley Temple curls, I know exactly why I pored over the album as a child, seeking comfort in its testimony to continuity, to victories over time. My faith was so innocent that knowledge was inevitably betrayal. To bite the apple was to know that photos didn't capture the present but only simulated the past. All along the album had been a graveyard and its images cenotaphs. "All photographs are memento mori," Susan Sontag says brilliantly in *On Photography*. "Photographs testify to time's relentless melt."

What I had thought a bulwark against time was itself time's creature, and not only photographs but the album itself. If photography began when my great-grandparents were kids, the album began when they were bearing their first children, in the middle of the last century. It began when celebrity photos the size of visiting cards became the rage and were collected, like baseball cards, into albums for the parlor table. For my great-grandparents these *cartes de visite*, as they were called, became "identity cards" that shaped their own identities as they composed their faces in imitation of their heroes and heroines for the camera's eye. Since exposure time was long, they posed stiffly and solemnly, creating for the next generation the iconography of the eternal couple and the sacred family in ascending ranks—backs straight, knees and lips together, eyes dead ahead. They did so at the very moment the Biblical structure of the Victorian family was suffering time's relentless melt.

By my time, the album was not the annunciation but the tombstone of my family clan. My mind's eye had conspired against me, for believing was seeing, not the reverse. It was I who'd created continuity, coloring the grass green between the graves. It was I who'd imagined the past and future of people I'd invented and re-invented from photos that were mere hicroglyphs in my family's Book of the Dead. All these people, not just my Marine brother or dead mother, were mysterious strangers, as unknown to me as I was to past images of myself. If images had power to reveal, they also had power to conceal, by fixing what was fluid, isolating air-brushed moments, falsifying truth.

In time I discovered how much they had concealed. In time I learned that my gentle sweet-faced mother was a suicide, her mother an iron-willed tyrant who ruled her twelve daughters from an invalid's bed. In time I learned that my ever-smiling father was blamed by my mother's family for her death. By living I learned that he had surrendered his children as hostages in the permanent cold war between his mother and his second wife. There were many secrets that I would never learn, that the images would never tell. While the generations continued their ritual poses—eyes front, saluting the camera with regimented smile—they now looked more and more like police lineups for suspected homicide.

If all photographs are, as Sontag says, "instant antiques," for my children the family album was as weirdly archaic as a snuff box or gramophone. By the time they were born, the flickering black box had replaced album and Bible as parlor totem. Instead of turning pages, my kids switched channels to snatch cartoons in animation or lives in constant motion. Our family lives imitated TV. We were always traveling, always on the move. Instead of seeing the world in flash-freeze moments, my children viewed Egypt, France, Greece with the roving eye of the videocamera, seeking constant change. Instead of the Kodak's "Hold it," the videocamera hollered, "Do something—move!"

They had done their best with speedier versions of the Kodak, from Instamatics to Polaroids, but my children rebelled early against the posed shot. At twelve, my son refused to have a professional studio portrait taken and demanded a series of action shots—dribbling, kicking, heading his soccer ball. The photographer, I remember, was perplexed. She was accustomed to head shots that could be framed and mounted like big-game trophies on the family wall.

Our nuclear family could never replicate the extended family portrait, which required a certain stasis. Both my husband and myself had reversed the Western migration of our ancestors and had lived in apostate exile in the East. Photo-opportunities for three generations were rare. What shots there were, posed old-style before some grandparental manse, reveal the strain. No longer serried ranks stand at attention in full dress. Our siblings and ourselves can scarcely mask the irony of our pressed-on smiles. Our assembled children look down, up, away. Those who face the camera, mug. Poses that once said, "This is the family eternal," now say, "Are you kidding?"

My own nuclear family rejected past for future, wiping the screen clean on a daily basis. Our place in the world was defined not by the factual particulars of where we were but by the projections of Universal Studios, a place we once had been as tourists, when visiting our children's grandparents in the California we had fled. We sought and found identity in the family icons of *Leave it to Beaver* and *I Love Lucy*, and when the fictive Cleavers and real Ricardos broke up, so eventually did we. As a family, our Nielsens had been overrated. Our time was no longer prime.

Divorce switched our category from sit-com to soap-opera and split the screen in four. We abandoned the sound stage we'd called "home" in search of new studios, new performances, seen through four separate view-finders. None of us had a fixed point of return. Fixed points were as antediluvian as daguerreotype. Conditioned now by fast-forward, none of us mourned officially the death of the family. There wasn't time for reruns.

In my new studio apartment, I tossed the album in a closet, along with boxes of photos unsorted since my father's death. Age ninety-two. Boxes he'd carted one way across the country, I carted another, in promise of "tomorrow." From time to time my adult children would visit me, from one coast or another, to paw through album and boxes, looking for clues to yesterday. In their round-faced baby lives, in mine, in the toothless bonneted grin that was unmistakably their father's. In white-bordered images of the four of us together, some of us large, some of us small, all of us strangers to ourselves.

Although the snapshot form was quaint as hoopskirts and pan-taloons in some forgotten attic, still my children searched because they too are image junkies. As if like me they believed one kind of magic could work another, as if the chemical reversal of negative to positive could somehow reverse what is to what was and what might be. As if the holding of translucent film to light could illumi-nate a dark truth.

But unlike me my children are sophisticates about the false, fleeting nature of images themselves. My children, after all, have watched our Kodachromes fade, our Polaroids vanish, the spines of our albums crack. Accustomed to the whirling collages of MTV, they are bothered not at all by chronological jumble, no more than they are bothered by shifting from one lodging to another, with no fixed abode, no single point of view. Their lives are improvised for hand-held camcorders that document their rights of passage, in and out of focus, in multiple perspectives, to be preserved in little boxed coffins stacked like albums on a shelf. They can tune in, tune out, at will. Their control is as arbitrary as it is remote. For the electronic connection, however invisible its waves, is always there. The eye of television, however blank its screen, is always open, scanning Heraclitus's stream.

As for me, I am a child of frozen poses. In a forgotten box, I re-cently came on a photo of myself posing in muslin skirt and wings, knock-knees carefully together, a starred wand in hand, Angel in a Christmas pageant. Age ten. Written on the back, in my father's aged hand when memory and mind were fading, is my name twice misspelled, "Bettie Fussel." Then two questions: "Who did she marry?" "Where does she live?" When I saw him, from time to time, in the nursing home where his flesh became translucent as film and the red-rimmed eyes turned slowly in, he sometimes saw me but never knew me. Decades ago, I'd slipped away from the image in his hand. Out of sight, out of mind, except for the little girl I'd left behind. Only the knock-kneed angel matched the image in his head.

Now I've left all my family behind or they've left me, parents on one end of the plotted curve and children on the other. But I've put them willfully together in frames on my bedroom walls, generation after generation, revealing bloodlines like X-rays of the heart. There's my son's nose in my father's face, my daughter's mouth in mine, her eyebrows in her father's. The puzzle of genes and chromosomes reads like a crossword that goes several ways at once—across, down, diagonal—and like an anacrostic conceals beneath the punning clues a hidden little message. In this one place, arbitrarily and without consent, we are all connected and, for a moment, standing in the middle, surrounded by my walls, I feel I know them all. These images are my familiars.

That illusion is their power. While we depart, they stay. They will stare at my children's children as they stare now at me, teasing me with wordless secrets, with stories I will never know, stories both ended and forever incomplete, challenging others to ask, Who were all these people? Who married whom? Which mother is whose child? Whose baby is that old man? I am faithful to my congregation of photos because we have been through so much together, and even knowing their deceits, I have surrendered gladly to their power.

They are my icons and my reliquaries. Now they frame me, shape how and what I see, shift my narratives, collect people as I once collected them. No longer content with a single room, the photos mount the walls of all my rooms, filling in the gaps between doorways, floors, and ceilings. Though still, these photos are on the move, moving my particular times, places, people, into a different dimension where all times happen at once, like a Byzantine chapel where kings, prophets, saints, and evangelists range from floor to ceiling in mosaic splendor. And at the top, overseeing all, the awesome black-rimmed eyes of God. Mere images they may be, but I'd be lost without them. Without them, I wouldn't have a prayer.

Ontario Review, 1995

Thanatopsis '83

HE WAS FRAMED. I shot him with my Olympic 972X on January 4, 1983, in the Riverside Convalescent Community Center. He was a sitting duck, as still as the California navel oranges spray-painted in acrylic on a field of green behind him. Like them, a *nature morte*. The carved beak of his nose, the thrust of his jaw were right for a Roman coin. Instead, immobilized in his wheelchair by the afghan that skirted him from waist to toe, he looked like Whistler's Mother. Was that right?

He never knew what hit him. He had been often shot and was most alive in ovals and rectangles, embraced by solid cardboard, under glass. He had been shot once as a boy, by T. Owen Foley, in Washington, Iowa, in 1904, behind a wicker table where he stood with his younger brother, Roy. They wore identical knickers, high-button boots, double-breasted jackets with gold watch chains threaded from buttonhole to upper left-hand pocket. Beneath the taming hand of each, immobilized upon the table, was an identical guinea pig. "The guinea pigs were won as a prize," my father had written on the back of the cardboard provided by T. Owen Foley, along with a fur rug and a painted backdrop of palms.

As my father discarded knickers for long pants, he turned toward science and became a dissector of guinea pigs. My Uncle Roy became a missionary in Brazil. They grew into men as upright as the stiff collars they had worn as boys. My Uncle Roy sent home framed pictures of Rio de Janeiro, worked in butterfly wings of tropic blue. My father put butterflies to death in jars before he spread their wings on cotton and impaled each thorax with a pin.

Uncle Roy brought Calvin and a portable organ to the savages of the Amazon. My father brought Darwin and a microscope to the natives of Riverside Polytechnic High. His classroom was a mortuary of pickled frogs and skeletonized cats. My father wore different colored sneakers which he bought at Woolworth's and he smelled strongly of formaldehyde. His favorite food was Del Monte canned peaches preserved in lemon Jell-O.

Uncle Roy came home once every seven years on furlough, bringing with him a wife and a boy and a girl, alike in age and sex to the boy and girl of his brother. The missionary and the scientist never quarreled, God and Darwin lived in perfect harmony in identical but separate frames. The millions of dead departed before Christ were unfortunate in their timing. The millions of dead born before Darwin were unfortunate in their ignorance. If the Bible impaled the sins of man, *The Origin of Species* exposed the skeletons in his closet.

Squatting in the dust of the backyard, we children posed for pictures, like silverbells and cockleshells, all in a row. The boys wore knickers and the girls sunbonnets, like the ones worn once in Washington, Iowa. Pater killed a chicken and Mumsie plucked its feathers and, after the apple sauce, we sang "I Come to the Garden Alone," accompanied by Aunt Evelyn on the upright Baldwin in the parlor. Sometimes father shot us standing on the patchy grass of the frontyard beneath the large framed black sign on our white frame house. The sign said ELIZABETH BLAKE HARPER D.O.

* * *

My stepmother, Elizabeth Blake Harper, Doctor of Osteopathy, pinned bodies to her treating table, where she preserved them by cracking bones. She shared my father's interest in the skeletal. When my tonsils grew too big for my throat, she cracked my neck first to the right and then to the left and told me I felt very much better.

She preferred the treating room to the kitchen, so it was my father who preserved tomatoes every summer, just as his mother had done. He put them in Mason jars in the basement, all in a row above the row of pickled frogs. One row was red, the other green.

Uncle Roy might conjure cockatoos, but the basement was my Amazon. Here beside the jars of living dead were cages of God's creatures live. Garter snakes and king snakes and an occasional rattler. When I cranked the wet wash through the wringer, the rattlesnake would shake his rattle as if he were a baby in a pen. We sought and found black widows in dark corners and sometimes found the turtle we had seized as desert booty. My brother Bob and I killed spiders with a fly swatter and fed the turtle iceberg lettuce, until he immured himself beneath a shelf and thriftily turned shell to coffin.

I did not like to touch the snakes and so I touched them. Even in the hottest August their skin was cold and wet. I liked instead the horned toads. My father taught me how to flip them on their backs and stroke their stomachs until they lay like corpses in your hand. They were not hard to hypnotize, their tiny fingers rigid and their eyelids sealed in ecstasy.

In the basement too were plant presses, where my father tenderly pressed wild flowers to death to preserve their sweet fragility. Life in the Mojave Desert was precarious at best, and the nectar they had hoarded from the sun was now sucked dry between gray blotters which took the imprint of lupine blue and ranunculus yellow.

While the Doctor of Osteopathy laid out patients on her table, the Bachelor of Science catalogued his plants, giving each a Latin name as in some Popish rite and filing them in drawers in the metal filing cabinet in the dining room. On top of the file stood a lamp, sent by Uncle Roy, carved from a single piece of Brazil-nut wood which we called "Nigger-toe." Tacked to the wall in my brother's bedroom was the petaled skin of a Brazilian python. We lacked neither flora nor fauna.

My missionary uncle promised life everlasting to the dying creatures of the Amazon. My scientist father killed the things he loved to keep them better. God had called them to do His work, which He had framed in Nature. The brothers laughed together when they met, remembering the guinea pigs of Washington, Iowa, the peach trees of Edgerton, Kansas, and Mumsie's old gray dobbin, Minnie. They laughed when Uncle Roy held up his hand to show the finger stump, the top joints missing since the day his brother mowed the lawn and did not hear him scream when the blades went snicker-snack.

Of my mother not a word was said. She was not remembered, laughing. She was not preserved in cardboard or under glass or between blotters. She had refused to be framed by either God or Nature. She had played Bach in the one-room garage that served as home among the oranges of Rivina Orchards, while the baby cried and little Bobby chased his pet red rooster in the yard. "List / To Nature's teachings," the poet Bryant said. But she chose to join the millions of the dead departed on terms that were her own. In the garden to which she came alone, the dew had long dried on the roses and the butterflies were pinned to cotton. She lay still on the floor, when her husband found her, with the poison in her hand, a perfect specimen except for stains of vomit which could be, and were, removed.

He filed her under "H" for "Hazel," her blossoms pressed and labeled. When Uncle Roy and Aunt Evelyn returned on their next furlough, his brother's family had removed to a house of larger frame. A treating table had moved in with the piano and the anatomist of bones had replaced the anatomist of fugal organs. In the heat of the day we ate fried chicken, drank Kool-Aid, and prayed together. In the cool of the evening we sang "When the Roll Is Called up Yonder" for our evening's grace.

My father was ninety-two when I shot him with my Olympic, but he didn't see my crime. His eyes were all gummed shut. His mind was elsewhere. What fields of butterflies, what deserts of gray and melancholy waste did he look in upon? And did he see a woman in muslin white as any cabbage butterfly, lying still upon the floor like a finger on the grass? Did he smell formaldehyde instead of urine? Did he dream of desert lupine or of bowls of shimmering Jell-O concealing peaches gold as the cockatoos of Rio? Or was he once again a boy in knickers and high-button shoes, standing upright with his brother, holding each his prize guinea pig as still as any bone, to be immortalized in cardboard?

Ontario Review, 1983

My Daughter the Painter

■

IT WAS MY 55th birthday and as I unwrapped the present my daughter had brought me, we looked at each other and smiled. The present was not a surprise because weeks earlier I'd sat still for her in a chair for a couple of hours, the first of several sittings, while she painted my portrait in oils. But she hadn't let me peek and now that it was finished, I was excited. I ripped off the covering paper and was shocked. It was not her style—post-Abstract Expressionist with a color palette of hot purples and livid greens—that flummoxed me. She'd done a number of portraits in that style and I'd admired them. Until she did mine. What I saw was not me, but the wicked step-mother of my childhood. What I saw was a witch.

I tried to hang the painting on my bedroom wall in the middle of the family photographs and paintings, but I couldn't. The image was too powerful and the face too malevolent. Was that really the way my daughter saw me? It was as if her eye had expressed what her mind had for decades suppressed. It was as if she'd painted from her gut, outflanking her brain. She was hurt when I finally had to explain that although I thought it a very good painting, to be honest, I couldn't bear to look at it. Surely, I said to myself, her vision was distorted by anger that I'd broken up the family when I'd recently divorced her father after 32 years of marriage and that she and her brother, although grown and in their 20s, had been hung out to dry. Still, this portrait was so much stronger than any of the photos displayed on my walls and archived in shoeboxes under the bed that I was forced to reexamine the faces I'd worn in our snapshot moments when we were all together.

I hauled out the shoeboxes and there we were in black and white—and kodachrome—filed by decades. The Polaroids were a washout, but otherwise I had a floor's worth of documents testifying to a happy nuclear family posed stiffly in ones, twos and threes, at home, abroad, at school, at Disneyland, at the beach, in London, France, Egypt, Greece. I'm seldom in them of course. Somebody has to snap the shutter. Occasionally my husband, a child or a friend would take my place behind the viewfinder, but mostly I was not in the picture. As my daughter put it much later in a more meaningful way, "You were always there, but not there, you know what I mean?"

Where was I in the radical sixties, when the phrase "nuclear family" evoked a mushroom cloud reflected in the eyes of a little girl doing a countdown with daisy petals? Because American families were exploding every which way, I preferred the Brit term "corn-flake family," which at least suggested that the family that poured milk together stayed together. I smugly assumed that my own symmetrical unit of two heterosexual adults with two children, one male and one female, would always be 100% homogenized. We were clones: all blue-eyed fair-skinned blond Wasps, with bony frames and toothy smiles in every shot. Revisiting those photos, however, I could see that when my son was about ten, he decided not to smile on command anymore, and while the rest of us grinned, he looked dead serious. I began to see, like the photographer in Antonioni's *Blowup*, that my snapshots were full of clues, hiding something.

Worse, I could see that I'd used photos as a cover. Friends told me that when I was playing the perfect wife, they'd seen me through a veil, as if I wore my smile like a funny nose and fake moustache. In defense I'd quote Oscar Wilde: "Man is least himself when he talks in his own person. Give him a mask and he will tell you the truth." Only I'd reversed that paradox to read, "Give him the truth and he will don a mask." Donning a mask, play-acting, had been as natural to me as sneezing, and I'd done both since my hay-fever childhood. When my children were young, we performed together on stage in our small town of Princeton, New Jersey. My eight-year-old daughter was willing, but I had to drag my five-year-old son from the wings to sing our *Mary Poppins* number, "Supercalifragilisticexpialidocious." When McCarter Theatre organized an amateur group of players directed by a musical-comedy professional, I was in suburban heaven. As a mother of two in my mid-30s, I was glued into a stripper bodysuit for the title role in *Gypsy* and watched my neighbors sneak into rehearsals to be shocked.

I put us all on show, a virtual-reality family like the Cleavers, if only Mom and Dad had swigged martinis while leaving everything to Beaver. The house we moved to when the children got too big for the first one was built entirely for show. It had been built on a cement slab, without a basement, since this part of Princeton was a reconditioned swamp and everyone who had a basement also had a sump pump working overtime. I felt a twinge of uneasiness because I remembered Saroyan's drunk in *The Time of Your Life* mumbling, "No foundation, all down the line." But I didn't dream it could apply to me. Still, I knew something was missing but what was it? We spent a fortune remodeling the ground floor into an entertainment suite of two living rooms connected to an elaborately equipped dining-room kitchen. While the second floor had a cubicle bedroom big enough for our daughter, our son had to tuck into a dormered room in the attic. I swore that a larger unfinished attic room would make a great family room for the kids, but of course we never finished it since the parent half of the family was entertaining friends Cheever style, as they drank their way home from swimming pool to swimming pool. When our house was chosen for some charity's annual Christmas House Tour, I made for the dining table a magnificent gingerbread house, glued together with the same sugar icing that shingled its frosted roof with gumdrops. It must have been hubris that drove me to set a candle inside the house so that light would shine through its little windows and doors until, of course, the icing melted, the roof imploded and the walls came tumbling down.

When for a year we rented a house in London on Trevor Square, we repeated the errors of our parenting ways. We'd picked an elegant 18th-century townhouse, with one room per floor, only this time our daughter got the attic bedroom and our son a cubicle in the basement. When we all came down at the same time with Hong Kong flu—as they called it in London, and no doubt called it London flu in Hong Kong—our housekeeper Phoebe ran up and down five flights of stairs dispensing cups of hot tea to four vertically layered mummies, who shared misery but not proximity. Even when we were in health, however, there was no place for a family to gather because both the dining room on one floor and the drawing room above it were crammed with Louis Quinze antiques far too valuable to sit on or eat at. I was touched that Phoebe gave my son a little blue lovebird in a cage to keep him company in his basement room.

I should have known the game was up when at the end of the seventies we took a final family trip together to Capri to celebrate our 30th wedding anniversary. The timing was tricky since my daughter by now had a job in advertising in New York and my son was going to college in the West. We bribed them with tales of beaches and night life in Capri to come with us for two weeks in June. But since we had friends who summered in Capri, we parents went out to dinner as usual while our grown children shifted for themselves. A photo taken by a pro in a Capri restaurant on the very night of our anniversary, June 18, when we did manage to eat together, tells it all. We're in a booth, my son and I on one side, my husband and daughter on the other. And when the photographer said "Smile, *prago*," mother and son mugged outrageously while father and daughter flashed perfect teeth on cue. The photo suggests what might happen to a family held together by meltable icing and the wholly inadequate frosting of clowning and forced smiles.

When confronted by my daughter's portrait just a couple of years later, I finally had to examine my own memories and the images they evoked. I had to ask myself whether I hadn't worn motherhood as a mask all through my thirties and forties in order to conceal what I really wanted to be—Cinderella permanently at the ball, not back home scrubbing out the fireplace. Typecast in the dual role of good wife to my husband and good mother to my children, I thought I'd performed well: managing the house, entertaining friends, driving the kids to ballet to ice hockey to soccer to French to piano lessons, keeping the schedule, comforting the husband, cornflaking the kids. But my passport brought me up short. "Occupation: housewife." I'd ignored the mystique of sixties feminism because it seemed abrasively anti-men. Still, I'd never seen myself as a mothering housewife but as a woman in full bloom, sexually desirable and just possibly ever so slightly available. When I embarked on an adulterous affair during my Gypsy Rose period, my wife-&-mother mask became as fixed as plastic surgery because now I had something not just to deny to myself but to hide from others. Beyond infidelity, what I was hiding from everyone was that I didn't know how to be a mother. I didn't know what a mother was. So how could I possibly raise a family?

All I'd known about were stepmothers, and in life as in fiction they were invariably wicked. I'd no memory of my blood mother, who'd died when I was two. What I did remember was wearing to church on Mother's Day a white rose pinned to my lapel, instead of the usual red one. Red meant mother was alive, white meant she'd "passed." I remember feeling special on this Day because I was the only child in my Bible Class with a white rose. My real mother had been a college teacher who'd never expected to have children, had had more than one "nervous breakdown," hadn't married until she was 40, and when she had three children bam-bam-bam and one of them died, she was too frail to cope and killed herself with rat poison in a garage in the middle of an orange grove. My father, desperate for a woman to care for his children, married an osteopathic doctor who'd chosen career over marriage in the late 1920s and was flabbergasted to find that in late middle-age she was saddled with a pair of young kids.

My imagination was crammed with images of wicked step-mothers, while I skipped through the forest as Gretel and Cinderella and Snow White. But where had all the good mothers gone? In a house without books, except for scientific texts, I grew up, with the movies and, yes, there was an occasional dumpling-and-apple-sauce mother like Spring Byington in *The Little Women*, but what girl in her right mind would identify with Marmee rather than Jo? All of my role models were independent glamour girls, not cookie dispensers for husbands and kids. Who did I want to be after Shirley Temple? Why Jean Arthur and Rosalind Russell and Katharine Hepburn and Betty Grable. Not a mother among them. When Barbara Stanwyck played mother, she was Stella Dallas, which proved that glamour girls should not be mothers. When Bette Davis played mother, she was either the terrifying Mrs. Skeffington or the evil Regina. Greer Garson managed to be a glamour mother who was nice, but she didn't count because she was English. The American movie mother I most warmed to was Aunty Em in *The Wizard of Oz*. The Spanish mothers Pedro Almodóvar paints in *All About My Mother* would have blown my bobbysox off.

My husband's mother was potentially a good Spring Byington mother, but in reality a wicked mother-in-law because she had one of her own in the Victorian matriarch who ruled the family roost. My husband wanted to escape both women because his feelings toward mothers and women in general were complicated and ambivalent. After experiencing firsthand the horrific realities of World War II, something in him felt that the Mothers of America had betrayed their sons. As soldier boys, never had sons needed mothers more, and yet never had the gap between returning wounded veterans and home-front aproned mothers been greater. My husband's family had produced a gendered lexicon as Victorian as his grandmother, but the war had fixed it as Natural Law. Women were meant to be either mothers or sisters, so when my husband took a wife, her job was to be both mother and sister to him—mother for comfort, sister for fun. When we had children of our own, unfortunately the mothering act had already been spoken for. I sometimes thought of him as my eldest child, but even with him I was a reluctant mother. I wanted not to be his mother but his mate, both friend and spouse, with children tossed in for good measure. Fathering, he knew, was foreign to him. "I never should have been a father," he once confessed to me as we were splitting up. In contrast, I always felt I should have been a mother, but it wasn't at the top of my list because I wanted to be so much more.

When the split came, my grown children let me know that while we may have shared time and space, my children and I, we did not share inner lives. While I remembered emotional intensity in relation to my husband, my son and daughter remembered an emotional vacuum in relation to themselves. Post-divorce that vacuum was filled with anger. My daughter fired her shots in machine bursts that were bewildering because unpredictable. My son burned with a slow fuse that made anticipated explosion the more devastating. I believe my children's sense of betrayal exceeded even my own, even my husband's, as all the doors in a houseful of corridors with tightly shut doors flew open at once. That their parents had not been sexually faithful to each other, that the facade of public entertainments covered shadowy private entanglements and deviant erotic undercurrents, our children would have sensed in uneasy and unspoken ways throughout their childhood, even as they shut their doors in self protection. Certainly as husband and wife, we kept our doors and our mouths shut, except when we argued. I remember my son in his late teens asking me one day, after the reticulated "discussion" my husband and I were having over the merits and demerits of some movie like *Citizen Kane*, "When are you and Dad going to get a divorce?" I was shocked into laughter. "Never," I scoffed. "You know how we are. This is just the way we talk."

But of course the way we talked excluded most of the things that mattered, which made the new open-door policy created by divorce the more shattering. The final straw was a memoir I published called *My Kitchen Wars*, about 20 years after my divorce, which was not recollected in tranquility. In it I told the story of my marriage as I remembered it and the discovery of myself as a writer. My children asked before it was published, "Are there any more surprises?" There weren't, but to make our hidden life public was to double for them the betrayal of the family breakup. I had not thought of my story as their story. So although I'd detailed the birth of each child, I'd skipped over the details of raising them because I felt they were old enough to tell their own stories and might resent my pre-empting theirs. I was right about that.

As it turns out, each member of my family has written a memoir. My husband, known for his many nonfiction books, wrote a first-person story about his discovery of the truth of war in Alsace after a comfy childhood in Pasadena. My son, a fledgling writer, wrote a coming-of-age story when he transformed himself as a competitive bodybuilder from a gangly Oxford grad to the Hulk. My daughter, a teacher-painter, wrote a survival story in the form of a graphic novel, conquering the ogres of breast cancer with cartoon humor and imagination. Maybe it's not odd that our memoirs don't overlap, except minimally, nor do they even contradict, although only in my own memoir do I recognize myself. In my husband's story, I barely exist. In my son's, I'm a suburban Mom offended by swollen abs and pecs. In my daughter's, I'm riskier than surgery when I drive her home from the hospital. Not a word from any of us about those smiling family moments in the photos. Maybe none of us could bear to look at them. We'd shared the same frame, but it was clear we'd had no group history. As each child said to me separately but firmly, "We were never a family."

That was a truth I found so hard to admit that I couldn't begin to try until I discovered what an unreliable tool memory is for getting any story straight. Curiously it was a comfort to learn just how quirky our brains are and that remembering is an ongoing process in which our brains make up stories. The stories mothers tell themselves need not be as psychotic as those of "The Munchhausen Mother," who physically inflicted upon her children the illnesses she fantasized so that she might star as The Mother Who Suffers. Nor do we need family therapy to document that remembered stories among family members are bound to conflict. Even so, I found that conflicting memories are sometimes a good thing. What I remembered from a trip my daughter and I took to the Galápagos was the mutiny I staged against the drunken captain of our leaking tub. Guilt, my default program, registered "Controlling Mother." What my daughter remembered was that despite her mother's terror of snorkeling in strange waters, she donned mask and flippers and went at it. I have a photo to prove it, but where I saw a masked mutineer, she saw a brave wimp.

In the age of the uncertainty principle, we know that any absolute divisions between memory and fantasy, fact and fiction, the observer and the observed are gone with the cosmic wind. Bombarded as we are by media hype and political propaganda, it is not so easy in 2006 to tell nonfiction from fiction in the wake of a million little pieces of illusionary weapons and faked redemption. God knows that even when our intent is not to deceive others, we are more than vulnerable to deceiving ourselves. Since memory is much more like an endless video with self-editing software than like a computer with storage files or a box of snapshots, "truthiness" is always problematic. Particularly when we've invested so much in software to keep our screens clean and our programs tidy.

Yet the uncertainty principle is what makes me, no matter how hopeless a mother, hopeful about my shattered family. I obviously can't change the past, but I can look at it differently. I can revise my memory of what I thought happened and of who I thought I was by looking through my children's eyes, by looking at our shared snapshot memories in a different way, just as I look at Netflix movies with different eyes now than when I was 5 or 25 or 75. I'm not the person I thought I was at any of those ages, certainly not the mother I thought I was and wanted to be when my children were young. Nor are my children who I thought they were. Now that they're middle-aged and I'm the age of my grandparents, it's painful to undergo the shock of the new—new images, new stories—but I know I must discard the bubble-wrap for truthier memories. I must see my children in the present with new eyes.

When I look now at my marriage memoir, I see that I'd fashioned a gingerbread house where I could play girl hero put in harm's way, looking for someone evil to shove into the oven. I'd gotten stuck in the glue of my own childhood narratives, and my daughter's portrait of me stripped away my mask of innocence. But seeing that is better than not seeing. Maybe if I pay fierce attention to what my grown-up children tell me, I can begin to revise the stories I have told to make myself look better than I am. Maybe if we pool our stories in some fantasized sometime and tell them to each other, maybe the three of us, even the four of us though we're scattered to the winds, can conjure for ourselves a group picture, not for display, where getting closer to the truth makes all of us smile, for real.

Vogue (unpublished)

My Son the Bodybuilder

■

AS I DEPLANED in the LAX terminal, I thought only in California would I see a monster like the one approaching from the distance—slow-thighed, arms flared by a massive chest, neck engulfing his jaw—an incredible hulk who parted the crowd like the Red Sea and kept on coming, kept on grinning. What was that grin supposed to mean? "Hi, Mom." I recognized the voice, if not the man. It was Sam—my son the bodybuilder.

All 6 feet 4 inches and 250 pounds of him bent over and gave me a kiss. In Valley-speak, it was awesome. I hadn't seen Sam for a year, and I couldn't stop staring, which was just what he wanted. He played it cool, picking up my suitcases as if they were paper bags. He could have slung me over his shoulder like a towel, this Samson, who a mere 30 years ago was born a perfectly normal Sam—weighing 8 pounds 10 ounces, measuring 16 ¾ inches long. I felt like a character in *Invasion of the Body Snatchers*, struggling to recognize in this mutant alien my own flesh and blood. My son had always had a Gothic imagination—he had devoured volumes of monster tales and reels of horror films—but who could have foreseen for that little boy a transformation as bizarre as this?

Bodybuilding was an unusual career choice for a young man who earlier had piled an Oxford degree in English lit on top of an American one—though *career* is, perhaps, the wrong word. Even a full-time bodybuilder is an amateur until he wins enough contests to make a name and, thereby, money from endorsements. Until then he scrabbles to pay for his own intensive training by training California's legions of the health-and-fitness crazed.

Not only was bodybuilding an odd career choice; it was downright deranged for someone like Sam, who hadn't lifted weights until he was 26. Most bodybuilders begin to train in their teens if they're going to compete in the big leagues for a Mr. Olympia or a Mr. Universe title. Sam in his early teens was known as "Little Wee," the smallest boy on the Lawrenceville, New Jersey, soccer team. At 17, however, his hormones went berserk and he grew four inches in one summer, six in one year. "I was a genetic freak," he says now, now that he's had his revenge on nature.

Nature, of course, includes his parents. As a child of suburbia, he was neither biologically nor culturally predestined to find delts, pecs, and traps a life's work. But what better way to declare independence from parental genes than to literally recreate every sinew, muscle, and vein? What more powerful way to say no—no to intellectual, academic, nonathletic, antifitness, fat and flabby parents—than to say it in body language, in the word made flesh? His body wasn't subtext, it was megatext—at once funny and astonishing and appalling and embarrassing.

The larger my offspring grew, the smaller I felt as proud mother. While other mothers spoke of their son the brain surgeon or the nuclear physicist, I pulled out photos of my son the bodybuilder and watched eyes roll and mouths drop. One friend to whom I showed a photo at lunch said, "Oh, God, not while I'm eating." Others asked discreetly, "Why is he doing this?" meaning "Why is he doing this to you?"

Four years ago when he began his bodybuilding I thought, Okay, he's paying his Freudian dues, only I wish he'd just sock his dad in the jaw and be done with it. It also occurred to me that he might be suffering from the Big Apple blues and boredom with a clerk's job in a publishing house that ignored his Oxford expertise and barely paid for the basement room he rented in Queens. He had joined a health club for survival, but when he found iron to pump, he found a new identity as he began to change shape slowly, but visibly, from the outside in. A boy who had been small for his age and had suffered a critical illness in childhood began for the first time in his life to feel safe because he looked so powerful. Now heads began to turn wherever he walked. I loved to walk with him on crowded streets, my hand tiny on his bulging arm, because I too felt safe and energized by the electricity in women's eyes and the awe in men's. Sam had created an image of power, and now all he had to do was to continue to fill it—by working out every day until he dropped and by downing 13 milkshakes until he gagged. When I saw how changing shape was changing his life, I knew he was right to quit his job and move to Southern California to follow his bliss—in the words of Joseph Campbell, a favorite of his.

His bliss was, of course, my despair; the arcane rites and lore of his profession gave him in every way the upper hand. With what pleasure did he indoctrinate me in muscle lingo: delts, traps, abs, pecs, and lats (deltoids, trapeziuses, abdominals, pectorals, and lastissimi dorsi)! How happily did he break me in on magazines like *Ironman* and *Flex*, on movies like *Pumping Iron I* and *II*, on biographies of Arnold Schwarzenegger, on shopping lists that included the Total Arm Blaster and the Triceps Bomber and ingestibles like Anabolic Mega Paks and Sugar-Free BIG, Weight-Gain Powder in

Vanilla Nut flavor! He even broke me of the habit of buying clothes for him because XXX-Large was eventually too small.

I came to see that this was not a rite of passage but an obsession costing, as T.S. Eliot said in a different context, "no less than everything." Sam had explained that it would take him five to seven years to build a champion's body, years of total dedication, discipline, and determination. Was that a clue? The regimen was so severe it was masochistic—each day two intensive workouts of two hours each, spaced between four bouts of force-feeding that boggled the mind but built muscle. A day's typical menu:

Breakfast at 7:00: five whole wheat pancakes as big as dinner plates—with syrup, three eggs, coffee.

First lunch at 12:00: three to four chicken breasts, two to three cups of brown rice, a pound of steamed broccoli, a pound of grapes, a quarter of a watermelon, a half-gallon of low-fat milk.

Second lunch at 4:00: repeat chicken, rice, steamed broccoli, fruit, low-fat milk.

Dinner at 8:00: a large steak, veal chop or fish; two baked potatoes; three slices of whole wheat bread; four bananas; at least one glass of low-fat milk.

Sam called this "maximum protein utilizations." I called it gross. But bodybuilding was not just about getting bigger, Sam explained; it was also about getting smaller. As he put it, it's about sculpting flesh the way an artist might mold clay or chisel marble. Body builders call it "cutting up"—stripping off the body fat, winnowing it from 15 to 20 percent of body mass (for an average male) down to 3 to 5 percent in order to achieve "definition." The aim is to become transparent, to make the invisible visible—unto every striation of muscle, tissue, artery, vein. Oiled and tanned (with Pro Tan Instant Competition Color), it's the body look that many gentle folk, especially women, find revolting. It's also the look the bodybuilder kills himself to achieve—kills himself through a system of binging and dieting that retains body mass while removing fat.

Before his first competition last fall, Sam lost 30 pounds in eight weeks, the last 14 pounds in six days. Bodybuilding is not—*not*, Sam repeats—about health and fitness. What bodybuilding is about is challenge, imagination and art, daring and risk, stretching the limits, "using weights to sculpt your body into forms previously thought incomprehensible other than in Michelangelo's paintings." It's landscape architecture, altering the course of nature by building a terrace here, a fountain there, exercising a biceps one way to lengthen it, another way to make a peak. You must visualize yourself as you want to be and then, millimeter by millimeter, fill in the frame, Samson among the Philistines.

I heard weird echoes of Sam's father the aesthete. I heard weird echoes of myself the chauvinist when Sam extolled bodybuilding over power lifting and the Olympic lifting as "the perfect democratic form." To the Eastern bloc, which excels in Olympics, bodybuilding was until recently decadent, Sam explained, narcissistic, a form of capitalist image consumption. To Sam, bodybuilding is gloriously American because it's a completely individual sport, embodying the virtues of self-reliance and self-improvement. "It's just you and the weight," challenging yourself, exerting total control, stretching what the body can do—"the battle is against yourself."

The battle also reveals the ancient paradox of democracy in which every man yearns to be king. "Above all," Sam believes, "bodybuilding is selling a fantasy, your own and other people's— the fantasy of California, of Horatio Alger, of Martin Luther King, Jr.; it's a literal embodiment of the American Dream." Look at Schwarzenegger, an ordinary guy from Austria who made it big on his muscles and his mouth, then hit America to become the Terminator and finally the husband of a Camelot princess.

But Sam talks less of fame and money than of integrity, intensity, passion—the words of his calling. Integrity means feeling every repetition when you're doing shoulder presses on the bench, side laterals on the cable, pecs on the butterfly machine, abs on the incline board, biceps on the cable preacher curl, legs on the hack squat machine. It means building sets of repetitions in pyramidal progression—following sets of 10, 8, and 6 with sets of 6, 8, 10, and 12, allowing only 40- to 60-second rests between each. You're cheating if you don't shock the muscle with each rep, and only you know whether you're feeling the shock.

Intensity means "refining one movement by repetition, like a diamond cutter refining a stone," concentrating, visualizing, blocking out everything and stopping at nothing. Including drugs. In bodybuilding, steroids are so common they're called "roids." Some magazine ads read, "Try our new 'roid' replacer." When I asked a professional trainer and gym owner about "roids," he defended them fully. "Competitive sport is not about health," he told me, "it's about excellence, about breaking world records, about having an extra edge, and steroids absolutely work." I had asked because when I saw Sam in L.A. he was on them. "No bodybuilder's going to say he owes his body to steroids, and he's right," said Sam, "but steroids help, and I leave nothing to chance."

At the beginning he had said, "No way." Now he said, "You get blacklisted if you talk about it, but it's everybody's dirty little secret and everybody does it." Steroids are legal although costly when obtained by prescription, so Californians get them cheap from Mexico. A lot of bodybuilders—but not Sam—make their living by selling them.

As Sam prepared for his first competitions—Mr. San Gabriel Valley and Mr. Golden Valley—he demonstrated the ritual poses, and I came to see bodybuilding as less a sport than performance art: living statues that move. The lights go down, the audience is suspended in darkness—"It could be Shakespeare," says the Oxford grad—music begins, and suddenly a guy, naked except for his briefs, steps onto the spotlit podium and for the next few minutes transports the audience into fantasy as he fleshes out his own dream of who he can be—a Hercules, an Apollo. It's the Platonic ideal in action, an incarnation of pure form.

Just before going onstage the actor gets set for his moment of ecstasy by pumping up, "flooding" each muscle of his body with blood. "You put yourself on a bench and start pumping out chest sets and suddenly your chest expands, puffs like a big bird. Your plumage bursts out with a burning sensation, like an erection. You start glowing and then, like the moment after orgasm, you feel both flooded and released." With such vivid descriptions did Sam remind me—and sometimes all too often, I might add—that by breaking the norm, by defying nature, by demanding the impossible, bodybuilding was a way to shock the bourgeoisie.

But I wasn't shocked until he said, "You go every day religiously to that one square room, the gym, and it's like communing with your Lord." I was shocked because I heard in Sam the rebel the words of his Puritan forefathers, those Bible-thumping Scotch

Presbyterian dissenters who left Scotland and Northern Ireland to commune with their Lord in the desolate prairies of Kansas and Nebraska. "I want to preach overcoming obstacles," Sam said, in the voice of his Uncle Roy, the missionary, who had communed in the jungles of Brazil. "God created us, but it's up to us to change ourselves"—this was Sam talking—"and I want to create something you've never seen before, something that makes you say, 'Holy shit.'"

Finally I understood. My son the bodybuilder was a preacher like his ancestors, a Calvinist acolyte of duty, devotion, and morality so extreme that nothing less than perfection would satisfy his craving for the absolute. Though a child of the '70s in his scorn for the Establishment, he was a man of the '80s in his need for something holy. "Our society says there has to be a dichotomy between mind and body, but to me, it's a sin not to develop both," Sam confessed. "What I'm doing is an affirmation of life, of life at the fullest, of being here now. It's very pure."

After I returned home to New York, Sam won the heavyweight title of Mr. San Gabriel Valley and came in second for Mr. Golden Valley. Right now he's recovering from his crash diet, is off the steroids, and wondering whether he's ready to compete for Mr. Los Angeles, ready to postpone the marriage and children that his live-in girlfriend longs for. He knows that his kind of passion is hard on other people as well as on himself, and perhaps he will find other ways to pursue his quest for perfection.

When I think of my son the bodybuilder, I see Sam at age four, setting off to nursery school in his knight's costume, which he wore every day for one year, a costume of knitted "chain mail" worn over black tights and under a tabard stitched with a red cross. He also wore a tin helmet with a visor and carried a cardboard sword and shield, spray-painted silver. With his mop of blond hair, his radiant skin, and his blue eyes, he was "a verray, parfit gentil knight." Who would have thought that the knight grown to bodybuilder would find himself by reincarnating my grandfather the prairie preacher?

Lear's, 1989

Nostalgia: Salad Days

AT FIVE O'CLOCK on November 1, 1949, we welcomed guests to our first cocktail party in the slum apartment we called home on Huntington Avenue, across from the Mechanics' Institute in Boston. Cocktail parties were why you got married, so you could join the couples club. If you were a couple, you were somebody; otherwise, not. For this occasion I had bought (I usually made my own clothes) a blue satin cocktail dress in Filene's Basement to introduce myself to my new husband's friends, mostly couples, at Harvard Graduate School. This was my coming-out party to validate me as half a couple, and I wanted to come out in style. Blue was conservative, but satin lent a bit of flash. Of course we served sherry (it was cheap as well as intoxicating) and Vienna sausages and clam dip on Ritz crackers. And, of course, as I turned to be introduced to somebody, somebody's full glass of sherry slopped down the front of my dress from cleavage to hem. If only I had been wearing that Claire McCardell apron.

It was two or three years before I could afford my first and only Claire McCardell dress, even though her clothes were relatively affordable because she used cotton instead of satin and silk. After all those war years of armored shoulder pads and nose-cone breasts and militarized suits, McCardell liberated women in the fifties from the strictures of our mother's girdle and June Allyson's waist. McCardell showed us who we desperately wanted to be: fresh and natural as a gingham apron, casual and easy as the matte-jersey dress beneath. During the war we'd been on hold, waiting—without meat, sugar, butter, gas, nylons, or men. Now we had everything at once, and we burst from our bottled-up selves like a French 75 of brandy and champagne.

So many explosive bubbles, so many contradictions and, as always, food expressed the change. My husband and I knew as little about real food as we knew about love, sex, or marriage. Salads (imagine it!) were to us a brand-new idea. Despite the fact that we were a California couple—he born in Pasadena and I in Riverside—we'd never eaten any lettuce greener than a slab of iceberg doused with Hellmann's mayonnaise or a pink bottled dressing labeled Thousand Island. My husband's mother was a carb freak, surrounding her dried leathery roasts with mashed potatoes, Parker House rolls, frozen lima beans, and frozen corn as prelude to ice cream, cake, and cookies, the grand climacteric of her culinary foreplay. Liquor was forbidden, but not fat, and God knows not sugar. Fresh fruit and veggies were suspect, unhealthy until frozen or canned. It was years before my husband would willingly eat rabbit-food greens, despite the fact that our wedding presents included not one but two large wooden salad bowls with matching individual bowls, and several pairs of silver salad-server forks and spoons to avoid wooden pairs that might appear too cheap. To make a dressing from scratch of oil and vinegar was a radical departure, so much so that I usually added a dollop of Heinz ketchup for thickness and sweetness and actually called it "French." For a very long time, our food had been as isolated and as bottled and canned as our lives.

But by 1950, we gals—I was 21 when I married and definitely a postadolescent girl, not a woman—were busting out all over, trying to be all things at once. We wanted to be housewives and helpmates for our wounded veterans back from the war. We wanted to be hostesses, sparkling in simulated diamonds and pearls, to show off our bare shoulders and pearly teeth. But we had to be cooks whether we wanted to or not. I'd never cooked anything more taxing than hot dogs and scrambled eggs, not because we'd had servants but because we were poor and went straight from Depression austerity to wartime deprivation. But housewifery wasn't enough. I wanted to be as learned as my husband so I could keep up my end of the literary argument with our academic friends. While he was finishing his four-year Ph.D., I wanted a one-year M.A. I foresaw that down the line I would need to feel less dependent, would want to get a job on my own, even though at that time only about a third of America's work force was women. To get into Radcliffe (no women at Harvard), I had to teach myself Latin and German from scratch, memorizing word cards hour after hour the old-fashioned way. To learn to cook was nothing in comparison to learning classic Latin declensions and barbaric German syntax.

In 1950, females were not the only ones scrambling to define themselves. The nation was caught in a time warp of old feelings shaken by new rhythms, new images, new events. Nat King Cole's "Mona Lisa" was soon to be undercut by the beat of a kid named Little Richard at the Tick Tock Club in Macon, Georgia. *Cheaper by the Dozen* was obliterated by the Oscar-night success of *All About Eve* and *Sunset Boulevard*. Mary Martin's *South Pacific* might still have been enchanting Broadway, but a few years later America's first H-bomb ended all enchanted evenings of an island in the real South Pacific. American forces crossed the 38th Parallel in Korea shortly after Senator Joseph McCarthy struck his first blow against

Communism in the 48 states. Sometimes I think we just couldn't let go the intensity of our wartime feelings, so we had to create new wars to justify them.

If World War II forced us to learn about countries on the far side of both oceans, we soon began to experience those countries firsthand by choice, embracing travel abroad as a prerogative of normal middle-class life. Claire McCardell was right there for us with the perfect travel dress. The one I bought in 1953 was of crinkled black cotton georgette, cool because cotton breathed, practical because black concealed stains, drip-dryable because the crinkles were permanent. And boy, was it glamorous. The top was designed as two separate pieces, which you crossed when you put your head between them, so that the dress had a Grecian-drapery effect with bare shoulders and a loosely gathered skirt. I traveled in that dress for the next 30 years. It packed like a handkerchief, shook itself out, and was instantly ready for any scene, from a dingy London pub to the Parthenon. I would still be wearing that dress had it not, over the decades, faded to gray, marred by an occasional indelible stain and unmendable tear. But it was the kind of dress that when it died you wanted to bury it, it carried so much of your life in its fabric.

It was also, of course, the perfect dress for performing the role of hostess-cook. I never wore aprons, because the ones that arrived in my kitchen were all gifts from well-meaning mothers and others, whether frilly tea aprons or commemorative holiday aprons or full-bodied smocks that made you look pregnant. I didn't want to be pregnant, not yet. I wanted to postpone that shift from girl to woman for as long as possible. I wanted to relish my moment of power when I could both stage-manage and star in my own kitchen drama, where I cooked as carefully in my dinner dress as if it were a theatrical costume, smug in knowing that it was cotton and easy to clean if somebody slopped a glass of sherry down my front.

Maybe resistance to conventional aprons was a statement about the unconventional tweaking of our roles. Yes, we were housewives and cooks, and eventually mothers, but we were also glamorous, sexy, smart, and fun. We broke down the rules of housewifery the way we tore down the walls between our kitchens and dining rooms to make cooking and serving the center of our stage. We wanted to open up the backstage to public view and to make our hard work look as easy and casual and graceful as a McCardell apron that looked like a dress. After the hardships of the war, we wanted to party hard, and we did.

There might be devastating new wars at home and abroad, but we were survivors who'd already had to reckon with the deaths of friends and lovers, not to mention the unimaginable extinctions of Hiroshima and the Holocaust. Shadowed by fear and ignorance, I had to learn how to couple just as I had to learn how to cook, studying the ingredients of marriage as if learning a foreign language, mixing our separate lives as if tossing a fresh salad, serving ourselves forth to the grown-up world as a couple, with all the energy and hope of a 21-year-old girl and a 24-year-old soldier boy, who would soon learn that sherry wouldn't get us through the next 30 years nearly as well as gin.

Vogue, 2005

Love and Mayonnaise

■

Had we but world enough, and time,
This coyness, Lady, were no crime . . .
My vegetable love would grow
Vaster than empires and more slow.

—FROM ANDREW MARVELL,
To His Coy Mistress (1650)

ALTHOUGH ANDREW MARVELL disapproved of vegetable love, I'm sure he would have understood my love of mayonnaise. The chemistry of this emulsion would have pleased him because it gives a lie to one of nature's truths: that oil and water do not mix. Marvell knew as well as anyone that lies breed love, just as Oscar Wilde knew that lies breed truth, what he called "The Truth of Lies." Even as a child, innocent of poetry, I had clear scientific evidence that some lies were more truthful than others and that oil and water did too mix. They did so in a jar that stood always to the right of my father's place, north by northwest of his knife on the oilcloth of our dining table.

The jar stood as the royal salt once stood on the damasked cloth of Louis XIV, not only as witness to the color of his blood but as evidence that water could turn into edible rock. My father's jar was rock of another kind. Among the treacherous waters of our meals, his jar was fixed and constant as Gibraltar. Since he slathered the contents of that jar on every dish from breakfast eggs and toast to noon-time bologna sandwiches to bananas to dinner mashed potatoes, boiled lamb, iceberg lettuce, and fruited Jell-O, I had no reason to doubt the truth of the label's assertion that Hellmann's Mayonnaise was "REAL" and, if refrigerated after opening, eternal.

My father offered a simple explanation for this impossible union of oil and water. He called it an emulsion, the suspension of one liquid in another against nature. In mayonnaise, he explained, vinegar or lemon is the liquid in which drops of oil are suspended and yet kept apart by a film of egg yolk which coats each drop of oil as it's beaten into smaller and smaller droplets. As more oil is beaten in, smaller droplets cut larger droplets down to size, subverting the natural commonality of oil. By such alchemy, translucent water, too, defies its nature to become thick and smooth as Devon cream. Naturally I fell in love with a texture that melted in the mouth when I put it on my peanut butter sandwiches and on my vanilla ice cream. Even as a child, I had a talent for gilding lilies.

That the emulsion, however miraculous, is also unstable is obvious to anyone who has tried to make mayonnaise himself and to preserve it. The union is fragile, subject to stress, the extremes of heat or cold, agitation, or simply the erosion of time, any of which may break its elements apart. But no such fears troubled the faith of my father in the miraculous power of technology to remedy all natural defects. While our family dining table was subject to intense stress and agitation, the labeled jar was lodestar to his passage through straights too narrow to leave room for doubt. The jar was as God-given as my grandfather's Bible or my grandmother's Postum. This mass-produced, chemically-stabilized artifact was a sign of God's and America's grace, purchased two for one in a store comfortingly named "Safeway."

When I fell out of grace and out of love with God and my father, I fell out with mayonnaise. I broke the family emulsion, which had never really taken, no matter how many arms had tried to force its hostile elements together by beating. I broke the emulsion before it broke me and was glad of it. Let water and oil pool separately as nature intended, I thought, and so they did for many unforgiving years, during which I scorned Hellmann's, as I scorned peanut butter. Kid stuff, I said. One stayed stiff in the spoon like Jell-O and the other stuck to the top of the mouth. They reminded me of the oilcloth on the table and the linoleum on the floor and the newspaper curtains at the window and the smell of poverty in the boiled lamb.

When I married, I fell into carnal and culinary knowledge and back into mayonnaise. Rejoicing in my newfound hedonism, I was reborn in the kitchen of affluence. Food, sex, marriage, and the family, this was a new emulsion and I defied the extremes of emotional heat and cold, agitation and time, to do their worst. I felt invincible as I learned to make mayonnaise in the French way, by the strength of my own right arm. If my father had been obsessed with keeping a much mortgaged roof over the heads of his discordant family, I became obsessed with filling my house with food. Not just any food, certainly not the canned and jarred goods of my parents' table, but glorious food made by me.

I was intent on mastering personal chaos by French craft. My kitchen overflowed with haute cuisine emulsions, the trickier the better—béarnaises, hollandaises, maltaises, beurres-blancs. But I separated out the gourmet fare for grown-ups from the junk the kiddies got. While the engines of my Osterizer and Cuisinart purred like B-17s, my children were grounded, consuming Hostess Twinkies and Hawaiian Punch and peanut butter and banana sandwiches slathered with Hellmann's, straight from the jar.

The kids were right to steer clear of my French whisks. My food obsessions were isolate, a monomania of my islanded self. I thought kitchen craft would be enough to keep together the warring elements of a husband and wife suspended in marriage. But my romance with Francophile sauces proved as illusory as the banquets set by Prospero on his enchanted isle to snare the conscience of "three men of sin."

An island scene undid me. In Greece, our family of four had rented a house for the summer on an island inhabited by a group of British eccentrics. They were a small band who had left England after the war in pursuit of Arcadia and God, then been converted to the Greek Orthodox Church by a dissident Oxford don. An isolated cove of this island was to be the paradise regained of a homosexual British blue blood, a Canadian engineer, an Oxbridgean professor and his Greek wife, bound together for a time in a Mariolatrous mayonnaise. Eventually, however, nature took its course. The blue blood seduced one too many boat-boys on his yacht, the engineer went to bed with the professor's wife, and the professor liaisoned with a young village girl.

I can't say that any of them jinxed directly the sauce I tried to will into being one burning August noon when we planned to celebrate the arrival of visitors with ice cold retsina and grilled lobster at a small taverna up the road. My contribution, and my nemesis, was the mayonnaise I insisted should replace the taverna's humble vinaigrette of lemon and oil. My jinx was the fact that one of the visitors had been my lover, whom I hadn't seen since we quarreled with some heat several months before and had vowed to keep silent and think cold thoughts ever after.

Tension was high in the kitchen of our primitive island house, which had two parallel steel railway lines running through it, connecting the bauxite quarry up the hill to the dock of splintered timbers and rocks at the front of our misnamed patio. Mussolini's army had occupied the village during the war and had shipped this ore to Naples to further the Axis union. When the oven heat of our cove became intolerable, we spoke of the ovens at Old Dachau. This day was such a day, a day of Dachau heat matched by the heat of an anger I could scarce admit, let alone voice. A lover's anger. A lover's heat.

I've never believed that mere body heat was the cause of my failure to whip together the heavy viscid green Greek oil with the yolks of some startlingly orange eggs. Was it the temperature of the air? Perhaps. The state of mind of the beater? No doubt. No whisks in this kitchen, only a fork and a perceptibly cracked bowl. I set to work as always, beating the yolks with a rotating motion of the wrist, squeezing in a few drops of juice from a thick-skinned lemon that bleached the yolks where the drops hit, adding a few chopped leaves of basil, a pinch of salt, a shake of pepper.

Pouring the oil, drop by drop, from the bottle in my left hand while agitating the fork with my right, I watched in horror as the oil stayed green and the yolks pale orange. The emulsion would not take. While others came and went, I beat oil into the cracked bowl on the kitchen table until my arm and shoulder ached. The children wandered in for nibbles before the long-delayed lunch, my husband chipped ice into his ouzo to keep an aesthetic distance from vulgar kitchen chores, our friends gossiped about some recent outbreak of ego or libido among the incestuous Brits, my ex-lover calculated his exact position by the latitudes of others and stayed clear.

And I still beat and five times started over, repeating each time the rescue operation of a new egg yolk in a clean bowl, designed to bring together what obdurately remained apart. I exhausted a dozen eggs, a liter of oil. I was beating still when the whole contingent left for the tavern, impatient with my mania and just plain starved for lunch.

I would show them. I would create with my own hands, despite the hellish heat, a wondrous basil-scented mayonnaise to set them all aquiver. I will triumph, said the Presbyterian apostate and adulterer. God's grace was not for her, nor God's commandments, but Greek hubris was. I tried once more, dumping in six yolks at once and for a moment it looked as if I'd got it right. I clapped a cover on the bowl and a hat on my head for the long hot walk to the tavern. I remember well how the sun hammered the top of my head, flattening me into the white dust of the bauxite, battering my pride, stripping me of everything but hate. I hated my lover less than my failure to do what I'd set out to do—escape one failed emulsion for another.

When I reached the table set under a wine-dark arbor, the crew was merry, having drunk much wine and eaten many lobsters. They greeted me with laughter amid orange-red carcasses. I could have died of sunstroke on the path and not been missed. I lifted the cover on my bowl and looked at the mess inside. I poured it over a heap of broken shells and watched the oil leach out and pool at the bottom, leaving a few clotted spots behind on shards of tail and claw. So much for mayonnaise. The party had gone on without me, something else had pulled their particles together while I had separated out.

I should have paid attention to this mayo moral, but I was slow to learn. My marriage broke soon after. Perhaps our union had always been a matter of suspended disbelief, like the union of my childhood family or of my father and myself. By the time I divorced, my father's mind had long since separated from his body, leaving it to pool and dribble in a nursing home. I put a blob of mayo on his Jell-O and he seemed pleased to eat it with his spoon. But I knew that no amount of whipping could have prevented over time the separation of his family or of mine. There had been too many extremes of hot and cold, too much agitation, or simply too much time.

Real emulsions, whipped no matter where, on a Greek or a suburban isle, were not meant to last forever, as nothing in nature is. Despite its label, the mayonnaise my father loved was fake. Chemical preservatives had subverted its "REAL" nature. Preservatives were by definition unnatural. But so was nature. So was love. I had found out, by doing, what Marvell and the poets already knew: that love's truth is the truth of contraries, *contra naturam*. The truth is that oil and water do not mix, except for brief and shining moments that defy nature, outwit chemistry, challenge time, and with a pinch of luck and a shake of grace, put to shame the artificial shelf life of our lies.

Culturefront, 1999

Home Free:
Of Keepsakes and God Pots

I KNEW ABOUT the Lacandon Indians of Chiapas and had seen them barefoot in their woven shifts in the market at San Cristobal, but I wasn't thinking about them when I shoved the yellowed remains of the dress I had worn at my wedding 32 years earlier into my daughter's bureau drawer. I wasn't thinking about anything but packing up and clearing out. Would my daughter ever wear this strapless organdy June Allyson pouf, scrunched next to the fake lilies of the valley, the remaining fingerless nylon glove, the clunky shoes with sweetheart tops? No way. Neither would I. With working-girl pennies, I had bought this calf-length number at B. Altman's to double as a cocktail dress, but it remained untouched after the wedding. So why did I keep it year after year, shifting it from closet to closet, basement to attic, house to house? And why, for god's sake, was I keeping it now, in a bureau I had packed with my daughter's ancient toys—miniature Steiff animals, G.I. Joe with all the accessories—at the very moment the family was splitting apart and I was packing up my marriage as well as my house? I laughed as I jammed the dress with both fists into its wooden coffin, and then I cried, and then I called my daughter.

I should have called the Lacandones, for they are experts in packing up and moving on. They have done so for the past 1,400

years, ever since their ancestors built and abandoned the temples of
Palenque, Bonampak, Yaxchilan. There are only a couple hundred
of these Mayan descendants left, but there they are, hanging on,
with gods and ceremonies intact, because they know the fragility of
temples and sacred objects, and the renewal powers of the jungle.
Stripped to the essentials, they know what counts.

They know that artifacts that are cherished gain power over
those who make and then cherish them, so that the users become
the used, tyrannized by their own creations. Every eight years they
ceremonially smash their god pots, the clay receptacles in which
they burn the fragrant resin they call *copal*. It's a tradition as old as
the ancient Mayans, who "murdered" their sacred pots by drilling
holes to render them useless and who ritually "killed" their temples
by destroying their carved images of men and beasts and gods. And
then, to deflect the power that cherished objects gain, the ancients
miniaturized them in symbolic fetishes, which they wore like bangles on wristlets and sashes and ear flares.

I needed a drawerful of bangles because my house and all within
it had ganged up on me over 25 years. It had become my "god house,"
stuffed to the rafters with god pots, but I had no ceremonies for
murdering pots or killing houses. Instead I was stuck with my own
instinct—to hang in, to hang on, to preserve at any cost. My husband had been the tosser, I the saver. We both went to extremes. He
tossed out checks and cred cards along with the junk mail. I saved
broken ashtrays, chipped teacups, even, so help me, human teeth.
I kept them in a basket of old buttons—my children's baby teeth
and my own silvered molars and hard-won wisdom teeth. Hard to
explain. I called them "bones," my own sort of fetish to deflect the
power of change, the fear of loss.

What had I *not* saved? I could chart my lost childhood from the objects I had kept 3,000 miles and five decades distant: an Orphan Annie spoon, a Dopey carved in soap, a china ballerina with one remaining leg, a diary with a single entry repeated for an entire year ("B.H. loves T.B.," the unfortunate initials of the boy I adored), a Copacabana cocktail napkin from an air force pilot lost over the Solomons. The attic of my house was a midden of such junk, my own layered on top of my children's—school notebooks, piano recital programs, "Picasso" finger painting, mice-nibbled popcorn strings, and used wrapping paper, fading and folding from ancient Christmases.

With the same mania, I saved jars, food, plants. Cupboards bulged with emptied jelly jars, sour cream glasses, mustard pots. Freezers burst with chicken bones and shrimp shells, asparagus peelings, garlic pressings, baggies of leftover sauce so old the labels had fallen off—all saved, just in case. Rooms crawled with scraggly geraniums, all stalk and no blossom, spider plants dropping from ceiling to floor, a rain forest of avocado trees sprouted from decades of saved seeds. Still, I clung.

I should have called my friend Karl, an interior designer whose clients often hired him not to make new but to clear out the old: to make up familial minds divided between husband and wife, parent and child; to be Solomon and split a credenza down the middle if necessary. He had filled and emptied many houses of his own, enjoyed them all, and never looked back. Nothing personal, he said, so why dwell on it?

For Karl, attics as well as memories should be tidied regularly, painted over, brightened up. The voice of reason, but to me, as unthinkable as child killing. I felt the same horror when a friend's house had burned to the ground one night, consuming all but the five members of her family, clothed in nothing but their pajamas and their lives. Without a moment of regret, my friend began to fill out the insurance forms for new paintings, towels, toys, draperies, walls, swimming pool. "Everything is replaceable," she said briskly, "nothing is unique."

Nothing sacred, either. No god pots there, just pots and pans, while for me even the cobwebs were particular. For me the house was not a disposable box but a cherished space condensing intimacy. Instead of packing up and clearing out, I had spent a year taking photos of the house, commemorating it as if it were a living person incarnate in the star crocuses in the spring, the cats chasing butterflies on the summer lawn, the leaves drifting from the tulip tree in the fall, the storm that iced its winter branches. Nothing was replaceable, everything unique.

"I hate this house," my daughter Tucky said when she came down from New York after I'd called her to help me out—out the door, out of the house, out of the deep freeze of my married life. What I had loved, she had hated. I was shocked. For her the house was ugly, anxious, tense. "We were never a family here, Mom. It was wrong from the start." For me the rooms were alive with family images— some of them bright as the Christmas tree strung with popcorn, others dark as baby Tucky howling all night because of an infected ear. For her the rooms were oversize trash bins heaped with parts of her life she'd left behind, parts of my life I'd hidden behind, all of which I'd clung to as if I were drowning. "Chuck the lot," she said. "We'll have a garage sale."

Compulsive savers don't have garage sales, but I was desperate. "Tags," she said. "We tag everything and advertise." She saw my face. "Everything, Mom—the *National Geos*, the old cracked 78s, the used light bulbs, my old drum set, the sour cream glasses, the basket of bones."

"Who would want them?" I asked.

"With the right price tag, everything sells," she answered.

The right price tag. What price was right for the little Victorian settee with the wobbly leg and tattered horsehair seat I had got with baby Tucky for $3 at a farmyard auction where the wife rocked on the porch in tears? Skilled in advertising, Tucky saw only selling potential. While I marked everything down, she marked everything up. Folks came while we were still double-marking battered pots, old shoes, scraggly geraniums. Our lawn looked like Faulkner's Snopeses in Yoknapatawpha County, as if the house had vomited its contents and was none the better for it. For me it was all junk and all beloved, but others made finer distinctions. Within an hour, the good stuff was gone, and at the end of the day the bad stuff was still there. We had to hire a dump truck to cart it away.

I was learning the hard way what the Lacandones know from birth—that the best way to preserve is to trash. Hopis, too, enact ancient cleansing ceremonies each year: The women sweep out their hearths and houses, break their pots, put out the fires to guarantee a bountiful harvest of corn and the preservation of their race. I had rejected even a housewife's spring cleaning, and nature took revenge. But still, my daughter and I were the women of the house, the custodians of tradition, and it was up to us to seek a ritual for cleansing. We found purgation in that garage sale.

With childlike glee, Tucky counted our nickels and dimes: We split the profits and then a bottle of champagne. After we had swept the floors, sucked up the dust, and tossed out the pot shards, we walked from room to room surveying the bare boards emptied of rugs, the hearths of ashes and andirons, the bookshelves of moldy books, the closets of toys and skeletons. The house sighed with relief and let us go.

The house was not to blame, my daughter found, making her peace. The house could not preserve, I found, making mine. We sat on the floor of the empty living room with empty glasses, stripped of our shared and unshared past. For me, the past was before and after Tucky. For her, there could only be an after Mom. It was a hard moment of truth.

All those years I'd never asked, "What really matters?" and so I'd tried to save it all—just in case. I'd missed the point entirely about the virtue of endings, the taught blessings of loss: leaves that fall, crabs that shed their shells, and Lacandones their pots.

"I can't believe the junk I've kept," Tucky said with a laugh when she dropped in on my New York apartment recently to say good-bye. She had cleaned out her apartment, five blocks from mine, in preparation for a move 3,000 miles away. A change of inner and outer space. "It's good to see where I was and good to know I'm not there now," said my daughter, clear-eyed as ever.

I showed her the latest addition to my windowsill. In the seven years since my move I'd saved avocado seeds, and not one of them had taken. But there, in a clay pot, was a new stalk two feet tall and growing fast. "Just don't collect a rain forest, Mom," she said.

"I'll try to remember," I said, fingering my wristlet of bones.

Lear's, 1990

On Murdering Eels
and Laundering Swine

■

MURDER WE MUST. If not cows and pigs and fish, then cabbages and rutabagas. We flay bananas, violate oysters, ravage pomegranates. Our lot is beastly and there's no help for it, for feed we must on creature kinds. Our hands are stained with carrot blood and not all the seas of Noah's Flood will wash them clean, not after God's pact with Noah: "Every moving thing that lives shall be food for you." That's a lot of territory in which to assert our puny manhood and decree that this is fit and this not, this food pure and that dirty. No, all that lives is food for man who, dead, is food for worms. That's the deal.

Some living things are harder to kill than others, even though some things beg to be killed. Snakes, for instance. Their very shape mirrors our throttled circumstances, the narrowness of our confines, the anguish of our passage. The same root, *ango*, generates *anguis* (snake) and anguish (pain). The same root generates *anguilla* (eel), a fish in snake's clothing. Its snaky form makes some eaters queasy and others ravenous, but to eat an eel you must kill him first and quite deliberately, with the zeal of an ax murderer, because he is well armed against us.

I have killed many snakes in the desert when it was their life or mine, but killing an eel in cold blood, on the fourth floor, in a New

York City apartment—that's different. The eel and I were already intimate, for I had carried him in my lap in a large plastic bag on the subway from Chinatown, and he had roiled against my belly as if I were pregnant with eels. Watching the bag slither with speed across my kitchen floor, I was afraid to deliver him. I was, in fact, deathly afraid of snakes.

My father had kept them in cages in our basement, next to the laundry tub, the newfangled washing machine, and the old-fashioned clothes wringer. Dumping laundry from tub to washer to wringer to basket for hanging on the line, I kept my eye on the snakes. Whether harmless as garters or lethal as rattlers, they were the Serpent *anguiformes*, the One cursed by God to creep without legs or wings on its belly, condemned without mercy to the darkness of a basement with a burnt-out bulb. Their skins, if you touched them, were cold as death and, though dry, wet as an oyster. Because of them I was damned, as my grandfather had read me in the Book of Genesis, "For the imagination of man's heart is evil from his youth." I was young and therefore evil. The logic was impeccable: the snake and I were kin.

Nothing in my basement past, however, had prepared me for murdering an eel. I needed time to think and threw the bag in the freezer overnight. When I opened the bag in the sink next day, he looked stone cold dead. When I turned the water on to remove the slime, he came suddenly to life. I grabbed a Chinese cleaver and tried to grab his thrusting head, but he was all muscle and I was not. With both hands I slammed the cleaver down on what might have been his neck but may have been his shoulders. A mighty whack barely nicked him. I whacked again as, tail thrashing, he tried to worm his way down the minnow-sized drain. "I'm sorry," I apologized with every whack, and I was. But I needn't have been because I had not even scotched the snake, let alone killed him.

I looked for a blunt instrument and found a wooden mallet that I used for pounding meat. I cracked the mallet on his head and the wood split, but nothing else. He was breathing heavily, gulping air that filled a pouch below his jaws. Was he strangling? I didn't want to know. Like Raskolnikov, I wanted him dead. Like Rasputin, he refused to die. I looked in the freezer for respite and held the bag open for him to slither in. He went halfway, then with a quick U-turn wrapped his tail around my arm and began to slither out. Engulfing him with a second bag, I flopped the works on to the ice trays and slammed the freezer door.

I needed time for research and reflection, my brain against his muscle. I consulted books. "To kill eels instantly, without the horrid torture of cutting and skinning them alive, pierce the spinal marrow, close to the back part of the skull, with a sharp-pointed skewer," William Kitchiner advised in the *Cook's Oracle* in 1817. "The humane executioner," he added, "does certain criminals the favour to hang them before he breaks them on the wheel." A kind thought, but what if the criminal refused to hang? Madame Saint-Ange, in *La Cuisine*, advised French housewives to grab the eel's tail in a dishtowel and bash its head violently against a stone or wall. So much for sentimental Brits.

Surely there was some practical, efficient, clean—American—way to kill. The best way to kill an eel, A. J. McClane wrote in his *Encyclopedia of Fish Cookery*, was to put him in a container of coarse salt. I poured two large boxes of coarse kosher salt into a large stockpot, pulled the eel bag from the freezer, and slid the mound of icy coils into the pot. Before they could quiver, I blanketed them with salt and waited. Nothing stirred. Salt, McClane said, also "deslimes" the eel, but my hands and clothes were already covered with an ooze that would not wash off. When I finally inspected my victim, I found the deed was done, his mouth marred by a single drop of blood.

Skinning was yet to come. McClane suggested I attach his head by a string to a nail pounded in a board. I had neither nail nor board. What I wanted was an electric 7 ¼-inch circular saw with a carbide-tooth blade. What I had was a pair of poultry shears. I pierced his thick hide and cut a jagged circle below his head, then scissored the length of his belly. With one hand, I held his head and with the other pulled back the skin with a pair of stout pliers. It was slow work, but the leathery hide finally slipped off the tail like a nylon stocking. Naked, he was malleable as any flesh.

With one clean stroke I severed his head and hacked him into lengths. He was a three-pound meaty boy, thick and fat. He was everything one could ask for in an eel. I put him in a pot and baptized him with white wine and vinegar, vegetables and herbs, and butter whipped to a froth. He was delicious, as fat eels always are, and crowned my murderer's feast with blessing. For the order of eels are in nature born and buried in salt. Enduring a lifetime's banishment to freshwater pastures and the long journey there and back, they return to their cradle in the salt Sargasso Sea to die in a burst of sperm and roe. "It is a covenant of salt forever": God's covenant with Levi matched the one with Noah. The salt that blesses and preserves also deslimes and kills. The eel and I were bound by the same double deal. His life for mine, salt our shared salvation.

A serpent dead, however, did nothing to scotch my deeper anguish. "Shit is a more onerous theological problem than is evil," Milan Kundera wrote in *The Unbearable Lightness of Being.* "Since God gave man freedom, we can, if need be, accept the idea that He is not responsible for man's crimes. The responsibility for shit, however, rests entirely with Him, the Creator of man." If murder is man's crime, shit is not. Shit is God's joke, yet shit we must even as we feed.

What was my relation to the ten pounds of frozen hog's guts, thawing and spreading like drowned Ophelia's hair, in my apartment bathtub? The chitterlings, ten times the length of my own inner tubing, were pastel yellow, white, and pink. They spread like dubious laundry, triggering memories of washing dirty socks and underwear in the bathtubs of innumerable French and Italian hotels that invariably forbade guests to launder. With guts as with underwear, it was better to do as a French cookbook instructs, "Take the stomach and intestines to the nearest stream or river." Women once washed guts as they washed linen, rising at dawn to carry their baskets of offal to the communal gathering place, to laugh and quarrel, a medieval poet said, as they washed "innards" at the stream.

It is laundry that connects pig's inwards to man's outwards. The ruffles on a shirtfront were once called chitterlings, "exuberant chitterlings," as Washington Irving said, "puffed out at the neck and bosom." Our foppish frills were once the ancients' omens, when offal was deemed awe-ful and the parts most worthy of the gods. A beast's inwards then put man in touch with the stars, the outermost circle of our confinement. But we who see in serpents no more than snakes, in guts no more than garbage, in destiny no more than a gambler's shake—to our narrow and straightened palates, chitterlings are the food of slaves.

I suppose it's the smell that does it, a pervasive stink that clings to hands and hair, slightly sweet, slightly sour, like dank earth turned over, like rotting bodies in a trench, like human shit. It rubs our noses in all we would deny. Washing guts, I found clusters of fat stuck to the inner lining, along with specks of what dignified recipes call "foreign matter." Some guts are thick and rubbery, others thin and limp as wet hankies. Guts are not smooth like plastic tubing, but gathered length-wise along invisible seams, to puff like parachute silk with gas. They are gathered the way a seamstress gathers cloth for ruffles. To reach the translucent membrane of the casing, I had to strip and strip again the clogging fat until, held to the light, the stretched skin showed leaf patterns, clouds, sea scum, palely mottled and beautiful. Only by laundering the guts of swine did I discover that shit comes wrapped in a layer of clouds trapped in a membrane resilient as nylon. Still, my lustrations were brief. Most of the cleansing had been done for me at the slaughterhouse, before the guts were frozen by the Gwaltney Company, a son of IT&T. The corporate master that sent me hog's guts puts satellites in space, making however inadvertently the cosmic connection of shit and stars.

From Lily of the Valley, Virginia, a slave's granddaughter told me that she cooks chitlins in their own yellow juice with onion and garlic and vinegar, until the guts are tender enough to chew. Chewy they are, rich on the tongue like all rejected vitals—heart, liver, lights, or haslet—all those messy innards that remind us uneasily of our own. "Cut them chitlins in small lengths, or knot 'em, and cook 'em up with collards or rice in the pot of chitlin gravy, or fry 'em deep in bubblin' fat until they float up crisp and light," she said.

Even crisp and light, a little inwards go a long way. They go a long way as vitals, en route to shitty death. Bre'r hog knows better than I the rhythm that melds eating and shitting in every moving thing that lives, in the dung birth and death of cabbages and swine, men and snakes. "We must pitch our tents in the fields of excrement," cried Crazy Jane, who liked the way my fingers smell, my stove, my bathtub. The smell of chitterlings clings to the air the way the taste of chitterlings sticks to the tongue. It is a lingering power that gives, my Lily of the Valley friend says, satisfaction.

But I am a child of deodorized air and Lysol drains. My pasteurized senses are not ready for the excremental smell of my bathtub. I poured "Fragrant Pine" bubble bath into the water and was ashamed to read the labeled contents: sulfates, chlorides, formaldehydes, succinates, and an ingredient called "fragrance." I am too sanitized for the fragrance of pig shit. I can turn murder into blessing by symbolic salt, but excrement into sacrament is a harder trick to turn. God owes me there. My guts are serpentine as a mess of eels, but the inward darkness of Genesis shakes out as farce. Farce is my Exodus. I know that after a lifetime's wandering through a wilderness of snakes and swine, no amount of murdering, no amount of laundering, will change my promised end as meat and gravy for rutabagas, pudding for worms.

Not for Bread Alone, 1992

Earning Her Food

∎

I'M A CITY girl from New York. I'm also 82 and half-blind, so what am I doing deer hunting with my son, Sam, at the end of October in Montana? We're in the foothills of the Swan Mountains near Kalispell, south of Glacier National Park. For the last four days, Sam and I have been tramping dawn to dusk over tree debris that loggers call "clear-cut." We haven't eaten since we left his cabin before dawn. Now it's snowing, and I'm wet, tired, and bloody cold.

Because Sam wanted to make sure I wouldn't blow his head off by mistake, I'd learned how to load and fire a .22-caliber rifle in September at a shooting range off Fifth Avenue in Manhattan. I found out you needed only one eye to line up the sights. But when I arrived at Sam's place, it wasn't a .22 he handed me but a .270 Winchester with a scope. He showed me how to haul it up, push it hard into my shoulder and jam my cheek along the stock, but the gun was so heavy I could barely keep it still. Even if I see a deer, I thought, how will I aim this wobbling bazooka?

Sam calls hunting "earning your food." Although I've spent a lifetime of buying, cooking, and eating food, this would be the first time I'd ever hunted and sought to kill. Others had always done that for me.

By noontime on this fifth deerless day, I have seen nothing but snowflakes and ravens. The air has been so milky that I fantasize coyotes, wolves, mountain lions, bears. Sam's pointed out the scat of all these, fresh and glistening, along with deer scat. But the white-tail stay invisible. I've liked the challenge, but I've also yearned to go home—not to Sam's cabin but to my overheated New York apartment.

This morning I vowed at breakfast that it was going to be today or never. I can't let Sam down, nor myself, nor even the deer. Somehow we're all in it together. But as we trudge across one more clear-cut hell, I say to myself, I will not cry. I'm like a Marine recruit on Parris Island, collapsing from heatstroke while his sergeant says, "Suck it up, Fatso."

By miracle the sun breaks out, lighting up the landscape like Christmas in Manhattan. Sam points. For the first time, I can actually see a doe with my naked good eye because she's no more than 40 yards away. This first week of rifle-hunting season, young deer are so innocent, they'll just stop and stare. They don't know that this is my only chance to hit one.

When I lift the gun and look through the scope, by chance she's right there presenting herself broadside. Weirdly the crosshairs are exactly on the target point, just behind and above her right shoulder. I squeeze. The gun booms and bounces. The target disappears.

"Great shot!" Sam hollers. I jump into his arms. My head is exploding as we embrace. "A double-lung shot," he says. "She didn't know what hit her."

I'm both elated and appalled. Extreme joy and extreme grief are locked like the crosshairs. "Now's the time to pray," Sam says. Even though I long ago abandoned my forefathers' Calvinist God, it's Him I thank for the fellow creature I killed.

The first rule in hunting is to dress the animal in the field, remove the innards and leave them for the crows, magpies, and coyotes whose territory we've invaded. Except for the innards you may want to eat.

Sam puts a warm, wet ball in my hand. I've cooked and eaten many veal hearts and chicken hearts, so I know a heart when I see one. But not one this newly cut out, dripping blood between my fingers. And certainly not this naked, without the euphemizing wrap of Cryovac. But I'm so hungry I could practically eat it raw.

After Sam hauls the dressed doe on his back to his truck, we drive to the Lower Valley Processing Company, where I choose to turn my deer into steaks, sausages, and jerky. Soon my freezer will be stuffed with venison. My deer's hide will go to a Montana tanner and then onto my Manhattan bed.

That evening when Sam and I sit down to dinner, we eat the heart. Most recipes say to slice and fry with garlic and onion, add barbecue sauce. I just use salt and pepper in order to taste the grilled flesh pure. Men use fire; other animals don't. But I have never felt the bonds of creaturehood so intensely.

I repeat the blessing my grandfather said before each meal, "Bless this food to our use and us to thy service," With gratitude, we eat.

New York Times Magazine, 2010

FOOD SAYS . . .

A Is for Apple

▪

I love his cabbage, gravy, hash
Daffy about his succotash,
I can't do without my kitchen man.

MAN OR WOMAN, those of us who spend a lot of time in the kitchen over cabbage, gravy, hash know that the language of love, whether sung by Bessie Smith or William Shakespeare, springs from every creature's first love, food. Far more than music, *food* is the food of love, for the alphabets of both are as primary and interchangeable as mother's milk and baby's howl. Kitchen men and women know that food cannot be reduced to chemistry because it is first of all a language, and not just our primal body language, but our primal symbolic form from which all other language springs. Food and speech, in fact, are as interchangeable as milk and howl, for we have but the one organ, mouth and tongue, to suck food in and blow words out. Eating, it could be said, is our way of tasting images, as talking is our way of tasting words.

"Would it not be better to have another orifice for food, and to keep the mouth only for words?" Elias Canetti asks in his essay "Crowds and Power." "Or does this intimate mixing of all our utterances with the lips, teeth, tongue, throat, all those parts of the mouth that serve the business of eating—does this mixing tell us that language and eating forever belong together, that we can never be nobler and better than we are, that basically, however it's disguised, all we say is the same terrible and bloody thing, and that revulsion and our gorge only rise if something is wrong with our food?"

Cooks as well as writers know that this ludicrous intimate mixing, the bondage of man's highest power to his lowest needs, is the human *plat du jour* that defines our fate and the language we use to express it. Cooks, in fact, are constantly engaged in acts of poetry, since food is the base, the *fond*, of our earliest myths and metaphors. Ancient religious myths invariably center on food metaphors extended into narratives, whether it is the precious cactus-fruit of the Aztec, the Promethean liver of the Greeks, the apple of the Hebrews, or the bread and wine of the Christian. The Biblical myth of the Garden of Eden makes the connection of language to eating painfully clear: God created the universe by speaking the Word, but man created human destiny by eating the one food that was off the menu.

Someone has said that the cosmos is conjugated by the verb to eat, in the active and passive mode. Not just the earth's food chain of sun eaten by grass eaten by animal eaten by man eaten by worm, but the cosmic energy chain of black holes eating stars and, in the wacky vocabulary of astrophysics, of machos eating axioms eating neutrinos eating wimps. The cosmic metabolism is as circular as the earthly one, but the Garden of Eden lacked metabolism just as it lacked hunger, for metabolism means change and hunger means pain. In the beginning there was no change, no pain. Adam and Eve had "every green herb for meat" without labor or want.

Man's story in Genesis begins not with hunger but with desire. In comparison to "desire," a soft Latinate word that speaks of "a feeling, directed toward the possession of something from which pleasure is expected," the word "hunger" is a Teutonic grunt that embodies the torment and ache caused by a terrible lack. After God created the grass, trees, beasts, fowl, and creeping things, each after its own kind, and after He created male and female, in His own image, only then did Eve desire: "And when the woman saw that the tree was good for food, and that it was pleasant to the eyes, and a tree to be desired to make one wise, she took of the fruit thereof, and did eat. . . ." The green herb was enough for animal need, but Eve was no animal. When she saw an image "pleasant to the eyes" and edible to the tongue, she desired it not because she wanted the immortality of the gods, but because she wanted their wisdom. Desire spells pleasure. Hunger spells pain. Eve ate for pleasure.

If A is for Apple, it is also for Appetite. The deepest principle of life, says medical scientist Leon R. Kass in *The Hungry Soul*, is not the code of DNA but the syntax of appetite and desire. The human desire to eat the sacred, symbolic of all that separates us from gods, is also what separates us from animals. Appetite, from Latin *appetere*, "to seek after," defines our human kind. When Eve sought after wisdom, knowledge, truth—the provenance of the Word—she found self-consciousness, separation, death—the provenance of the flesh. The inextricable mixing of both together, visions and divisions, is the provenance of humanity. For the poet and mythmaker, food is a natural bridge for the divisions between Word and flesh, for food as language is image and substance, intelligible and concrete, just as the act of eating is a ready-made plot for tragi-comic reversal. Seeking pleasure in her food, Eve found pain. Seeking union, she found separation. Seeking glory, she found shame. Every meal, by embodying the gap between *want* and *is*, repeats the plot of our initial kitchen-opera.

And it is that generic plot, giving flesh to the mysteries of our dilemma, that shapes the way we eat images, taste words. The pastoral drama of Genesis, by supplying an ideal garden with real fruit, whets our appetite for both. The pastoral romance of the Song of Solomon, by making a real garden incarnate the ideal body of the beloved, excites our desire for both:

> *A garden inclosed is my sister, my spouse, a spring shut up, a*
> > *fountain sealed.*
> *Thy plants are an orchard of pomegranates, with pleasant*
> > *fruits, camphire, with spikenard,*
> *Spikenard and saffron, calamus and cinnamon, with all trees*
> > *of frankincense, myrrh and aloes, with all the chief spices.*

Instead of cabbage, gravy, hash, the poet sings of pomegranates, saffron, cinnamon, but his song of love is no less a recipe for healing the gap between *want* and *is* than Bessie's prescription for the blues. Despite the divisions between word and flesh, the poet in his singing can make our olfactory nerves tingle, our mouths water, our tongues taste each word as they pop images against the palate like pomegranate seeds.

How odd to find New Testament poets rehashing the metaphor of the Garden of Eden in the Garden of Gethsemane, and even odder to find them rehashing Solomon's metaphor of the garden-banquet of the beloved in the banquet of the Last Supper. Christ in the Garden of Gethsemane is an emblem of the tree of life and of the fruit that hangs thereon, and is in himself "a garden inclosed." Both bride and groom, the beloved of his disciples, Christ is also in himself the entree of the Last Supper and the wedding cake of the Marriage Feast.

Food and love come together in remarkable ways at this cannibal table. As G. Feely-Harnick details brilliantly in *The Lord's Table*,

Christ by presenting himself as the Paschal Lamb subverts the earlier Feast of the Passover and the dietary laws of Leviticus that followed Adam's expulsion from the Garden and Noah's rescue from the Flood. In Leviticus as in Genesis, the law of God's Word is embodied in actual foods, dividing the permissible and the forbidden, separating different "kinds" of animals in order to separate different "kinds" of human beings. The Levitican laws, which sanctified and purified God's Chosen by separating blood from flesh, implemented Noah's Covenant that allowed people to eat all living things, but forbade blood because blood belonged to God alone.

Christ's Covenant, however, upsets both Noah's ark and Eden's apple cart. The man whom Jewish priests called "a glutton and a drunkard" because he hosted an egalitarian table, open to sinners and priests alike, perverts the traditional meaning of animal sacrifice by serving up himself to all comers, Gentiles as well as Jews. In commanding his followers to chew on his flesh and drink his blood, in the ultimate union of eater and eaten, Christ caps the miracle of turning water into wine by turning a baguette and *vin ordinaire* into God's flesh and God's blood. For the Christian, once God's Word became incarnate in Christ's flesh, the interchange of bread and wine with flesh and blood is as intimately mixed as language and eating. To eat Christ and drink his blood is to devour death itself. "So he who eats me," John quotes Christ's words in his gospel, "will live because of me."

The Word made Flesh is a stunning development of the narrative that began with Eve's eating an apple. "The Last Supper is horrifying by itself," Feeley-Harnick remarks. "But in the context it is merely the last in a long series of culinary disasters." The disastrous *déjeuner sur l'herbe* of the Old Garden is redeemed by the horrific banquet of the New, where the paradoxes of food and love accumulate like multiple courses at a feast. The terrible bloody business of lips, teeth, tongue, and throat rending and swallowing God's flesh and blood, in an act of *love*, changes the stakes in the intermixing of speech and food.

These are the stakes W.H. Auden, speaking as a poet-cook, plays with in his poem "On Installing an American Kitchen in Lower Austria":

> *Then surely those in whose creed*
> > *God is edible may call a fine*
> *Omelette a Christian deed.*

Poets and cooks are alike engaged in Christian deeds if their belief runs that way, for they know that an edible God, no less than an omelette, requires the breaking of eggs. Even those whose gods are not edible know that an omelette redeems the destruction of eggs in the way that a blessing redeems the devouring of the mother hen, whether the eater is Christian, Jew, or Muslim. Since we can preserve life only by destroying it, we are all in need of blessing. "Bless this food to Thy use and us to Thy service" was my Grandmother Harper's Presbyterian prayer, spoken before each meal. The words redeemed her hunger.

Even if I do not repeat her words, I know that every meal, store-bought or home-cooked, is nature's gift, God-given, like Eve's Garden, which we violate by eating. I know too that every meal is a culinary disaster because desire is as different from hunger as image from substance in our muddlements of food, sex, and love. The novelist Georges Simenon, notorious for the sheer volume of his sexual affairs, justified them by his quest for a real "ideal" woman, one just like his mother, the woman with whom he discussed all the way home from his wedding "the best way to make French-fried potatoes."

Anyone who has cooked, made love, or written down words knows that our rituals of food, sex, and language are bulwarks against loss, exile, pain, fear—medicine for mortality. Eating, like sex or poetry, is one way to seize the day. Our recipes, our menus, our poems are diagrams designed to stop time, arrest the moment, and by exploiting transiency transcend it. "Haddock and sausage meat," Virginia Woolf noted in one of her last *Diaries* before her suicide. "I think it is true that one gains a certain hold on sausage and haddock by writing them down."

But no recipe, no poem, can match the scenario in our heads, no more than a real garden can match Paradise. Asked once for his favorite food, Federico Fellini answered, "The Zuppa Inglese of my grandmother." He proceeded to list the ingredients, explained how to layer them one by one, how to sprinkle them with the anisette liqueur *mistra*, and how to cover them with whipped meringue placed in a cone shaped from a page of the newspaper *Corrière Padano*.

"That is an important detail because the cake had just the slight flavor of the newspaper," he said. "It is therefore impossible to duplicate, because that newspaper is no longer in business. *The New York Times* is not right at all. *Corrière della Sera* is closer. But really, you must go to a library and steal a page of *Corrière Padano*. The other flavor you need is of my grandmother's thumb over the bottle as she sprinkled on the *mistra*."

No recipe has better expressed the absurdity of all recipes in their attempt to recreate a particular moment, condensed in a particular dish, tasted on the tongue and in the heart, recoverable in the imagination but never in real life. But still, many of us collect recipes the way we collect books and records, all of them fragments shored against our ruin. In America many collect recipes the way some cultures collect fetishes, to ward off evil, cast spells, induce love, stop time dead in its tracks.

The higher and more complex our technology, it seems, the lower and more magical our purposes. Forever puritan, America as a culture continues to struggle against the wages of sin, but we do so with the enfeebled language of nutri-babble and gastroporn. Alternating between flagellation by diet and death by chocolate, today we are as prurient about forbidden fats as our New England ancestors about forbidden sex when A was for Adultery. But if fat is our pornography, perfectibility is our pathology. In the Middle Ages, gluttony and lechery were called sins because they were "perverted loves," expressing self-love, self-worship. Such loves we call virtue in the holy name of health and self-improvement.

To the credible, no claims are too great for the curative powers and spiritual virtues of our nutritionists. Harvard's diet-guru Jean Mayer, who proclaims that his *Diet for Living* "will help improve our physical looks and emotional well-being and will help to prolong your life," echoes the rhetoric of faith healers from the time of Jethro Kloss in *Back to Eden*: "Wrong habits of eating and the use of refined and adulterated foods are largely responsible for the intemperance and crime and sickness that curse this world."

What an odd reading of Eden's apple, which apparently would have been okay to eat if it had not been chemically sprayed. Certainly our diets are magical attempts to reclaim Eden and free us from fear, a fear we now attach to the whole world of food. Rationalizing our fears in biochemical jargon, we babble of low-density lipoproteins, serotonins, endorphins, *E. coli* 0157, and binge on oat fiber, omega-3, beta-carotene, kombucha tea. Even as we define ourselves by our power to consume, sexually and gastronomically, we are consumed by the power of industry and technology to engineer our appetites and hungers. The new Eden offered us in the pages of *Food Technology* is "an orchard of imitation fresh fruit flavors." Where technology is God, consumers, as Ross Hume Hall once wrote in *Food for Nought*, are processed as much as their food.

In our processed desires, we labor not to acquire but to rid ourselves of food altogether, and of our animal need for it, because we have lost our place in the world. We confuse the vows of poverty and chastity with the vow to eat no meat. We confuse the martyrdom of sainthood and salvation with anorexia and bulimia. Our food obsessions reveal the sickness of our food language, which is a language of despair hopelessly at odds with the facts. If we do not eat, we will die. If we do eat, we will die. That is the lump that sticks in our craw and that no nutriceutical can cure.

While the need to feed does not change, our appetite for the wisdom of words can change animal need into human desire. No words can change the biological fact that the same mouth that speaks eats, whether we hunger and thirst after righteousness or power, after holy or perverted loves. But we are more than biology, just as food is more than chemistry. Words can change the form and substance of our lives the way cooking changes eggs to omelettes or grain to bread.

Not the green herb nor the raw apple, but bread is the distinctive food of human beings and the proper continuation of Eve's alphabet. Our fall into hunger is the leaven of our desire, as intimately mixed as grain, yeast, and fire. Bread is made by the sweat of one's brow, but by grinding grain into flour, leavening it with a ferment, transforming and preserving it by fire, Eve made "kitchen men" of us all. A loaf of bread, a jug of wine, is food for any creed if we eat our images, taste our words with the kind of pleasure that turns cooking fires into the fires of love, turns omelettes into offerings, turns the pain of our mutual dependency into an appetite for song:

> When I eat his doughnuts
> All I leave is the hole.
> Anytime he wants to,
> Why he can use my sugar bowl.
> I can't do without my kitchen man.

Culturefront, 1996

Acknowledgments

TO A GARDEN of Eves who at one time or another have traded bites with me: Nancy Oster, Joan Tapper, Elizabeth Mitchell, Dawn Mobley, Felicia Campbell, Meryl Rosofsky, Fern Berman, Annette Grant, Joyce Carol Oates, Sally Singer, Becky Saletan, Gloria Loomis, Theo Stephan, Melissa Clark, Amy Dickerson.